Liberature

A Book-bound Genre

I0540781

topomo

Liberature

A Book-bound Genre

Katarzyna Bazarnik

Jagiellonian University Press

SERIES
Topographies of (Post)Modernity. Studies in 20th and 21st Century Literature in English

LANGUAGE EDITING AND PROOFREADING
Chrissie van Mierlo

REVIEWERS
prof. dr hab. Tadeusz Sławek, prof. dr hab. Marta Gibińska-Marzec

SERIES EDITORS
Katarzyna Bazarnik, Bożena Kucała, Robert Kusek

SERIES ADVISORY BOARD
Šárka Bubíková (Univerzita Pardubice), Mirosława Buchholtz (Uniwersytet Mikołaja
Kopernika), Finn Fordham (Royal Holloway, University of London), Johan Jacobs
(University of KwaZulu-Natal), Zygmunt Mazur (Uniwersytet Jagielloński),
John McCourt (Università degli Studi Roma Tre), Claudia Marquis (University of Auckland),
Krystyna Stamirowska (Uniwersytet Jagielloński)

COVER DESIGN
Marcin Klag

With the financial support of the Institute of English Studies at the Faculty of Philology,
Jagiellonian University in Kraków, and the Faculty of Philology

ISBN 978-83-233-4201-4
ISBN 978-83-233-9565-2 (e-book)

www.wuj.pl

Jagiellonian University Press
Editorial Offices: ul. Michałowskiego 9/2, 31-126 Krakow
Phone: +48 12 663 23 80, +48 12 663 23 82, Fax: +48 12 663 23 83
Distribution: Phone: +48 12 631 01 97, Fax: +48 12 631 01 98
Cell Phone: +48 506 006 674, e-mail: sprzedaz@wuj.pl
Bank: PEKAO SA, IBAN PL80 1240 4722 1111 0000 4856 3325

Contents

List of illustrations 7

Acknowledgements 11

Introduction 13
   Necessary confession 13
   Generic constraints 14
   Zenon Fajfer and _____'s *Mute-Eye-Late* 16
   Overview of the content 20

PART ONE: INBETWEENNESS

Hybridity 25

Liberature: an appendix to a dictionary of literary terms 31

PART TWO: LIBERATURE AND RELATED CONCEPTS

Literature in the form of the book 41
   Liberature and the artist's book 41
   Book is a meaningful space 45
   Book is a navigating device 50

Conceptual metaphors in liberature 57
   B.S. Johnson: breaking through the walls of fiction 57
   William H. Gass's material metaphors 62
   Books are buildings 65
   Book is a body 70

Poetics of presence 77
    Presentification 77
    Literary work is an event 80
    Book is a performative space 85

Liberature and multimodality 87
    The Intermedia 87
    Liberature and concrete poetry 90
    Liberature and multimodal literature 96

PART THREE: THE QUESTION OF GENRE

Genre trouble 109
    A "venerable error" 109
    A demise or regeneration of the (literary) species? . . . 111

Categorising and (re)conceptualising 123
    Ideas and shadows 123
    The idea of liberature or what is a concept?. 126
    A theory of liberature 132

Dimensions of genre 135
    Structural, rhetorical and thematic dimensions 135
    Does liberature have a thematic dimension? 137

Genre functions 145
    Genre as a (proto)type 145
    Literary soleras: sommeliers 148
    Literary soleras: winemakers 154

Classifying and cataloguing 157
    Patching the system. 157
    Forms of knowing 160

Conclusion 165
    Liberature: what's in the name? 165

Bibliography 171

Author and subject index 191

List of illustrations

Fig. 1. Zenon Fajfer and Katarzyna Bazarnik *Oka-leczenie*
[Mute-Eye-Late] (2000)   17

Fig. 2. Zenon Fajfer (Courtesy of the author),
an excerpt from "~~lyric, epic, dramatic,~~ liberature" (2010b: 43) . . .   44

Fig. 3. Adam Thirlwell's (Courtesy of Visual Editions; photo Marcin Klag)
Kapow! Unfolding pages stretched like a sheet of cloth (2012) . . .   50

Fig. 4. B.S. Johnson *The Unfortunates* (Polish and English editions) . .   51

Fig. 5. "A window into the future (and the past)" in B.S. Johnson's
Albert Angelo (2004b [1964]; photo Marcin Klag)   62

Fig. 6. Zenon Fajfer (Courtesy of the author) "Actaeon"
(excerpt from *ten letters*, 2010)   94

Everything in the world
exists in order to end up as a book.
Stephane Mallarmé

...books are buildings;
and therefore they exist like other objects –
they are a space in space...
William H. Gass

A book is a machine to think with...
A.I. Richards

Genre (...) is a universal dimension of textuality.
John Frow

Thoughts without content are empty,
intuitions without concepts are blind.
Imannuel Kant

Acknowledgements

I would like to thank the Institute of English Studies and the Faculty of Philology at the Jagiellonian University in Krakow for the financial support that made the publication of this book possible. I thank warmly my reviewers: prof. Marta Gibińska-Marzec and prof. Tadeusz Sławek for their valuable comments, advice and overall support, the more precious because offered during the holiday season. I am grateful to all my colleagues from the Comparative Literature and Culture Section, who have given me much encouragement, stimulating ambience – and friendship: Izabella Curyłło-Klag, Beata Piątek, Ewa Kowal and Robert Kusek; among them Bożena Kucała deserves my special gratitutude for her unfailing support. Warm thanks are also due to Agnieszka Przybyszewska, Piotr Marecki, Monika Górska-Olesińska, Anna Nacher for many inspiring discussions about print and electronic literature. My international colleagues, and friends: Kathi Inman Berens, Finn Fordham, Caroline Warman, and Jolanta Wawrzycka deserve my equally deep gratitude for providing me not only with hours of inspirational conversations, but also with a generous supply of books, materials, and free lodgings in Oxford.

Many other people have generously given me their interest, advice and support – I am grateful to all, but for the sake of space I can mention only a few: prof. Krystyna Stamirowska, prof. Elżbieta Tabakowska, prof. Wojciech Kalaga and prof. Jerzy Kutnik. The students of my modern literature seminar 2014/16 were stimulating, passionate (and patient) intellectual companions over the final year of writing this book – thank you, Monika, Karolina, Sabina, two Natalias and two Olas, Basia, Kasia, Iwona and Magda. My thanks are also due to the staff of the Faculty of Philology Library (thank you, Ania, Monika, Beata and Teresa), who have patiently assisted me with home and inter-library loans. Chrissie van Mierlo has my deep gratitude for her discerning editing and proofreading of the manuscript. I am equally grateful to the staff and editors of the Jagiellonian University Press who have demonstrated inexhaustible patience in the making of this book, and most professional assistance in preparing it for the printing press. And thank you, Marcin, for clothing it in style.

Finally, and first of all, thank you, Zenon, for many hours, days and years of passionate discussing, and living. This book would not have been born without you. I hope its siblings, Dante and Kazik will forgive their mother for having to share their time with it.

And to my mum: *dziękuję, że jesteś*.

Introduction

Necessary confession

Before I begin, I am obliged to make a confession. The present monograph is the fruit of miscegenation between a scholar and a creative writer, and its subject – the eponymous *liberature* – is the product of a similar trespass. Beside my academic publications, I am the co-author of two books: *Oka-leczenie* [Mute-Eye-Late] and *(O)patrzenie* [Ga(u)ze], written jointly with Zenon Fajfer. The concept of liberature, featuring in the title of my book, was in fact first proposed by this poet and my artistic collaborator, in an article with the provocative title "Liberature. Appendix to a Dictionary of Literary Terms" (Fajfer 1999).[1] In his essay, which combined the zest of an artistic manifesto with some theoretical reflection, Fajfer suggested a new and distinct literary genre. It would denote a kind of creative writing that fuses text with its physical form into an inseparable whole in the space of the book. The name of the postulated category, in which he fused Latin *liber* (the book) with "literature," also hints at writers' liberty to use their material as freely as necessary. Linguistically, his coinage was a hybrid word, just as works he described or envisaged could be seen as combinations of different arts, but – as he has always stressed – with the unquestioned dominance of the literary component.

So my hybrid position corresponds well with the hybridity of my subject. I admit that I am speaking here both as a creative writer and a literary scholar, a theorist of the genre to which I have contributed. Such

---

[1] The article first appeared in Polish in the literary journal *Dekada Literacka*, and accompanied "Booksday," the exhibition held as part of the 2nd Krakow Bloomsday conference in 1999. Further quotations are from the English translation included in Fajfer's bilingual collection, *Liberature or Total Literature. Collected Essays 1999–2009* (ed. and trans. by K. Bazarnik, Krakow: Ha!art, 2010).

a situation, though not so rare in the academic world,[2] is nevertheless an uncomfortable one. In my defence I should perhaps quote Christine Brooke-Rose, my more eminent predecessor in this practice, who in her preface to *Stories, Theories and Things* offers the following disclaimer:

> [...] the novelist can often throw an aura of doubt or humour or particular perception upon theory. The book [...] is in fact about this connection, about how the critic and teacher reads also as writer and how the novelist writes also as theorist, aware of the fundamental inseparability of elements that critics and teachers have to separate, even rejoice in separating, pin-pointing, for the purpose of this or that type of analysis, though some try to refound them into large universal systems which the novelist knows can only hold in a precarious suspension of disbelief. (Brooke-Rose 1991: 1)

Like the British writer-scholar, I also strive to balance "ideal definitions of form and formal definitions of ideas," while sometimes offering "statements of position, confessions, autobiographies, greater aims, interpretations, glimmerings of overall themes. All are protean, capturable for brief moments in language, but already changed even into their opposites another brief moment later" (ibid.). I admit that my argument oscillates at times in a similar manner, and that my final conclusions are rather tentative descriptions than unqualified statements. And though I have tried hard to maintain a matter-of-fact tone, and keep the roles of the artist and theorist apart, this has not always been easy, or possible.

Generic constraints

As I have indicated above, the separation between the artist and the scholar is my aim and ambition in this monograph. Conventions of the genre call for a distanced, objective style, and little, if any, personal information. Of course, I am aware of the norms of scholarly decorum one of which is enunciative erasure. Enunciative linguistics describes *effacement enonciatif* as a consistent strategy of avoiding personal pronouns and subjective phrasing that would allow the reader to identify

---

[2]   Examples could be numerous, suffice it to list a handful of names from different cultural backgrounds: Christine Brooke-Rose, Jacqueline Rose, Inga Iwasiów, Raymond Federman, Milorad Pavič, William H. Gass, not to mention Umberto Eco and J.M. Coetzee.

the speaking voice with that of the author. Thus, "deictic subjectivity" is replaced with "modal subjectivity" that bespeaks the "commitment to what is said" as universally true, irrespective of the identity of an actual speaker (Rinck and Boch 2012: 117–119). Or, to paraphrase T.S. Eliot's utopian call, the mind of the critic should function as "the shred of platinum," activating the critical reaction but itself remaining neutral. This may partly or exclusively operate upon the experience of the (wo)man herself; but, the more perfect the critic, the more completely separate in her will be the (wo)man who creates and the mind which investigates: "the more perfectly will the mind digest and transmute the passions which are its material" (Eliot 1975: 38). As Fanny Rinck and Françoise Boch note,

> [e]nunciative erasure is a linguistic feature: discourse is never actually cut off from the situation in which it is produced. However, enunciative erasure is exploited by theoretical discourse as a way of objectivising what is said by presenting it as independent from the situation of production; it is a discourse that is centered upon its object (the 3rd person is predominant), without deictic terms (traces of the I-here-now) and that aims to give universal truth value to what is being asserted. (Rinck and Boch 2012: 118)

But objectivised discourse does not automatically ensure any inherent truthfulness or genuine objectivity; it is a rhetorical strategy aimed at persuading the audience of the soundness of the argument. Following Catherine Kerbrat-Orecchioni, Rinck and Boch remark that objectivity should not be confused with neutrality as the impersonal tone does not imply a lack of position (ibid.). An individual perspective is always there, only it is hidden under impersonal constructions. The author's attitude can be inferred from lexical choices, modal statements, and other stylistic nuances. Perfect impartiality is a fantasy upheld by a specific register and institutional authority. Hence, while accepting the impersonal voice as the required style, I share the view that it is a stylistic-rhetorical construct, and that the enunciative act always occurs in a specific situation. One always speaks from an individual position, no matter how hard one tries to veil this. And my position is *in-between*, something that is so vividly represented by the central, transitory codex of *Oka-leczenie*. I have come to accept that – take it or leave it – I speak from a hybrid perspective. This is something I neither can, nor want to, avoid, since, as Brooke-Rose remarked about herself (1991: ix), the roles of writer and scholar are deeply interconnected, and perhaps fundamentally inseparable.

But with time I have also realised that this kind of crossbreeding may in fact be an asset. For example, it may open up vistas that can be easily overlooked when one is limited to a single perspective. Working on *Oka-leczenie* and later *(O)patrzenie* gave me a unique insight into writerly practices, while efforts to get the books published provided me with knowledge about the function of the author, the opportunities available in the process of book production, and the limitations faced. These experiences have proven invaluable in explorations of works written by writers who seem to have shared a similar attitude to literary matter. So, hesitatingly, I embrace this opportunity: I am speaking from *in-between*, striving to observe scholarly decorum, but, simultaneously, incorporating references to my own creative work in order to argue and demonstrate some points, in the hope that my hybrid discourse will appear acceptable.

Zenon Fajfer and _____'s *Mute-Eye-Late*

When Zenon formulated his idea of liberature, we had already been involved in writing a story about death and birth, closeness and distance, speech and silence. That collaboration began with two voices initially individualised, but finally merging into one. Paradoxically, our focus on language and the search for unity resulted in a book that consists of *three* discrete codices, joined by the covers of a triple-volume binding, in a manner that suggests an uneasy sense of oneness.[3] The unconventional form of the work (entitled *Oka-leczenie*, which could be rendered as "Mute-Eye-Late" or Mute-I-Late"[4]) is related to its content. The primary plot takes

---

[3] In the German tradition this book form is called "ein Mehrlingsbuch." The multiple volume binding was usually applied in order to bring together several prayer books, religious songbooks, and the Gospels, and was not uncommon in the 16th and 17th centuries in Germany, the Netherlands, France and the British Isles (cf. Christoph B. Schulz 2015: 136–141). I have been unable to identify a Polish equivalent for this kind of multiple volume binding.

[4] *Oka-leczenie* is a pun on the word "okaleczenie" (literally: "mutilation," "maiming," "wounding" or "hurting") and the phrase "oka leczenie" (which means "healing of the eye"). The insertion of the hyphen, dissecting one word into two, produces a paradoxical effect: when the word "mutilation" is cut into pieces, its meaning turns into its opposite. Related to this is the title of our other jointly written book, *(O)patrzenie*. On the one hand, it means "dressing a wound," and on the other, "the state in which something appears no longer attractive because one has got used to it (as if by looking at it for a long time)." The brackets around "O" defamiliarise the ordinary word, drawing the reader's attention to its ambiguity. This effect is enhanced by the iconic shape of the brackets, which "wrap" the separated, initial letter. Thus, without going beyond language, these titles

place in the oncology and maternity wards of a hospital, and the two "outer" volumes contain two series of conversations. One is led by a family surrounding a dying father, the other by a couple going through labour. The two liminal moments of human life are connected by a sphere of in-betweenness, a moment laden with emotional intensity that is on the verge of communicable experience, "elusive, between the tear and the breath" (Fajfer and Bazarnik 2009: lxiv). Each of the three situations is located in its own textual space, that is in a separate codex. Still, they can be interpreted as forming one story, since the codices are joined by their covers in a kind of "bookish" accordion in which none of them seems privileged, and each can function as a beginning.

Fig. 1. Zenon Fajfer and Katarzyna Bazarnik *Oka-leczenie* [Mute-Eye-Late] (2000)

The unconventional form of the book finds its parallel in an unconventional literary form. In the two "outer" parts there are no descriptive passages, no traditional narratorial summaries or commentary; they contain only dialogues in which speakers are distinguished by different typefaces. The conversations constitute the "visible" text. But beside the visible, "surface" narratives, the book also contains "invisible" texts, i.e. streams or "undercurrents" of language issuing (perhaps) from the consciousnesses

alert readers to the significance of the visual and tactile codes at work in these books, just as the hybrid term "liberature" signals the importance of the book in literature.

of the mute figures – the dying man and the baby – with whom the surrounding people are not able to communicate.[5] As Zenon explained, devising the invisible texts he wished,

> ...for the impossible: to render the very moment of death, the moment when the man is exactly In Between – when he has not fully died yet but is no longer alive, when both worlds overlap in the mind of the dying person, accompanied by his relatives unaware of what's going on... [and] to express the other impossibility – the moment of birth, when It is still There, but It will be Here in a little while, emerging from the Invisible into the Visible. (Fajfer 2010b: 37–38)

The "invisible" texts can be accessed by reading the initial letters of the visible dialogues. The procedure should be repeated several times on text thus decoded, until the reader reaches a final, single word. It is as if the word lies at the bottom of a multilayered textual structure. Technically, this is a kind of multilayered acrostic, or to be more precise, multilayered notarikon.[6] Metaphorically, it is as if the visible text were folding in or fading away, becoming reduced to one word, or perhaps even one letter. This description refers to the direction of reading. In writing, the process occurred in reverse because the subsequent layers of text were written from the bottom up. It was as if they emerged or emanated from a single word in several steps of unfolding. Hence, Zenon called it the emanational form.

The two stories in the outer codices are mostly written in the emanational form, but they also contain letters that turn into images, or images made out of letters (which we have called sign-poems) as well as figural texts, i.e. the blocks of text form different shapes. A similar oscillation between writing and image is present in the middle codex, which constitutes a kind of transitory space between the hospital stories. It is filled with two kinds of handwriting, which resemble an electrocardiogram or encephalographic waveforms. At first glance it looks like asemic writing, yet as one turns the pages one begins to distinguish emerging words,

---

[5] For more on the genesis and function of the emanational form see Fajfer "Towards Literature" (2010k: 97–106).

[6] A notarikon is a form of acrostic in which all the letters of one word can be developed into a sentence or phrase (as in an acronym). Conversely, if all the initial letters of a sentence or phrase are put together, they form a word (cf. "Notarikon," def. 1 in Sol Steinmetz's *Dictionary of Jewish Usage: A Guide to the Use of Jewish Terms*, 127–129). In the emanational form, all the words of the sentence that has been formed in this manner are further developed into another layer of text. *Oka-leczenie* contains four tiers of such overwritten texts. For an animated demonstration of the form see the online version of Fajfer's "Ars Poetica" (2007a and 2007b; access: 3 November 2015).

which finally form a legible, handwritten text on the last page. The combination of these various kinds of writing (and print), visual elements, the (black and white) colours, and the pagination, as well as the structure of the whole book, constitutes a complex semantic code,[7] complementing the linguistic one. It is a story told through words, through their visual form, and through the structure of the book.

The mutual relationship between the work's authors is also inscribed in its architecture. *Oka-leczenie* simultaneously underlines the unity of its parts, and implies their distinctness. The material form of the book acts out its double authorship; once a complementary writerly duo that has now separated, with the roles of the poet and the scholar becoming more distinct. Sixteen years ago, when Zenon wrote his "manifesto," he attempted to fuse these functions. He reflected on our own creative work and that of other writers, nonchalantly blurring the boundary between academic and literary discourse. Later he continued to theorise about, and comment upon, liberature, but he has gradually withdrawn from this activity and devoted himself entirely to poetry.

For me such a convergence of positions has always been uncomfortable, though I am guilty of a similar trespass. Despite the fact that the idea of liberature was a spin-off from our creative collaboration and passionate theoretical discussions, I did not co-author Fajfer's seminal article. I refrained from doing so because I felt uneasy with its truculent, manifesto-like style. I felt it was unsuitable for a researcher, as I considered myself to be. More importantly, I was convinced that his theoretical propositions – with which I generally sympathised – needed more grounding in research. I knew from my readerly experience that there were writers who had exploited the materiality of writing in deliberately meaningful ways, and wondered why this had been little commented on. Indeed, the practice was usually described as eccentric or experimental, if not simply dismissed outright. I was inclined to agree that such works should indeed be gathered into a distinct category and, like Fajfer, I found that literary studies was in need of more comprehensive tools that would allow it to deal satisfactorily with such works. It seemed to me that this body of work may in fact form an 'other' tradition, parallel or complementary to the mainstream one in which books are seen merely as "transparent vials" holding the precious content of "human

[7] For more extensive interpretations of the book see Kalaga "Tekst hybrydyczny" (2010b), Przybyszewska "Close Reading of the Liberatic Canon. On *Oka-leczenie* by Zenon Fajfer and Katarzyna Bazarnik" (2014a) and Matuszyk "Liberackie ciało i jego *Oka-leczenie*" (forthcoming).

spirit" (Milton in McKenzie 1999: 32). It was also evident to me that the concept Zenon proposed entailed some sort of categorisation. But at the same time I felt that his generic proposition might need a different theoretical basis than the normative, historical, tripartite generic classification that he simultaneously attempted to attack and utilise.[8]

As it happened, the idea of liberature struck a chord with some scholars, especially those involved in researching the visuality of literature, as well as electronic literature, which sixteen years ago was only just emerging as a creative practice in Poland. With time the term has come into use, but, even for those who have found the idea useful, the generic status of liberature has remained the hardest bone of contention. No wonder then that the question of genre, mentioned in an off-hand manner in the conclusion of Fajfer's 1999 "manifesto," is central to many articles mentioning or discussing the concept. My present monograph is an attempt to respond to the controversy once more, reevaluating my previous arguments in the light of recent research on genre, and relating liberature to other, similar concepts that have emerged in textual, new media and communication studies.

Overview of the content

I begin by briefly recollecting the points Fajfer raised in his seminal article. This serves as a springboard to my theoretical explorations of "material" literature, and the development of my own description of liberature. I want to make it clear that my purpose is neither a historical survey nor a comprehensive, critical reading of Fajfer's evolving and sometimes contradictory views on liberature over the years. Agnieszka Przybyszewska has already done this in her monograph *Liberackość dzieła literackiego* (Liberarines of the literary work; 2015). Rather I treat Fajfer's ideas as sources of inspiration for my own theoretical reflections on "literature in the form of the book." In doing so I select some of his comments concerning the literary medium, writing, space and time, and the book in order to demonstrate how these can be related to other, similar concepts. I indicate how liberature is indebted to modernist explorations of the materiality of writing, drawing on Jerome McGann's notion of the bibliographical

---

[8] Cf. especially Z. Fajfer, "~~lyric, epic, dramatic~~, liberature" (2010d) and "Liberum Veto? (an authorial commentary to my article 'Liberature. Appendix to a Dictionary of Literary Terms')" (2010i).

code. I discuss how liberature differs from the artist's book which emerged in the era of Modernism as a distinct, though highly heterogeneous kind of artistic practice. This is further addressed in reflections that consider overlapping questions of spatiality and materiality in literary discourse, as well as the experiential dimension of reading. Here, with recourse to cognitive poetics, I demonstrate how some of the conceptual metaphors of self-reflexive writers have materialised in their books, and how this literary practice can be related to the longing for "presence" described by H.U. Gumbrecht. I also flag affinities between liberature and other recently developed, related concepts such as N. Katherine Hayles's *technotexts*, Jessica Pressman's *bookishness*, Lori Emerson's *readingwriting interfaces*, and Alison Gibbons' analyses of multimodal literature.

As I have already said, I do not intend to write a thorough history of "materially meaningful writing," though I am convinced that this would be an exciting and necessary project. This is because I am more interested in pursuing the bone of contention noted above: Fajfer's initial impulse, sustained with hesitation over the years, to frame liberature as a (literary) genre. While sympathetic to his arguments about the significance of visual, typographic, and other "material" codes in literary works, some scholars have found this aspect of his proposal to be in need of modification, untenable, or simply wrong, chiefly because the criteria he offered as generic markers were too liberal to be functional in any serious sense. Yet I am convinced that the controversy can be partly resolved, or at least alleviated, if genre itself is rethought in line with recent research that takes into account functional, sociological, and culturally oriented approaches. Described by John Frow as "a universal dimension of textuality" genre is, after all, deeply grounded in cultural practice (2015: 2). So in the third, final part of the book I ponder such questions as why Fajfer's concept happened to be formulated in terms of genre, and how the generic framework can be viable for liberature defined "simply" as "literature in the form of the book." In other words, I attempt to explain why I still consider it sensible to speak about liberature as a genre, rather than about the liberariness of certain works, or liberatic poetics. Along with describing the formal, rhetorical and thematic dimensions of the genre, I briefly mention its sociological dimension, evident in its institutional presence: "Liberature" is also the name of an established imprint, as well as the name of a reading room, holding a special collection, in the main library of Krakow.

PART ONE

Inbetweenness

Hybridity

Admittedly, to begin with hybridity is a perplexing prospect, not least because it connotes an impure mixture, infertility, monstrosity, that which is an eye-sore. On the other hand, in the light of several of the responses that *Oka-leczenie*[9] (the first work that came to be know by the name of liberature) provoked, there seems to be no better option. Some critics, asked to review the book, admitted to mixed feelings and doubted if such an amalgam of language, typography, images, and unconventional binding could make any coherent sense at all. One reviewer explicitly described it as "neither fish nor fowl nor good red herring [or to use the literal, word for word translation: "neither dog, nor otter"]," declaring helplessness in the face of such a (monstrous) hybrid (Cuber 2003). The colloquial metaphor is suggestive of the reading since the etymology of "hybrid" can be traced back to a mongrel, something that apparently comes from the ancient Greek, and means "an insult or outrage, with special reference to lust" (Warren 1884: 501). Investigating the numerous semantic fields of the original Greek word, Josef Kuře adds to the definition a frighteningly impressive list of vices: "vainglory, pride, superciliousness, arrogance, profanation, maltreatment, high-handedness, degrade, abuse; [...] debauchery, revelry, offence, malefaction, crime, injustice," and concludes that "[t]here are not many Greek words that have such a broad palette of negative meanings as *hybris*" (2009: 12). Mythological hybrids represent a whole spectrum of monsters: from Minotaur, Chimera, Harpies, to seductive mermaids, centaurs, fauns, and the devil. And even in the case of angels and amiable divinities, such as Ganesha, there is still something uncanny about them. (Some liberatic books combine different arts, media, and materials, appearing strangely non-bookish.) In biology, the term denotes the (usually infertile) offspring of parents of different

---

[9] "Eyes-ore" was the first, tentative translation of the title. Another, more often used, is "Mute-Eye/I-Late."

species, genera or, rarely, families. (Indeed, the generic status of libera-ture has sometimes been described as an abortive idea.) Perhaps hybrid cars have more positive connotations due to their environment-friendly nature? But they still fall behind petrol-fuelled vehicles when it comes to acceleration, maximum speed, and the price, too. (Liberatic works can-not be easily scanned and speed-read, for sure. Fortunately, though a lit-tle more expensive that "ordinary" books, the price of trade editions is not prohibitive.[10])

On the contrary, in philology hybridity connotes creativity, and nu-merous fruitful combinations bear witness to this fact.[11] Linguistically, the hybrid word is a compound made up of elements from two or more tongues: examples range from 'miniskirt,' 'television,' 'biography,' 'soci-ology,' 'genocide,' 'dysfunction,' 'impartiality' to 'xenophobia,' and the eponymous 'liberature.' The extent to which such hybrid words permeate language is now evident; enriching, nuancing and enchancing the way we express thoughts and ideas. In the Bakhtinian sense, many hybrid words are the voice of the classical past, the living presence of so-called "dead" languages – Latin and Greek – in contemporary tongues. Other hybrids, such as 'allurement,' 'slogans,' 'looter,' 'thuggery,' and 'sugar-coated,' are traces of contact between different languages, often with a colonial prove-nance, constituting a kind of subversive presence of the Other in the Eng-lish language. English itself, with its mixture of Anglo-Saxon and French, and its extreme openness to loanwords, is sometimes called "a hybrid tongue" (Hitchings 2009: 2, 9). Numerous other languages could be de-scribed in these terms as well.

Comparable combinations of different semiotic codes and systems of notation are characteristic of liberatic works. The semiotician Wojciech Kalaga described this in terms of hybridity, and discussed how different semiotic modes are combined in such works in a "verbivocovisual pre-sentment" (Joyce 1989: 421), crisscrossing not only different literary forms, styles and registers, but also other arts (Kalaga 2010a). An en-hanced sense of crisscrossing is reflected in the descriptive name he of-fers when he calls liberature "a hybrid transgenre" (Kalaga 2010b: 76–77). But literature need not be "contaminated" with alien elements for

[10] See, for example, the price list of "Liberatura," a series issued by the Polish publisher Ha!art (http://ha.art.pl/sklep/index.php?k6,ksiazki-liberatura). Also relevant are books published by the London-based Visual Editions (http://visual-editions.com/).

[11] See also Dorota Gonigroszek's insightful, corpus-based study of the semantics of the word, "*Hybrid cars, hybrid theories, hybrid nails*. Corpora analyses "hybridized" with psy-cho-and sociolinguistic investigations."

hybridisation to occur. In literary genre studies, Ireneusz Opacki considered hybridity to be the major generative force in the emergence of new genres, "a determinant of the evolution of poetry" (2000: 121). He described the dynamism of generic transformations in terms of a political power play (and a celebrity culture, perhaps). In the hierarchy of a given historical moment one genre dominates the literary scene, and achieves the status of the "royal genre," which exerts a powerful influence on other forms that "follow" its style, engendering them and lending its own distinct features (122). This pushes us to consider the etymology of the term itself, which entails an evident valorising hierarchisation.

In Latin "hybrid" meant "the child of a free man and a slave,"[12] which points to an imbalance between blended elements. (In liberature this could be redefined in terms of the literary dominant.) This hints at the dominance that characterizes the relation of coloniser to colonised, especially given that Roman slaves usually came from colonised peoples. Homi Bhabha, who theorises hybridity in a political and cultural context, points to its origin in "an intervening space." This is a space of mixture, syncretism, or confluence, a site of simultaneous confrontation and fusion of different traditions, sensibilities, and languages, which consequently becomes "the space of intervention" (Bhabha 1994: 7). For the American-Indian scholar, hybridity is then,

> ...the sign of the productivity of colonial power, its shifting forces and fixities; it is the name for the strategic reversal of the process of domination through disavowal (that is, the production of discriminatory identities that secure the 'pure' and original identity of authority). Hybridity is the revaluation of the assumption of colonial identity through the repetition of discriminatory identity effects. It displays the necessary deformation and displacement of all sites of discrimination and domination. It unsettles the mimetic or narcissistic demands of colonial power but reimplicates its identifications in strategies of subversion that turn the gaze of the discriminated back upon the eye of power. (112)

Its creative energy comes from a reversal of perspectives, and from *différance* entailed in the fact that it is unsettlingly impossible to repeat or imitate the word and world of the Other. With regard to discourse,

[12] "Hybrid." Oxford Dictionaries site. Oxford University Press, http://www.oxforddictionaries.com/definition/english/hybrid?searchDictCode=all (access: 19 February 2015).

hybridity happens in an "'in-between' reality" and is the outcome of the pressure of colonial power on local speech (13). What emerges here is a blended voice that is neither fully that of the hegemonic culture, nor that of the subalterns. Bearing traces of its double origin, this strange, new language (mis)translates, disfigures, de-forms, and (con)fuses the language of authority with the seemingly subjugated idiom (cf. 33, 37–38). By picking up and (re)using the language of power, the colonised are able to reassess and redefine both themselves and the colonisers, while at the same time presenting them with a disturbing image in which the conquerors can hardly recognise themselves.

Bhabha discusses the dynamics of hybridity in a cultural and political context, but let me apply these ideas to the world of writers and critics, since a comparable reciprocal relation may illuminate the circumstances in which Fajfer formulated his idea. In Bhabha's argument a daring act of "looking back" into "the eyes that fix you in a formulated phrase" (Eliot 1963: 15) is a significant gesture, triggering a process of redefinition, because it challenges the accepted "vectors" of gaze. No longer does the coloniser look *down on* the subordinated subject with "the force of authority," and the colonized *up to* the master. Rather they look *at* each other on equal terms. While they are *at* it, a third space emerges between them in which they are on the same level. They are *in* it, they share it, though it does not belong exclusively or fully to one or the other. Even if it is potentially charged with hostility,[13] it is a different, third space constituted *in between* their 'I's/eyes. The dynamics of gazing, constituting the space of in-betweenness, is captured in *Heart of Darkness* when Marlow exchanges glances with his helmsman hit by a spear: "Something big appeared in the air before the shutter, the rifle went overboard, and the man stepped back swiftly, *looked at me* over his shoulder in an extraordinary, profound, familiar manner, and fell upon my feet" (Conrad 1994: 65; emphasis mine). When he falls down, and his blood soaks Marlow's shoes, the narrator is forced to look down. "The man had rolled on his back and *stared* straight *up at* me; both his hands clutched that cane," he describes. But at this moment the vectors of gaze are changing: "He looked *at me* anxiously, gripping the spear like something precious, with an air of being afraid I would try to take it away from him. I had to make an effort to free my eyes from his gaze and attend to the steering" (66). At the moment of death, the black man's gaze is directed not *up to* but

---

[13] Note how the idiomatic phrase "at it" connotes aggression, violence and sexual domination, evoking a similar cluster of associations entangled with colonial domination.

simply *at* the whites; it poses an unspeakable question and holds a mirror up to them, reflecting their images back. In "the vacant glassiness" of his eyes, they see the same hollowness which Marlow identifies in Kurtz:

> We two whites stood over him, and his lustrous and inquiring glance enveloped us both. I declare it looked as though he would presently put to us some questions in an understandable language; but he died without uttering a sound, without moving a limb, without twitching a muscle. Only in the very last moment, as though in response to some sign we could not see, to some whisper we could not hear, he frowned heavily, and that frown gave to his black death-mask an inconceivably sombre, brooding, and menacing expression. The lustre of inquiring glance faded swiftly into vacant glassiness. (67)

The symbolic structure of dominance seems to be maintained by their physical positions, but the redefinition of the relationship, initiated by their cooperation on board the steamer and sealed in the final exchange of gazes, is reaffirmed. It has left an indelible mark on Marlow, who admits that he is "not prepared to affirm the fellow [Kurtz] was exactly worth the life we lost in getting him. I missed my late helmsman awfully, – I missed him even while his body was still lying in the pilot-house. [...] And the intimate profundity of that look he gave me when he received his hurt remains to this day in my memory – like a claim of distant kinship affirmed in a supreme moment" (73). The exchange of gazes effectively reverses the established hierarchy of significance; it makes Marlow declare that the subaltern's life is worth more than the coloniser's. The experience of the wound, the gaze, and the death let him see "with the other eyes."

Liberature: an appendix
to a dictionary of literary terms

Incidentally, the question of gaze is also central to Fajfer's work. As a theme it features in the titles of his individual and collaborative books: *Oka-lecze-nie*, *(O)patrzenie*, *Spoglądając przez ozonową dziurę*, *Powieki*, and *Widok z głębokiej wieży*; which mean respectively: "healing/hurting of the eye," "(over)looking," "looking through an ozone hole," "eyelids," and "a view from a deep tower." It is also at the heart of his programmatic, emanational poem "Ars poetica," whose "invisible" lines spell out the urge "to see with your eyes, differently, to have other (different) eyes, to go, to see but with your and my eyes" (Fajfer 2007b)[14] as if to erase the distance between different individual selves in order to merge them into hybrid I's/ eyes. So perhaps it was no coincidence that the poet turned his gaze towards literature's Other.

Whoever should be cast in the role of coloniser and colonized here, it so happened that Fajfer spoke from a position of in-betweenness. Although he has always considered himself a creative writer, by provocatively entitling his essay "Liberature. Appendix to the Dictionary of Literary Terms"[15] (1999) he ventured into the foreign land of theorising. The title suggested

---

[14] Also anthologised in *Electronic Literature Collection vol. 3*, http://collection.eliterature. org/3/work.html?work=ars-poetica. For the English translation see *Techsty. Magazyn 3* (2007), http://techsty.art.pl/magazyn3/fajfer/Ars_poetica_english.html (access: 3 November 2015).

[15] See footnote 1. An English translation of the article first appeared in *Liberature*, a 32-page booklet prepared by Fajfer and the present author for the 5th International Symposium on Iconicity in Language and Literature, held jointly by the Universities of Krakow and Amsterdam in Krakow in March 2005 (Bazarnik and Fajfer 2005b), and then in Fajfer's bilingual collection of essays *Liberature or Total Literature* (2010a). All references are to this more easily available edition. Additionally, the article has been reprinted in English in vol. 2 of *Vlak Magazine*, a journal of contemporary poetics and the arts (2011), and it appreared in Danish in *Den Blå Port, tidsskrift for litteratur* (Fajfer 2008).

it was to be a scholarly text, a gloss of critical terminology, and an addition to the toolkit of analytical concepts. But the essay opens with a truculent tone, full of colourful comparisons, sweeping statements, emotive vocabulary, and a rhetorical question concerning the alleged "exhaustion of literature" (Fajfer 2010b: 23–24). Stylistically, it resembles an artistic manifesto rather than a restrained scholarly article. It has no apparatus, no footnotes, nor bibliography. Only after a passionate introduction does the argument move to more critical and philosophical reflections in which the author poses a series of questions concerning the medium of literature, form, space and time of the literary work, and the book.

Employing definitions from a popular, comprehensive dictionary of literary terms as a foil,[16] Fajfer argued for an acknowledgement of what he believed had been overlooked by scholarly analyses, namely the semantic potential of the materiality of language. He asked:

> 1. Is language the only medium of literature? Or could an actual piece of paper be such a medium as well, a piece of paper that the writer is going to cover with black writing? Or perhaps, for some important reason, the page should be black and the writing white? Who said that the colour of the page must always be white? This is only a convention that writers automatically follow. (24)

As he claimed, this aspect of literary writing had been largely ignored in criticism[17] due to a "Cartesian split" between books' material bodies and their immaterial content (Fajfer 2010b: 23–24, 25). Around the same time N. Katherine Hayles, in her 2002 work *Writing Machines*, raised the point in very similar terms. She noted that, while some modernist works and even legal cases might belie the fact, the predominance and hence transparency of print had resulted in ignoring "the specificities of the CODEX book when discussing literary texts. With significant exceptions, print literature was widely regarded as not having a body, only a speaking mind" (Hayles 2002: 32). For Hayles and Fajfer this likewise

16 M. Głowiński, T. Kostkiewiczowa, A. Okopień-Sławińska, J. Sławiński, *Słownik terminów literackich* [A Dictionary of Literary Terms], 2nd enlarged and corrected ed., Wrocław, Warszawa, Krakow, Gdańsk, Łódź: Ossolineum, 1989.

17 Admittedly, it was marginally present in some Polish theoretical reflections, signalled as potentially worth exploring by Stefania Skwarczyńska, Henryk Markiewicz, and tackled in discussions of the modernist avant-garde (Rypson 2000) and concrete poetry (Sławek 1989). Agnieszka Przybyszewska notes that it was also commented on by Polish bibliographers such as Janusz Lalewicz, Teodor Zbierski, and Karol Głombiowski (2015: 297–316).

leads to a situation in which the literary work is identified with "an intellectual construction" (which can be understood as an Ingradenian intentional object) communicated through disembodied, dematerialised discourse. Yet, as the American scholar argues, the materiality of literature has a semantic dimension, which she sees as an emergent quality resulting from "interactions between physical properties and a work's artistic strategies" (33). The writer may activate this aesthetic and semantic potential if he or she wishes. It also entails the reader's involvement "with the work and the critical strategies she develops – strategies that include physical manipulations as well as conceptual frameworks" (ibid.), a description which echoes Fajfer's claims about the significance of the book and the presence of the reader.

While pondering the nature of the literary work, Fajfer further postulated that literature's material features can be integrated into the writer's rhetorical repertoire. Alongside stylistic choices, decisions concerning the selection of specific fonts, typography, layout, pagination, presence or absence of illustrations, kinds of paper, and the overall architecture of the book have a bearing on what a work expresses and how it is understood:

> The above-mentioned Polish dictionary of literary terms defines "form" as an established model according to which particular literary works are created and "literary work" as a meaningful creation in language (an utterance) fulfilling the criteria of literariness accepted in a given time and culture, and, in particular, the criterion of congruence with generally accepted standards of artistry. Do these definitions also encompass a reflection on the physical shape of the book? Do the shape and structure of the book constitute an integral part of the literary work, or are they only the concern of printers, desktop publishers, binders, and editors, and a matter of complying with generally accepted standards?
>
> [...]
>
> Shouldn't the shape of the cover, shape and direction of the writing, format, colour, the number of pages, words, and even letters be considered by the writer just like any other element of his work, an element requiring as much attention as choosing rhymes and thinking up a plot? (Fajfer 2010b: 25)

For him all material aspects of inscription may be implemented as auxiliary means of expression. When used deliberately, they function as a "material rhetoric" that needs to be read along with figures of thought and speech expressed through words. In short, like some writers and poets before him,[18] Fajfer calls for the self-conscious use of non-verbal, material means of expression, as well as for the unity of the "physical and spiritual aspects of the literary work (...) [that] should complement each other to create a harmonious effect" (25). In other words, a hybrid discourse that combines within the space of the book literary and other semantic codes, should, in Fajfer's call, be recognized as legitimate.

Fajfer's reflections are obviously in tune with some of the ideas expressed in the practices and programmatic writings of the early twentieth century avant-garde, futurists, constructivists, concrete poets, American and British postmodernists. Alongside them he grants a prominent place to Stephané Mallarmé, James Joyce, Laurence Sterne, and William Blake as radical visionaries of the Book who transgressed and expanded boundaries of poetic expression.[19] In doing so he does not stick to historical order but picks those who, in his opinion, transgressed and expanded the boundaries of poetic expression. All these writers demonstrate how the visual and material features of texts can function as a parallel code to language, complementary to or dialogic with it. Describing it as a code reliant on "the symbolic and signifying dimensions of the physical medium through which (or rather *as* which) the linguistic text is embodied"

---

[18] For poets and writers anticipating liberature in different ways, see Bazarnik and Fajfer's "A Brief History of Liberature" (2005a). In this article we mention Egyptian hieroglyphs coordinated with the space of the tombs, ancient classical visual and figural texts, magic squares, or other combinations of text and image, as well as works characterised by carefully designed compositions, such as Dante's *The Divine Commedy*, or George Herbert's *The Temple*, Sterne's *Tristram Shandy*, Blake's illuminated books, such as *The Marriage of Heaven and Hell* symbolically addressing the union of the material and the spiritual, Mallarmé's poetry, especially his unrealised project of le Livre, Marinetti's words at liberty, dadaists' mocking jests, Apollinaire's *Caligrammes*, Cendrars and Delaunay's *Prose of the Trans-Siberian Journey*, Przyboś and Strzemiński's *Z ponad*, as well and 20th century concrete poetry and postmodernist fiction. Similar, holistic approach to the book is also evident in works of Stanisław Wyspiański, Bruno Schulz and James Joyce (these are discussed in Kamisińska 2006; Kato 2012 and 2014; and Bazarnik 2002a, 2007a, and 2011). All of them exemplify McLuhan's adage "medium is the message". This is also discussed by Przybyszewska in her comprehensive monograph *Liberackość dzieła literackiego*, in which she analyses connections between contemporary writers, and functional typography, concrete poetry, artists' books, and last but not least, electronic literature, testing the extent of any potential overlap.

[19] He often mentions them in his essays on liberature and, with the exception of Blake, he devotes whole articles to them: "Joyce – Unwelcome Guest in Plato's Republic," "The Muse of Liberature (or Who's Afraid of Widow Wadman)," "Two Throws of the Dice or The Special and General Theory of Liberature" (with the present author) and "~~lyric, epic, dramatic~~, liberature" (the last two feature Mallarmé). Theatre artists were another important source of his inspiration, something that I discuss in the chapter "The book as a performative space."

(McGann 1991: 56–57), Jerome McGann called it the bibliographical code. The textual scholar argues that the physical appearance of a book *always* carries some meaning, but it is usually dictated by publishers. It embodies their set of motivations, principles, and ideologies, and is typically utilised to serve their marketing and promotional aims, while it is very rarely used by writers.[20] That is why he considers published documents as objects of social, collective, though traditionally uncredited, authorship (ibid.).[21] In *Black Riders: The Visible Language of Modernism* (1993) McGann argues that modernism marks an unacknowledged turning point in authorial use of the bibliographical code for expressive purposes. He demonstrates that such an authorial form was in fact a consistent and fairly widespread strategy among modernist poets, who used "expressive book design" to expand "spaces of signification" (McGann 1993: 80). According to the scholar, this was a significant cultural moment when creative writers (mostly poets) began to consider the physicality of the book as part of their literary projects.

Perhaps that is why Fajfer's concept of liberature is so closely entangled with modernism (Ranocchi 2012: 33–34; see also Bazarnik 2014). The Polish poet stresses that in order for a work to be described as liberatic, the semiotisation of the physicality of a work must result from writerly choices, motivated by expressive and aesthetic purposes, and not from other agents involved in book production and distribution. Emiliano Ranocchi identifies this as the desire for an "homogenised" language (2012: 33), i.e. a style that successfully hybridises its multimodal components. So choices regarding the material features of the book are not "accidentals" that can be freely changed and modified in subsequent editions by a new production team, but "substantives"[22] deliberately shaped by the author of

---

[20] See also Bazarnik "Introduction: Modernist Roots of Liberature" (2014).

[21] It is typically only the author of the text who is identified as "the author" on the book cover. However, the situation is clearly more complex than this, as reflected in copyright law. For example, in the UK copyright protection also covers layout, font, and the format of a text for 25 years after publication (cf. NTU Library "Copyright for Researchers" 2014). Obviously, different editions of "the same text" are sometimes protected by copyright law, an acknowledgement of the editor's "authorial" contribution to the shape of the text.

[22] In "The Rationale of Copy-Text" W.W. Greg defines substantives as "readings of the text, those namely that affect the author's meaning or the essence of his expression." By contrast, accidentals pertain mainly to the form of presentation and do not affect authorially intended meaning. Greg does not, however, treat the two categories as entirely distinct and absolute, admitting that "there is an intermediate class of word-forms about the assignment of which opinions may differ" (1950/1951: 21). Moreover, authors may change substantives, whether verbal or non-verbal. For example, this might

the *text* who, as a consequence, becomes the author of the *book*. Otherwise, Fajfer remarks, "one would have to agree with Raymond Federman and admit that one shares the authorship of one's masterpieces with the editor, typesetter, and manuscript reviser; and what writer would like to do that?" (2010b: 25). He is strongly attached to the idea of individual authorship, and feels "the deep need of a single creative mind" (Ranocchi 2014: 111), which can be reasserted by taking control of the material form of the text, and which Ranocchi associates with the modernist concept of the autonomy of the artist.

When the writer assumes their responsibilities, and deliberately exploits the materiality of language, he or she employs material rhetoric as a consistent writerly strategy. However, material rhetoric has been defined not only as a publishers' or writers' practice, but also as "a mode of interpretation that takes as its object of study the signification of material things and corporeal entities – objects that signify not through language but through their spatial organization, mobility, mass, utility, orality, and tactility" (Dickson 1999: 297). Informed by sociologically oriented bibliography, as well as textual and communication studies, such an approach consists of reading closely "not only the disembodied content of rhetoric", "but also the embodied texts, the material elements of their production and distribution." It examines how editorial decisions and publishing practices influence the ideological content of published texts (Collins 1999: 546). So it is a comprehensive interpretive strategy that embraces decoding a text, reading its stylistic and physical texture, as well as considering the contexts in which the work functions; in sum a kind of culturally and historically informed multimodal analysis. Related to it are other critical strategies derived from studies of perception in the fine arts, which in turn inform cognitive stylistics, studies of the grammar of images and visual design, studies of the intermedia, new media and electronic literature, which have evolved into multimodality studies, medium-specific analysis, and somatic criticism, as well as sociologically informed analyses of literature.[23] All of the above of-

---

■

occur when a text is revised, and the wording altered, during the preparation of a new edition. I borrow Greg's distinction here because it usefully illuminates the role of the author in text production.

[23] I return to this point later, and for now simply flag significant names who are pertinent to literary studies: for the aforementioned studies in multimodality see part 2 of the present book along with N. Katherine Hayles' *Writing Machines* (2002), Jessica Pressman's *Digital Modernism* (2014), and Lori Emerson's *Reading Writing Interfaces* (2014). See also Adam Dziadek's *Projekt krytyki somatycznej* (2014), and

fer tools and concepts necessary to read and interpret the works of authors who deliberately go beyond purely verbal expression and employ material rhetoric.

Fajfer's manifesto was, firstly, a call to acknowledge the distinctness of the organic union of content and form, of literature and the book, and, secondly, a call to analyse this material using such critical procedures as those mentioned above. He pointed out that this should involve interdisciplinary tools, combining an analysis of the materiality of writing with traditional literary concepts. Amongst these concepts, genre plays an important (though controversial) role. Fajfer closed his seminal essay with the suggestion that we should recognise liberature's generic distinctness:

> Be it called literature or rather liberature, the matter of terminology is of secondary importance. This is a concern for theoreticians, not writers. Perhaps we could find a compromise solution, for example, acknowledge that beside the three major literary modes: lyric, epic and dramatic (which, by no means, suffice to describe the richness of literature), there is one more that may be called "liberatic" that would include all the kinds of works discussed above. But, whatever the case, I believe that this fourth, still officially unacknowledged, mode will infuse new life into literature. This genre may be the future of literature (2010b: 28).

Fajfer's claims regarding the physical dimensions of literature may have seemed bold or provocative at the turn of the millennium. But he can now be viewed as another voice in an international chorus of writers, scholars, and researchers who have acknowledged this important layer of literary writing. Therefore, before I tackle specifically the most contentious question of liberature's generic identity, in the following chapters I explore some analogous reflections. My aim is to demonstrate how material rhetoric has informed some (often not so) marginal works, and how an awareness of this rhetoric has gradually percolated into literary studies.

Agnieszka Przybyszewska's *Liberackość dzieła literackiego* (2015). With regard to the sociology of literature, Pierre Bourdieu's *Rules of Art: Genesis and Structure of the Literary Field* (1995), and the work of C. Miller, C. Bazerman, and A. Bawarshi concerning genre as social practice, provide some relevant context.

PART TWO

Liberature
and related concepts

Literature
in the form of the book

Liberature and the artist's book

Fajfer's claim that liberature ought to be understood as a distinct *literary* genre is perhaps more understandable when one realises that that was intended to counteract an identification of his material poetics with the kind of material rhetoric that features prominently in artists' books.[24] This fuzzy, highly heterogeneous, and inclusive field of creative practice can, like liberature, trace its roots to innovative modernist publications,[25] William Blake's artistic individualism embodied in

[24] Indeed, initial responses to prototypical copies of *Oka-leczenie* proved that critics trained to ignore the materiality of literary discourse felt rather helpless. Either they openly admitted this, or they suggested that the work was nothing more than an artist's book; an object perhaps interesting to look at, but not to be read (cf. Cuber 2003; Jankowicz 2003).

[25] Johanna Drucker has written extensively and informatively about this; see her *The Century of Artists' Books* (1994, reissued in 2004), *The Visible Word: Experimental Typography and Modern Art, 1909–1923* (1994), and *Figuring the Word: Essays on Books, Writing, and Visual Poetics* (1998). Other scholars exploring modernist book art include Marjorie Perloff in *The Futurist Moment: Avant-Garde, Avant Guerre, and the Language of Rupture* (1986, new ed. 2003) and her other publications, as well as Megan L. Benton with her essay on "The Book as Art," in *A Companion to the History of the Book* (2007). Lisa Otty explored this topic in her PhD dissertation "Signals and noise: art, literature and the avant-garde" (2008) and her entry on "Small Press Modernists" in *The Aesthetics of Matter. Modernism, the Avant-Grade and Material Exchange* (2013). Gunilla Hermansson also contributed a piece on "Expressionism, Fiction and Intermediality in Nordic Modernism" to this collection. Finally, Torben Jelsbak's *Ekspressionisme: modernismens formelle gennembrud i dansk malerkunst og poesi* (2005) is also relevant.

the book, and a long tradition of visual and figurative poetry. Present in many languages, the term has culturally-specific, and often mutually exclusive, referents and connotations. In Poland, the artist's book is strongly associated with the visual arts (Rypson 2000; Dawidek Gryglicka 2012). Simply put, the term refers to a self-contained, autonomous artistic work expressed through or inspired by the form of the book, which is historically grounded in the rich tradition of the Polish literary avant-garde, and the strict control of printing technologies in communist Poland.[26] Importantly, the artist's book may include text (in the conservative sense of a verbal message), but this needn't be so. This qualification is more relevant to the American or Polish traditions of book art, and contestable in the context of the French *livre d'artiste*, which refers to a joint composition by a poet and a painter, often inspired and coordinated by an editor and typographer.[27] So in it text is an important component, the feature *livre d'artiste* shares with liberature. In the artist's book, moreover, there is no need for the text to be authored by the person who designs, illustrates, and makes the work. The work can be a typographically innovative presentation or artistic adaptation of someone else's text, a found text, or a textual collage. Furthermore, the semantic and literary dimensions of the text may be of little or no importance to the meaning of the work, as in Zbigniew Sałaj's *Miękka książka* (Soft Book), which is in fact closer to a book-based sculpture or installation.[28]

But generally speaking, regardless of local differences, artists' books are considered to be hybrid forms that are situated between literature, the visual arts, sculpture, installation, and even the happening.

---

[26] Piotr Rypson has discussed this fascinating topic in several publications, and this subject definitely requires further, separate studies; something that is beyond the scope of the present book. Suffice it to briefly mention here that, due to censorship restrictions, access to printing equipment was restricted to visual artists. They moreover needed to obtain permission to purchase paper, ink, etc. Dawidek Gryglicka's impressive study of text in visual arts in post-1970's Poland contains much relevant information, too.

[27] For more of the French perspective on the artists' book see Anne Moeglin-Delcroix, *Esthétique du livre d'artiste. Une introduction à l'art contemporain* (1997). See also Jean Khalfa *The Dialogue Between Painting and Poetry: Livres D'artistes, 1874–1999* (2001), and Elza Adamowicz "The *livre d'artiste* in the twentieth-century France" (2009).

[28] Sałaj's work can be seen on-line in the Polish Book Art Collection, see: "Polska Książka Artystyczna z Przełomu XX i XXI wieku," Muzeum Książki, Łódź, Poland, http://kolekcja.bookart.pl/info/viewpub/tid/4/pid/89.

As Johanna Drucker explains, they can have diverse shapes, use various materials, "participate in every possible tradition of book making, every possible 'ism' of mainstream art and literature, every possible mode of production, [...] every degree of ephemerality or archival durability" (2004: 14).[29] As Drucker contends, the category is so broad that "[t]here are no specific criteria for defining what the term covers," and it is "as little bound by constraints of medium or form as those more familiar rubrics 'painting' and 'sculpture'" (ibid.). Despite her broad approach to the artist's book, Drucker would most likely exclude Sałaj's book-based works from the category, and classify them as "book-like objects" or "sculptural book works," because she is convinced that their "legitimate identity is in the realm of sculpture where the book-like object loses its functional identity as a book and becomes a formal and metaphoric icon serving a distinct – and different – aesthetic agenda" (2000; 2004: 361–362).

Although Drucker and Fajfer would probably agree on this point, in fact they address two related, but non-identical, phenomena. Despite some striking similarities between liberature and artists' books – such as a liberal approach to conventions, materials, modes, and media – liberature is narrower in its generic claims and affiliations. Fajfer has always insisted that liberature should be understood as a kind of book-bound writing with a clear literary dominant, in which all other dimensions are subservient to the linguistic code (2010l). In other words, the theoretical motivation in proposing liberature was to distinguish a group of literary works whose authors have intentionally shaped the physical form of the work for expressive purposes. Such works are separate from other forms of literary writing, wherein the author is unconcerned with this (Bazarnik 2009). So liberature is better understood as a kind of "expanded" literature, aware of its spatial, embodied nature, and of the semantic dimension of the material form, often demonstrating "self-awareness" in self-reflective or metatextual comments. It is the art of the word, grounded in written (or printed) verbal communication. And though it may hybridise other arts and media, it prioritises language as its major semantic code (Fajfer 2010d: 43). As Fajfer poetically puts it in another manifesto-like article:

---

[29] See also Chappell's "Typologising the artist's book" (2003), and Phillpot "Books, book-works, book objects, artists' books" (1982).

Word is the substance of literature.
When we say the word, we stress its sound and sense,
when we write the word, we (sometimes) also mean its **appearance**.
Space
is hardly ever taken into consideration, if at all.
However, in order to come into existence in time
the word needs   space.
Space belongs to it as much as its

shape,

soUnd

and

meaning.

The word thus conceived is the substance of

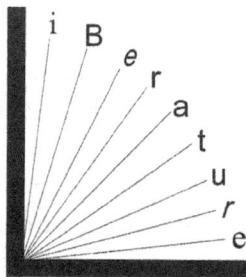

Liberature
or total literature
in which the text and the space of a book constitute an inseparable whole.

Fig. 2. Zenon Fajfer, an excerpt from "~~lyric, epic, dramatic,~~ liberature" (2010d: 43)

He goes on to say that, in this kind of writing, "[t]he physical object ceases to be a mere carrier of text; the book does not contain a literary work, but it is itself the literary work" (2010d: 44; original emphasis). Hence, a helpful rule of thumb in distinguishing between liberature and the artist's book is to check if the author affiliates her/himself with literature. If they do, their works should be considered literary (even if they radically depart from the conventional codex), and consequently may be regarded as liberature.[30] Fajfer has aptly demonstrated this with his own "bottled" poem *Spoglądając przez ozonową dziurę* (Detect Ozone Whole Nearby, 2004). As I have argued elsewhere, here Fajfer disagrees

[30] See especially his two essays: "(N)on Description of Liberature" (2010f), and "How liberature redefines the artist's book" (2010l).

with Clive Phillpot, who considers "a writer's book" to be an abortive idea (Bazarnik 2011: 53–54). Phillpot is convinced that it was the book artists who contributed most to "the revitalisation of the books as art […] and to the development of the visual and verbi-visual languages articulated within the book form" (Phillpot 1986). But the history of literature offers sufficient examples to refute his claim. Moreover, Fajfer and I are convinced that such critical blindness with regard to the existence and importance of such works, stems partly from the lack of a term that could point to their specificity (Bazarnik 2005b). Unlike the artist's book then, liberature foregrounds the fact that it is "literature in the form of the book."[31]

Book is a meaningful space

This seemingly unequivocal statement, however, calls for a reflection on the book. Accordingly, in the conclusion of his "Appendix," Fajfer implies a reevalution of the book in the context of literary writing. Noting that the codex has become its staple form, he envisages other options available to writers, if only they would care to think about them (this point he develops in his later articles).[32] This is because, in his view, one should think about the book as a space to be traversed; a space that offers the reader the opportunity to choose an individual textual path. This, in turn, determines the spatio-temporal shape of the world evoked by the text, and brings into play the reader's temporality as a meaningful factor (2010b: 27).[33] But even the traditional codex, when treated with consideration, can offer different possibilities. This is demonstrated by Cortázar's *Hopscotch*, in which several reading paths (hence, several different plots) are suggested in the table of instructions provided by the author. The book thus conceived can, as a consequence, no longer be seen as a transparent container for meaning, or a semantically neutral vehicle for the signifier (Bazarnik 2012b). Rather it is the space of embodied inscription that participates in the production of sense. Its physical construction (shape, format, pagination, etc.) and internal setup (divisions into volumes, chapters, sections, paragraphs, or verses, etc., as well as their typographically

[31] The phrase was used in the title of the talk we gave at the conference "Traditional and emerging formats of artists books: Where do we go from here?" at the School of Creative Arts, University of the West of England, Bristol, UK, on 10th July 2009.
[32] See Fajfer "Liberature: hyperbook in the hypertext era" (2010e), and Bazarnik and Fajfer "A Brief History of Liberature" (2005a).
[33] See also my article "Chronotope in Liberature" (2010a).

Literature in the form of the book

45

marked borders) become akin to architectural structures that combine practical, aesthetic and symbolic functions. So Fajfer explains, "[i]t does not have to be an all-embracing Book, but it should at least be a Book embracing the whole of... the book, in which all the elements, not only the text, are meaningful" (2010b: 28). In other words, it is the sum total of conceptual and material elements that make up a literary work. Hence, the other name he also used was "total literature," a collocation that evokes rather unfortunate overtones, which I address later.

Liberature, the hybrid name he coined for the postulated genre, points to the fact that such spatialised, multicoded writing is inextricably bound up with the material form of the book. He envisaged it as a book-bound type of literature, with the provision that the form of the book needn't be limited to the codex. Basically, the term can be extended to any material object that serves as the space of inscription. But this entails the fact of reproducibility: the liberatic book is not a unique, single copy; it is a democratic object of which a number of copies can be manufactured. Such a book embraces historical forms such as the scroll, the codex, the leporello, a bunch of unbound sheets collected together, or folded, or rolled, or bound in any way imaginable, yet forming a materially discrete, self-contained, conceptual entity. It may consist of a collection or constellation of loose pages, cards, or signatures, as in the case of the book-in-the-box (also called "shuffle literature," see Husárová and Montfort 2012). It is by no means limited to one-of-a-kind artworks, but is intended to be reproducible.[34] This may be another feature distinguishing it from the artist's book. Its form is contingent on verbal content, so the liberatic book becomes a function of meanings communicated by the text. And this is a reciprocal relationship since the shape of the book nudges the reader to follow the text in particular ways. So additional meanings emerge from specific distributions of text in and across the space of the material book, suggesting that it should be treated as a navigating device rather than as a container. This is also related to a broader question, studied by communication scholars, anthropologists of writing, and designers, who recognise that "[t]he point is that meanings aren't just in the written text, but partly come from where the text is physically placed in the world. Language in space and time" (Hamilton 2005: 378).

The space thus determined can be described as compositional space.[35] It is one of four types of iconic space distinguished by C.D. Malmgren in

---

[34] This is put into practice by the eponymous imprint of the Krakow-based publishing house Korporacja Ha!art, edited since 2003 by Fajfer and the present author.

[35] I discuss this in more detail in the article "Liberature: a New Literary Genre?" (2007b).

his study of postmodern American fiction. He defines the iconic space as the space of inscription, "involved in the fact that [the] speech act must be recorded on some sort of physical medium" (1985: 39). This space owes its name to the fact that the material features of literary discourse, which function as signifiers, remain in a relationship of resemblance with the signifieds conveyed by the text. Its subtypes, i.e. the alphabetic, lexical, paginal, and compositional spaces, are generated though a specific arrangement of printed language on the writing surface, motivated by senses that are verbally communicated. The most common, "default" type of compositional space is established when consecutive pages contain a chronologically or causally ordered sequence of textual units. This type of the compositional space is materially realised in the form of the codex, that is, as a set of bound, progressively numbered pages, with lines of text running from left to right (in scripts based on Latin, Greek and Cyrillic alphabets; and from right to left in Arabic, Hebrew, and Japanese scripts), from the top of the page down to the bottom. This material form prompts readers to follow the text in a linear fashion, from the first page to the last. As a widely used convention, it has become so transparent that it is considered irrelevant to both the concretisation of a fictional world, and interpretations of literary texts.

But it is worth noting that phenomenological approaches to reading acknowledge, covertly, this sequential space as a space that supports the gradual unfolding of discourse, such as the linear progression of plot, and understand it as a meaning-generating device. For example, Wolfgang Iser remarks that: "[i]f one regards the sentence sequence as a continual flow, this implies that the anticipation aroused by one sentence will generally be realized by the next, and the frustration of one's expectations will arouse feelings of exasperation" (1972: 284). So the reader's experience, when he or she anticipates a continual flow, is enhanced when the default compositional space is realised in the form of the codex. Conversely, "feelings of exasperation" are often evoked by "experimental" texts in which readers encounter works that are deliberately fragmented, going against the easy flow. This experience enforces "the search for connections between the fragments; the object of this is not to complicate the 'spectrum' of connections, so much as to make us aware of the nature of our own capacity for providing links" (285). When the reader perceives incongruity between the form of the book and the compositional structure (space) of the text, this makes him or her seek explanations, interpretations, or justifications. Of course, though Iser does not mention this, fragmentariness can affect not only the grammatical, narrative or stylistic strata, but also the typographic and spatial arrangement of the text. Unconventional page layouts in combination with some discursive, metatextual elements, as well as interventions in the material structure of the book, subvert this default space. The reader therefore becomes involved in determining their own paths through a text, increasing their awareness of their own anticipations and interpretive involvement. Thereby they engage in shaping a sequence of narrative units in a way that is different from reading "traditional texts," becoming aware of the space of the book as an embodiment of the compositional space of the work (Malmgren 1985: 45–49).

To support his argument, Malmgren quotes Raymond Federman, who explains that devices that draw the reader's attention to the compositional space can "liberate the fiction so that it may invent, create on the spot its own syntax as it progresses" (Federman in Malmgren 1985: 48). In fact, remarks by Fajfer – questions and appeals that are included in his "Appendix" – echo, and enter into dialogue with, Federman's propositions as put forward in "Surfiction." The French-American novelist likewise postulates that it should be "the writer (and not modern printing technology) who must, through innovations in the writing itself – in the typography and topology of his writing – renew our system of reading" (Federman 1981: 9). He is convinced that if the novel, the genre which preoccupies him most, is to become an art form, "we must raise the printed word as the medium," "the printed word as it is presented on the page, as it is perceived, heard read, visualised (not only abstractedly but concretely) by the receiver" (10). Not only does Fajfer agree with the proposition that the spatial and visual features of print can be used as a vehicle for meaning, complementing linguistic senses, but (as stated above) he also notes the semantic potential of the very materiality of the writing surface.

Malmgren's iconic spaces can be understood in terms of texture, which cognitive poetics conceives as "the experienced quality of textuality" (Stockwell 2009: 1). In my view, this concept allows readers to handle both linguistic variants of style, along with visual and material dimensions of language. As Peter Stockwell explains, "[l]iterature draws attention to its own condition of existence, which is its texture" including "a sense that the materiality of the object is noticeable alongside any content that is communicated through it" (Stockwell 2002: 167). He states that, when reading, we encounter a literary text in ways analogous to visual, spatial, and tactile experiences. So, for example, when seemingly minor elements are perceived as "disproportionately significant" – either due to their higher frequency, or position in the layout, or due to some other, non-verbal features – they become foregrounded, perceived as more prominent, hence, "larger" or "closer" (or more intense) than other aspects of the mental representations that are triggered by the text. This creates the effect of "depth, proximity and intimacy." These impressions can be enhanced, or even literalised, by typography, font size, graphic elements, and colour, i.e. the elements determining the alphabetic, lexical, and paginal spaces. Stylistic differences, shifts and changes that are easily noticeable, are perceived as movement. This also contributes to the feeling of texture, and reciprocally "motion itself also creates textured variation" (167–168), which can again be enhanced by material rhetoric. Danielewski's *House of Leaves* is a vivid example of this. Passages concerning the heroes' descent into underground corridors contain little text, prompting the reader to quickly turn the pages, as if in imitation of the characters' hurried pace. Similarly, reading slows down when the pages are fully covered with text. In this work the varied pace and direction of reading, dictated by typography, combine with stylistic diversity in order to produce an intensely rich and dynamic impression of texture.

So, in works resorting to material rhetoric, textural effects are achieved by both linguistic and physical features of discourse presentation; and in liberatic works the whole book possesses a distinct texture. For example, a shift in textual deixis, signalling the transition to a new mental space, might be actualised by a single word or phrase. The verbal effect of this can be enhanced by layout and typography, for example if these elements would appear in a large font, and in the empty space of an otherwise blank page. The impression of movement can be transposed into a physical manipulation of the book. Following Elaine Scarry, Stockwell describes, for instance, a type of "imaginary motion" that "involves seeing the text as a cloth (hinting at the textile origins of texture...), which can stretch out, fold and tilt images according to the shifting perspective of the focaliser" (Stockwell 2002: 174). This type of metaphoric movement is physically realised in works such as the original 1913 edition of Blaise Cendrars and Sonia Delaunay-Terk's *La Prose du Transsibérien et de la petite Jehanne de France*, and Anne Carson's *Nox*. Both were published in the form of a concertina that was several meters long. The reader must spread the work out like fabric, or fold and unfold it sheet-by-sheet, in order to read the text. Other examples include Fajfer's poem "Balcony," which folds out of an otherwise typical codex; Radosław Nowakowski's *Sienkiewicza Street in Kielce* (which extends into a 10.5-meter-long model of the eponymous street), and Adam Thirlwell's *Kapow!* in which the reader needs to unfold several pages, and turn the book around, in order to read patches of text that are interwoven into the main storyline (see Fig. 3). Even a cursory glance at the unfolded sheet of Thirlwell's book brings to mind a stretched roll of fabric, which almost visualises the dead metaphor of "weaving a story." The material form is in tune with the subject of Thirlwell's narrative: the work deals with the events of the Arab spring, and the unfolded part of the book might remind us of an arabesque flying carpet. At this point in the book, the narrator provocatively plays with stereotypical images of eroticized, "Oriental subjects," as the unfolded passage contains a story about a lustful maidservant, her mistress, and a donkey (Thirlwell 2012: 76–78).

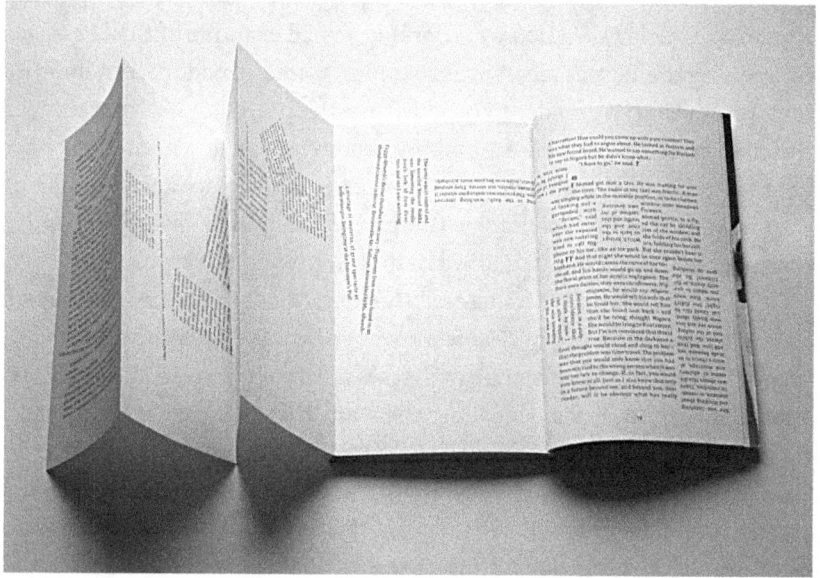

Fig. 3. Adam Thirlwell's *Kapow!* Unfolding pages stretched like a sheet of cloth (2012)

Book is a navigating device

As suggested by *The Penguin Dictionary of Literary Terms*, such deliberately shaped, material spaces of the book, and spaces within the book, can be also perceived as punctuation devices ("Punctuation" 1999: 712),[36] adding elocutionary force to text that has been thus segmented. By no means, however, does the relationship between the spatial segmentation of the text in a book, and the spatial model of the fictional world, rely only on resemblance. Of course, sometimes their relation is almost iconic as, for example, in B.S. Johnson's *The Unfortunates*. The story is about physical

---

[36] Besides typical punctuation marks, the entry includes the following "physical devices": presence or lack of interword spacing, pagination and foliation, *mise-en-page*, and the book itself.

disintegration due to terminal illness, and is inscribed in a disintegrated codex: a bunch of unbound booklets placed in a box (see Fig. 4). But in other cases the shape of the book deliberately complicates the coordinates of the relationship, drawing the reader into a game, of sorts, that is similar to the one experienced in modern theatre, especially in performances that engage the audience as active co-participants. Tensions, incongruities, and gaps may be generated by juxtaposing the linguistic message with non-verbal elements, thereby suggesting different interpretive possibilities, connotations and emotions. The mental spaces generated by the linguistic layer can fuse, overlap, clash, or come into a dialogue with meanings generated by the layout of text and its distribution in the book, be it a codex, a leporello, a scroll, or some other less conventional space of inscription.

Fig. 4. B.S. Johnson *The Unfortunates* (Polish and English editions)

Katherine Hayles notices the relation between the text and its "embookment" (or to use Jacek Ladorucki's phrase "inlibrisation"), and proposes that we call this relationship a "material metaphor." She claims that the term foregrounds the "transfer of sense" between words and the shape of the book, or "a symbol (more properly, a network of symbols) and material apparatus" (Hayles 2002: 22). Because the modification of the physical form of the book significantly "transforms the metaphoric network structuring the relation of word to world" (23), the expressive potential reaches beyond the text the book contains. The book, created according to the principles of material rhetoric, becomes a discernible device for "entering" the fictional space, or an "interface" through which the audience can navigate it. Moreover, Hayles explains, "the materiality of inscription thoroughly interpenetrates the represented world" in a way inseparable from literary effects (130). Observing that this kind of relationship may occur regardless of the medium, she proposes the term "technotexts" to describe creative works (print or electronic) that investigate the technologies and other means of their own production, and in doing so "mobilize reflexive loops between [the work's] imaginative world and the material apparatus embodying [those creations] as a physical presence" (25). Her term does not discriminate between different technologies, and the media that are related to this technology, because Hayles recognises that any mode of production is capable of creating this effect. In this sense, liberature can be seen as a subcategory of techotexts, embracing works realised in the medium of the printed book. As noted above, in such a text additional meanings emerge from its spatial distribution in a deliberately composed space, suggesting that the book is better understood as a navigating device than as a container.[37] This leads us to reconsider the book in terms of the interface.[38]

In digital humanities, the interface is defined as a set of material devices, the operations of which serve to communicate between two systems. The interface encompasses hardware and software: keyboards, monitors, the mouse, the joystick, voice recognition devices, motion sensors, etc. as well as specific operations performed by the individual using them (Therrien 2014: 305–306). As Carl Therrien explains, the interface does more than merely enable the user to access content in a rather passive manner, since "[t]he interface can project the user in specific make-believe scenarios where embodiment is defined precisely: primary actions [...] on the interface are mapped onto actions in a virtual world [...]. Depending on the affordances of any given interface, these mappings can be more or less isomorphic in terms of motor activation" (305). The isomorphism between the user's manipulations and the character's movements represented on screen corresponds to the iconic relation between the compositional space and the reader's handling of the physical book. Understanding the book as interface illuminates its potential for spurring the reader on to more robust, physical interactivity, and a more embodied act of reading.

[37] Johanna Drucker in *Diagrammatic Writing* (2013a) and Jay David Bolter in *Writing Space* (1991) treat this subject.
[38] I am grateful to Piotr Marecki for this suggestion.

This is related to an effect described by Hayles in relation to techno-texts. She remarks than the exploration of a text's materiality brings about a "dynamic interactivity through which a literary work mobiliz-es its physical embodiment in conjunction with its verbal signifiers to construct meanings in ways that implicitly construct the reader/user as well" (Hayles 2002: 130–131). Effectively, the reader becomes part of the represented world; much like what happens in games, or in liberatic works. The navigability of the text, via the interface of the book, implies that, in reading, such a work can be "composed" in more ways than one, thereby activating specific semantic paths. To paraphrase Aarseth's de-scription of cybertext, the book is "a machine for the production of va-riety of expression," enriched by an added paraverbal dimension, which means that the work itself fulfills his criteria for ergodic literature (Aar-seth 1997: 1). As Aarseth points out, ergodic works give readers a great-er sense of agency than occurs when reading "traditional" literature, an observation that effectively calls for the reconceptualization of readers as users. Wojciech Kalaga notes this potential in liberature, and postu-lates a similar redefinition:

Such a text enforces a reading which is nonsequential, nonlinear, and which enforces (more or less conscious, more or less contingent) decisions of choice. The reader, whether he likes it or not, takes over a large portion of the au-thor's responsibilities; the author himself, on the other hand, abdicates from the position of an absolute creator, the final authority on meaning and as-sumes the role of a "designer of the experience of response"[39] and his position

[39] Kalaga's original footnote is worth quoting here in full because it hints that liberature offers an opportunity to re-open a philosophical discussion on the ontology of the lit-erary work: "Liliana Bieszczad, 'Sztuka w epoce cybernetycznej: pomiędzy estetyzacją rzeczywistości a ontologizacją sztuki' [Art in the Cybernetic Era: Between Aesthetiz-ing Reality and Ontologizing Art], in: *Piękno w sieci. Estetyka a nowe media*, ed. Krysty-na Wilkoszewska, Kraków: Universitas, 1999, p. 95. Cf. Roy Ascott: 'The revolution in art which prompts these questions lies in the radically new role of the artist. Instead of creating, expressing, or transmitting content, he is now involved in designing con-texts within which the observer or viewer can construct experience and meaning.' Roy Ascott, 'From Appearance to Apparition: Communication and Culture in the Cyber-sphere,' *Leonardo Electronic Almanac*, Vol. 1, No. 2. October 1993."
Tadeusz Sławek, reviewer of this volume, pointed out to other philosophical vistas that call for a more in-depth response: the construction of subjectivity, and socio-political consequences ensuing from aesthetic choices made by liberatic authors and their audi-ences. These broad and complex questions are well worth discussing in another, book-length study.

is "'reduced' to one of the many co-creators of the work."[40] The recipient, as Ryszard Kluszczyński has put it, "turns out to be a fragment of the same structure/process that he appeared to be 'external to, a fragment that is decisive both of the shape that this process eventually assumes and of the sense that it realizes'."[41] The role of the reader described in this way exceeds the classical distinction between the Dionysian and the Apollonian reader: the reader of liberature, to a greater or lesser degree, becomes an interactive and aleatory recipient. (Kalaga 2010a: 18–19)

In a similar vein, Lori Emerson has recently proposed the term "readingwriting" to redefine (electronic and printed) literature that requires readers to actively choose a direction of reading, and hence to co-create the ensuing textual path. She describes this as "the practice of writing through the network, which as it tracks, indexes and algorithmizes every click and every bit of text we enter into the network is itself constantly reading our writing and writing our reading" (2014: 163). Another important feature of readingwriting, which is shared with technotexts and liberature, connects to the laying bare of the material mechanics of the reading process, exposing the seeming transparency of the physical medium, and "making visible the invisible, taken-for-granted media that delimit what information we can and cannot access" (177). In her view this ultimately entails a radical redefinition of the very concept of literature itself (164). Her bold claim echoes Fajfer's conviction that readingwriting grounded in the book form perhaps requires a different label than that of "literature."

These various proposals for new terminology – liberature, technotexts, readingwriting (as well as bookishness and multimodal litrature, which I discuss later) – attempt to grasp the same kind of idea: the specificity of writing entangled with its own materiality. The derivations of these terms illuminate different aspects of the idea. With regard to liberature, its Latin root hints not only at the book as the technological space, but also at the liberties granted to both author and reader. Admittedly, however, the shift from an authorially determined, single direction of textual flow, to a partly undetermined readerly track, may be perceived as intimidating

40 Kalaga's original footnote: "Liliana Bieszczad, 'Sztuka w epoce cybernetycznej', p. 95."
41 Kalaga's original footnote: "Ryszard W. Kluszczyński, 'Interaktywność – właściwość odbioru czy nowa jakość sztuki/kultury'" (Interactivity – a Property of Reception or a New Quality of Art/Culture) in: *Estetyczne przestrzenie współczesności*, ed. Anna Zeidler-Janiszewska, Warszawa: Instytut Kultury, 1996, p. 145."

rather than liberating. Or at least things might feel uncomfortable. Kalaga describes this in terms of an aporia: "an obligation" to make "a free choice" that involves the reader being forced to make choices, just like what happens when reading an electronic hypertext (2010a: 17–18). Commenting on the ergodicity of the cybertext, Aarseth acknowledges a similar risk. He points out that ergodic choices may result in unsatisfactory textual paths, that is in readings that the user perceives as a failure (Aarseth 1997: 4).

This is because both cybertexts and liberature constitute a challenge to reading habits, to readers' expectations, and to protocols of knowing *how* texts mean. This may be perceived as liberating or frustrating. And it is in tune with Johanna Drucker's observation that, in texts of this type, "[t]he 'structure of knowledge' becomes a 'scheme of knowing' that inscribes use as well as provoking it" (2013b: par. 36). As a consequence of this the "user-consumer is replaced by a maker-producer, a performer, whose performance changes the game" of reading (ibid.). So liberature appears as a kind of print literature that lays bare the illusion of a single, univocal reading that is implied by the familiar shape of the conventional codex, i.e. the sequential order of bound pages. By resorting to materially engineered indeterminacy, it undermines the seeming transparency of print, and the codex in particular. Variations on the codex form, and divergences from it, as well as radical departures from the traditional cuboid shape of the space of inscription, challenge the transparency of the medium and powerfully attest to the potentialities of the book, and the paths that lie beyond it. Unconventional "bookish interfaces" expose our ways of structuring knowledge, and consequently expose the preconceptions that underpin more conventional book forms. They remind us that forms of presentation are also already forms of interpretation.

Conceptual metaphors in liberature

B.S. Johnson: breaking through the walls of fiction

The book as an architectural structure, and the book as a human body, are two pervasive conceptual metaphors underlying liberatic works. The material rhetoric of these conceptual metaphors goes hand in hand with ways of structuring discourse, and this sometimes involves the visualisation, or literalisation, of spatial conceptualisations of linguistic forms. The relation "between the spatialized form of the language and the conceptual system, especially the metaphorical aspects of the conceptual system" (Lakoff and Johnson 2003: 138) is translated into, or reflected in, the physical shape of the text. This is because these two conceptual metaphors structure the way we speak about texts in general. Literary works seen as material embodiments of ideas must be close to architecture, the most material of arts,[42] and the one, moreover, which requires the audience to actively move in and around the architectural object. Since many writers who have resorted to the rhetoric of materiality draw explicit parallels between them, let me mention two of them who are particularly relevant to my subject. One is B.S. Johnson, a British novelist well known for his unconventional exploitation of the technological space of the book. The other is William H. Gass, an American philosopher, essayist and writer who is deeply preoccupied with "habitations of the word."[43]

In the "Introduction" to a collection of short texts, *Aren't You Rather Young to Be Writing Your Memoirs?*, B.S. Johnson points out that writers

---

[42] I also discuss their relation in Pound's *Cantos* in "Introduction: Modernist Roots of Liberature" (2014).

[43] This is the title of one of his collections of essays (Ithaca and London: Cornell University Press, 1985).

can learn much from architects insofar as in writing, just as in designing buildings, artists should consider their goals and available means. As Johnson explains, the "architecture of the book"[44] needs to be connected with its subject matter. Repeating the dictum of Louis Sullivan, "the father of modernist architecture" he declares that "form follows function" (B.S. Johnson 1973: 16). Johnson insists that his "formal innovations" in typography, and the structure of his books, are the result of the search for adequate expression. He claims that he uses the means available to him as a *writer* (not a book designer or visual artist), but he also admits that sometimes the novelist must "borrow, steal or cobble" from other media in order to invent "forms which will more or less satisfactorily contain an ever-changing reality" (16–17). So, for example, when he wants to convey the impression of a flow of memories stirred by accidental, external stimuli, he chooses to disbind the codex, and offers *The Unfortunates* as loose, unnumbered signatures in a box, convinced that his readers will be able to feel the intended randomness and fluidity of the experience thus inscribed. Then, as much as he is driven by the mimetic motivation "to embody present day reality" (21), he is also driven by the experiential potential of material rhetoric. He believes that by using it he is able to communicate something that cannot be expressed in words alone: "Where I depart from convention, it is because the convention has failed, is inadequate for conveying what I have to say. The relevant questions are surely whether each device works or not, whether it achieves what it sets out to achieve…" (ibid.).

With this in mind, it cannot be a coincidence that Johnson casts an architect as the protagonist of his second novel, *Albert Angelo* (1964). The eponymous persona appears to serve his purpose well for the majority of the narrative, which follows a five-part structure: Prologue, Exposition, Development, Disintegration, and Coda, corresponding to the elements of a classical tragic plot. This holds good until the end of part three. At this point the omniscient, extradiegetic narration describes Albert's idling at the drawingboard, and slips into free indirect speech with the hero as the focaliser:

Nearly seven weeks' summer holiday lay ahead of him in which to work; and he could not work today, always tomorrow was the day he was going to

[44] The phrase is used as the subtitle of *Od Joyce'a do liberatury* (From Joyce to liberature), the first collection of essays featuring Fajfer's newly coined term.

work. Part of the trouble, he thought, was that he lived and loved to live in an area of absolute architectural rightness, which inhibited his own originality, and resulted in him being — OH, FUCK ALL THIS LYING! (B.S. Johnson 2004b [1964]: 163)

The sudden, emotional narratorial outburst breaks down the illusory walls that exist between the fictional world of the novel, the world of the implied author, and that of the implied reader. This is executed verbally (through a swearword), and a series of deictic shifts[45] that conceptually "transport" the reader from one level of the fictional world to another, and through material rhetoric. Graphically, the exceedingly elongated dash suspends the flow of the narrative, arousing expectation and curiosity. This is immediately followed by the sudden shock of the rude, violent outburst of frustration. At this point the reader is confused as to the source of the outburst: does it come from the eponymous architect irritated by his creative block, or is this is a different voice shouting at her? (The effect is achieved by the use of capital letters and the enlarged font of "LYING!"). But the following pages do not bring any explanation, only prolonged suspense. There we see a practically blank spread, containing only the title of the next part "FOUR: Disintegration" in the top right corner (164–165).

This is exactly the moment of a complex shift in perceptual, textual, and compositional deixis. These typographic gestures corroborate the suspicion that the shout comes from the heretofore "polite" omniscient narrator of the traditional, realistic novel, who has now shed the mask of impersonality. They redirect the reader's attention from the fictional world to "the textuality of the text," and enhance the reader's experience of the texture of the work. The reader must suddenly abandon the mental space where Albert's story has unfolded, as the discourse literally undergoes a crisis; it can't go on, and almost disappears into three pages of emptiness, after which it resumes with the same words:

— fuck all this lying look what **im** really trying to write about is writing not all this stuff about architecture trying to say something about writing about my writing **im** my hero though what a useless appellation my first character then **I'm** trying to say something about me through him albert an architect when whats the point in covering up covering up covering over pretending

Conceptual metaphors in liberature

[45] For the typology of deixis see Stockwell 2002: 41–55.

pretending **i** can say anything through him that is anything that **I** would be interested in saying

— so an almighty aposiopesis

— **Im** trying to say something not tell a story telling stories is telling lies and **I** want to tell the truth about me about my experience about my truth about my truth to reality about sitting here writing looking out across Claremont Square trying to say something about the writing [...]

(167–168, emphases mine).

This time the reader realises that the utterances must be pronounced by a figure other than Albert, one who has emerged from behind the mask of the omniscient voice. The mental representation of Albert's world, which the reader has built up in vivid detail, is now shattered to pieces. In keeping with this, the conceptual metaphor of the story as a crumbling building is visually enhanced by a series of paragraphs, of differing lengths, that are separated by blanks. The text looks fragmented: "this device you cannot have failed to see cracking, ill-fitting at many places, many places," "such a mess, such a mess, so many loose ends" (168, 176). A sense of disintegration is strengthened by the aforementioned shift of the perceptual deixis,[46] and this further complicates the identity of the speaker. The deictic centre established at the end of "Development" is readjusted, moving from Albert's studio to the narrator's study. What's more, the narrator merges with the implied author, which is signalled by the transition from the lower case "im" to the capital "I" (compare: "**i** can say anything through him that is anything that **I** would be interested in saying" in the first paragraph of Disintegration.) This unmasked "I" then offers the reader some details that prompt us to identify him as B.S. Johnson himself, in an attempt to do away with fictionality by destroying the boundary between the implied and the real author.[47] This speaker is a highly self-conscious, theoretically

[46] Stockwell defines perceptual deixis as "expressions concerning the perceptive participants in the text, including personal pronouns (...), demonstratives (...), definite articles, definite reference (...); mental states," which according to him, as part of reference, determine a mental representation of a world viewed from the perspective of the agent of perception (2002: 45). See also Stamirowska (2006: 71–76) for a detailed analysis of personal pronouns as signals of shifts in the narrative perspective.

[47] Cf. Stamirowska (2006: 79). However, I would be cautious about simply identifying "the writer" with B.S. Johnson, as I suppose we could still distinguish between the Author who is so dramatically dramatised, and the actual person who wrote the book. It can be argued that even such a frank, self-revealing attitude is just anoth-

well-informed figure, who openly discusses his desire, even compulsion, "to tell the truth about me about my experience about my truth about my truth to reality" (167), which:

> — Is too
> — Is about the fragmentariness of life, too, attempts to reproduce the moment-to-moment fragmentariness of life, my life, and to echo it in technique, the fragmentariness, a collage made of the fragments of my own life, the poor odds and sods, the bric-à-brac, a thing composed of, then.
> [...]
> — And also to echo the complexity of life, reproduce some of the complexity of selves which I contain within me, contradictory and gross as they are [...].
> (169, 170)

At the end of the first paragraph the sentence suddenly breaks off, a device that is explicitly identified as aposiopesis – a rhetorical figure indicating exasperation or speechless rage. But its effect is simultaneously undermined by naming the device. More metatextual comments are then added in justifications for other devices, allowing the author to lay bare the mechanisms of fiction, in order to nullify them. As a consequence of his desperate belief in "conveying truth" through the medium of the novel, the writer even resorts to physically damaging the book – he cuts out "the future-seeing holes" that appear on two subsequent pages (175; see Fig. 5 for the holes in pages 149–152). Hence, we witness a material metaphor with a curious twist. The hole is a kind of demetaphorisation: by looking through the actual "window" in Johnson's "house of fiction" the reader gains insight into a future that is – literally – in sight. Thereby she is made acutely aware of the constructedness of Johnson's work, of its concreteness, its objecthood, of the material reality that she is holding in her hands.

----

er role, as the appearance of this authorial voice at this point in the composition of the novel is controlled by yet another agent, who could be called the Arranger. The concept was suggested by David Hayman in order "to designate a figure who can be identified neither with the author nor with his narrators, but who exercises an increasing degree of overt control over his increasingly challenging materials." The concept was developed in order to explain some idiosyncrasies in the texture of *Ulysses* (Hayman 1970: 70). It is further discussed by Hugh Kenner in "The Arranger" (2004: 17–32).

Fig. 5. "A window into the future (and the past)" in B.S. Johnson's *Albert Angelo* (2004b [1964])

Yet the non-verbal device defies an easy, unequivocal interpretation. The holes can just as easily be understood as a window into the past, since the passage that is visible through the opening is in fact an excerpt describing the murder of Christopher Marlow in a drunken brawl. Moreover, when one looks backwards through the "window," it shows only a blank, as if the past were a text still to be written down. This problematises the status of this snippet of text as a "vehicle for conveying truth" and a symbolic "piece of evidence" for the foreshadowed crime. Although the dramatic description hints at Albert's tragic end, its intertextual status simultaneously underscores the artificiality of Johnson's story, showing that it is a patchwork of different texts, not a uniform "autobiographical" narrative. This prompts us to think of the material book as an "interpretative interface," to use Johanna Drucker's phrase, mobilising "a critical network that exposes, calls to attention, its made-ness – and by extension, the constructed-ness of knowledge, its interpretative dimensions" (2013b: par. 41). Consequently, this also implies "the shift from conceptions of interface as things and entities to that of an event-space of interpretative activity" (ibid.), the point I develop below when discussing the performative dimension of the book.

William H. Gass's material metaphors

William H. Gass, an author equally sensitive to material rhetoric, raises the same questions about the interrelation between form, function, and thematic content while investigating the tropes of the text. Gass contends that the visual and spatial aspects of print constitute a particular challenge; one that may provide writers with a "new and adequate notation for the novelist's investigations, one which will permit new effects, new meanings to be articulated" (1997f: 152). Like Johnson and Federman, he focuses on the novel as a genre that is especially hospitable to material rhetoric,[48] although he also mentions other genres. He notes that, along with stylistic choices regarding the selection of "sounds, sequences, syntax, shapes, symbol," authors can make choices about the material and compositional features of the book (153). This becomes especially evident when the larger trope dominating a text is that of a building.

The adoption of this conceptual metaphor complicates the status of the literary work as an aesthetic object. While Gass takes a phenomenological approach to reading, he disagrees with the views of Roman Ingarden, a philosopher who disregarded an understanding of literature's material foundation as a semantically significant stratum (Ingarden 1973: 12–14). Developing the analogy between the novel and architecture, Gass states that:

> The printed text exists as a whole, all at once, as the rooms, stairways, and floors of a building do; and our first reading is like our first visit to the Palace of the Popes at Avignon; perhaps where an informed and garrulous guide leads us here and there as seems best: one step, one hall and doorway, one religious relic at a time; but it remains a building whose relation to the clock – like the Escorial – is only phenomenological. Novels are books, and books are buildings; and therefore they exist like other objects – they are a space in space (Gass 1997a: 153).

Here Gass draws our attention to a subtle tension between the work's ability to "transport" the reader into imaginary, mental spaces, and the concreteness of the text which lets the reader orient herself in layers of the fictional world, with the help of the spatial coordinates of the book.[49] As the essay progresses, he goes on to describe how a text can be experienced through the act of reading, and conceptualised as a geometrical figure: a circle in the circular *Finnegans Wake* and a hopscotch board in

---

[48] Ian Watt had already suggested that the novel is a genre whose development was facilitated by print. The connection between the extended narrative form and the technology of print was expounded by Maurice Couturier in *Textual Communication: A Print-based Theory of the Novel* (1991). For more recent studies see Alison Gibbons *Multimodality, Cognition and Experimental Literature* (2012), and Grzegorz Maziarczyk *The Novel as the Book* (2013).

[49] For example, this can happen when we use chapter and page numbers to remember specific moments in the story. James Joyce creates a link between the pagination, and the events described on a particular page, to particular aesthetic ends in *Ulysses*. In *House Mother Normal*, B.S. Johnson does so as a spatio-temporal indicator (cf. Bazarnik 2011: 39–41, 77–81).

Cortázar's eponymous novel. Likewise, various visual devices – such as colons in Juan Goytisolo's *Makbara*, or a picture of a tombstone in Katherine Anne Porter's short story "The Grave" – function as ambiguous symbols that are instrumental in interpreting these works (Gass 1997a: 153). For Gass, the literary text (in its printed form) is thus constituted by both fictional *and* material space, explored by the reader through imagination and the senses.

As a practicing writer Gass also provides us with an object lesson in this kind of material poetics.[50] This can be seen in his novel *The Tunnel*, which is about W.F. Kohler, a history professor who simultaneously investigates Nazi Germany, and his own life. The novel is narrated verbally and materially through the carefully planned use of physical features of the bibliographical code. As the author explains in detailed notes for the work, the novel is "manufactured and presented to the public as a book, and it [is] a real book, no doubt about that, but it must not be a book *symbolically*. Symbolically it is a heap of pages on various topics which the narrator has shuffled together. This must seem to be the case although at another level the work is tightly organized and determined" (Gass [nd.]: par. 2). Without this organisation, "the building would fall down" (Gass in Schenkenberg 2007). The "tight organization" consists in a skillful fusion of objective historical discourse with autobiographical writing, personal notes, scribbles, and doodles. Moreover, the narrative design also embraces all paratexts: "[t]he cover of the book, the dust jacket, the endpapers, the title page, and so on." These, along with the format and size, "are intended to be functional parts of the text" (Gass [nd.]: par. 3). The material, typographic, and spatial features of the book are thus used to create the impression of entering the work as if it were the eponymous tunnel, making the reader "feel, as he or she doubtless will, as if they are crawling through an unpleasant and narrow darkness" (par. 7c). So, for example, the dustjacket "should be completely empty and dark like outer space or the inside of a cave." The size of the book should be noticeably larger than is typical, so that the reader will feel as if he or she is "holding a heavy really richly textured lump of darkness" (par. 5). Different fonts have a function too, and they work to suggest a tone of voice,

[50] Gass's fascination with the materiality of literature extends to the embodied voice. This is evident in his essays, creative writings, and the audiobook of *The Tunnel*, which features Gass himself as the reader. The audiobook edition consists of three CDs, with 45 hours of reading in the mp3 format, and is complemented with a booklet that describes the material features of the printed book (see the Dalkey Archive website for the book at: http://www.dalkeyarchive.com/product/the-tunnel-read-by-william-h-gass/).

or an attitude, or to mark out different parts of the book. Consequently, "the material character of the book itself" is, in Gass's words, "another kind of muse" (par. 16). This muse had an earlier incarnation in *Wille Master's Lonesome Wife*, another of Gass's liberatic works that is discussed in more detail below.

But perhaps the most notorious literary work thematising the book as an architectural artefact is Mark Z. Danielewski's *House of Leaves*.[51] Described as an experimental horror, concrete fiction, a multimodal novel (Gibbons 2012: 46–85), "a networked novel" and "a print novel for a digital age" (Pressman 2006), "a textual artefact" (Bray and Gibbons 2011: 2), and a media collage, this 700 page, heavy brick of a book tells of a haunted house whose dimensions make "the whole [thing] just a hopeless, structural impossibility" (Danielewski 2000: 361). Like *The Tunnel*, the novel foregrounds its materiality and bookhood through layout, typography, narrative structure, paratexts, format, and size. Danielewski's literary *tour de force* is a prime example of "architexture," an amazing materialisation of the Jamesean metaphor of the house of fiction. Paraphrasing a self-mocking commentary attributed to Harold Bloom, one might say that *House of Leaves* "is so pointedly against symbol, the house [the book] requires a symbol destroyer [...] ...thus through this trope [one might] succeed in securing poetic independence no matter how lonely, empty, and agonizing the final result may be" (360).

Books are buildings

As Hayles and Alison Gibbons aptly demonstrate, the "poetic independence" of Danielewski's book is deeply rooted in its materiality (Gibbons 2012: 65–71), something which is used to enhance the emergent conceptual blend HOUSE = BOOK.[52] In this context, it is interesting to note that cognitive analysis reveals how a sense of the object's material substance is bound up with the conceptual metaphor of the literary work as a work of architecture. Exploring the metaphor AN ARGUMENT IS A BUILDING,

---

[51] Another one could be George Perec's *Life Instruction Manual*. A second, revised Polish edition appeared with the Liberatura imprint of Korporacja Ha!art Publishing House.

[52] See also the following chapter: "Crossing Thresholds and the Exploring Reader of *House of Leaves* by Mark Z. Danielewski" in Gibbons' *Multimodality, Cognition and Experimental Literature* (2012: 46–85). Also relevant is Hayles, chapter 8 "Inhabiting House of Leaves" in *Writing Machines* (2002: 108–131), and part I "House of Leaves" in *Mark Z. Danielewski* (ed. by Joe Bray and Alison Gibbons, 2011).

George Lakoff and Mark Johnson list its following fundamental aspects: content, progress, basicness, strength and structure (2003: 99). The same elements are also discernible in the metaphor A LITERARY WORK IS A BUILDING. Let us consider the expressions:

> *the house* of fiction, narrative *structure*, a lyrical *piece*, a *labyrinthine* text, *a maze* of words
>
> The text of the novel is set in two *columns*.
>
> It *is based on* an episode from the author's life.
>
> It is *a solid piece* of writing.
>
> Strange characters *inhabit* this novel.
>
> Too much of the story was *built on* a worn out plot.
>
> The book was fun enough to make up for the lack of *substance*.
>
> The plot is *weak*, it does not have enough *content* to *support* such a long novel.
>
> The text engages in a poetic *deconstruction* of the sonnet.
>
> Shakespeare, a *foundation* to the English poetic tradition.

These phrases indicate that the literary work is perceived as an assembled, concrete structure: a maze, a stately home, a museum, a temple, possibly a monument or a memorial. Of course, these structures have different functions, and thus evoke slightly different connotations, something which may be relevant to readings of specific works.[53] What I want to stress at this point, however, is connected with Lakoff and Johnson's observation that generally "in the BUILDING metaphor (...) the content is not in the interior; instead *the foundation and outer shell constitute the content*" (100, emphasis mine). In other words, the metaphor implies that form *is* content, and content *is* form. This is different from the conceptual metaphor of A CONTAINER, also frequently used with reference to books. The container metaphor suggests that content is separate from its material form, that is, can be easily removed from it and transferred into another receptacle without any loss. What the building metaphor says about the relation between content and form may explain why some writers emphasise the concreteness of their books, and why they are prone to the metaphorical reversal described above in connection with *Albert Angelo*. If literary texts are (like) buildings, then pages, covers, the spine, paper and fonts can be perceived as their constituents, elements that are on a par with words. B.S. Johnson understood this almost

---

[53] Gibbons, for example, discusses how Danielewski's book evokes a complex conceptual blend of HOUSE, LABIRYNTH, and BOOK (2012: 66–67).

literally: "subject matter is everywhere, general, is *brick, concrete, plastic*; the ways of putting it together are particular, are crucial" (1973: 16; emphasis mine). Gass voiced something similar in the above quoted image of the novel as a palace.

Exploring the conceptual metaphor, Gass also draws attention to the ways in which the literary work can be experienced as a spatial object. The physical manipulation of the book – opening it, leafing through its pages, turning it about – coupled with the book's concretisation of a fictional world, enhances the impression that the book is experienced as an imaginary structure; somewhere the reader enters and penetrates as if it were a building.[54] When the work's physical form diverts from the codex (e.g. it is presented in an unbound form), the reader (re)assembles the text as if it were a model kit, acting as model maker or builder. This is why Gass implies that, from a phenomenological perspective, literary works that foreground their materiality are perceived in a way that is similar to architecture. Interestingly, Ingarden, a phenomenologist who, as was mentioned above, generally refused to acknowledge the semantic aspect of the material foundation (and therefore its ontological significance in any kind of art), admitted that architecture was a special case. According to the philosopher, a building is simultaneously an intentional object that "refers back not only to the creative acts of the architect and the reconstructive acts of the viewer, but also to its ontic foundation in a fully determined real thing shaped in a particular way" (Ingarden 1989: 263). Its material qualities such as wall surfaces, spatial arrangement of elements, and light effects are intended to bring about "the appearance of the work's physical shape," in order to make it conceptually *and* physically accessible to the recipient (269). Likewise, in architecturally composed literary works narrative structure, stylistic features, typographic arrangements, page surfaces, and the physical form of the book are intended to facilitate our perception of it as a material object (Bazarnik 2010c). If reading requires us to engage in some non-standard physical manipulation of that object, this enhances the reader's grasp of the compositional space, a concept that is also embodied in the text.

Such literary works come to be understood as "monumental, total, semiotic objects." As I have noted in "Modernist Roots of Liberature" (Bazarnik 2014: 11), Vicki Mahaffey resorts to a similar architectural metaphor when she describes an approach to editing that "seeks to produce

---

[54] For example, Christoph B. Schulz describes similar effects in the first edition of Carroll's *Alice* (2015: 262–275).

[an edition of a text as] a kind of literary monument." She argues that this privileges the author ahead of other agents involved in book production:

> An understanding of texts as monumental implicitly upholds a canonical view of literature, and it favors certain kinds of authority: the authority of the author over that of his or her readers, the authority of the individual over that of the public, the authority of the genius over collaborative production and reproduction, the authority of preservation over decomposition, and the authority of the conscious will (intention) over the authority of unconscious need and desire (chance). (Mahaffey 1991: 178)

This chimes with Fajfer's description of liberature as "total literature" where every element is controlled by the writer. But his use of the adjective was inspired by modernist theatre practices of Edward Gordon Craig, Stanisław Wyspiański, and Tadeusz Kantor (Fajfer 2010d: 47), artists informed by the idea of *Gesamtkunstwerk*, though wary of its implicit, totalising ideology.[55] His description emphasises the role of the author as the agent responsible for both the linguistic and material shape of his or her text (though, let me stress, not quite for the shape of the textual path taken by the reader).[56] Admittedly, "total" has probably been a rather unfortunate choice, as it disturbingly smacks of totalitarian regimes, imposing the only "correct" way of writing, reading, interpreting, and living.[57]

[55] In *The Mask: A Periodical Performance by Edward Gordon Craig*, Olga Taxidou makes an interesting comment about "totality" of Craig's theatre. She claims that he falls between its two tradtions: one represented by Artaud as the artist emodying the sub-conscious, and the other by Brecht, who emphasised the role of the artist in the body-politics. As she notes, Craig's theatre was "[n]ot extreme, nor modern, nor political enough to embody either." Her description of "[a] performance that is not really a performance, modern but not modern enough, political but not really" (Taxidou 2013: 191) bears uncanny parallels to some comments about Fajfer's liberature, exemplified in books that are not quite bookish, and himself as an avant-gardists who constantly brings up tradition, the author who denounces any political commitment, yet fights fiercely for the autonomy of art and the artist.

[56] Emiliano Ranocchi also notes Fajfer's emphasis on the instrumental role and authority of the author, connecting it with the modernist concept of the autonomy of the artist (2012: 33–34).

[57] This point (if not outright criticism of seemingly totalitarian fantasies entailed in the project) has been raised by often sympathetic readers and critics, including Tadeusz Sławek, one of the reviewers of the present book (cf. also Jankowicz 2010). Although what was at stake in liberature, as Fajfer and I saw it, was rather a project of (w)holistic writing and reading, and inclusiveness rather than alienation, we were BLIND to the disconcerting connotations of this WORD. So we are willing to admit that its application was too LIBERAL. For Fajfer's latest comments on liberature as total literature

Yet, as Kalaga and Drucker have pointed out, this kind of "total" approach to one's work need not result in a "totalitarian" reading. On the contrary, the range of choices offered by liberatic works indicates that any given reading is always incomplete, fragmentary, and partial; an exhaustive, "total" reading is an illusion. Besides, Ranocchi grants that, rather than corroborating the totality of the unified object, liberature acknowledges its frailness and provisionality (2014).

Authorial control over the design of a book may concern the selection of various elements: the choice of paper, typeface, (colour and kind of) ink, perhaps printing technology, kind of binding, layout, and typography. If this happens, such selections are considered to be aesthetic, semantically charged decisions, as was the case with Joyce choosing a particular shade of blue, and white lettering, for the cover of *Ulysses* (Slote 2004: 12), or with Pound's editions of the *Cantos* discussed by McGann (1991: 106–112 and 129–152; 1993: 76–80). Gass compares such an attitude to that of a conqueror crossing borders to expand his dominion, indicating a similar drive to increase control over one's work beyond mere words: "a place beyond the asterisk, if not beyond the stars" (1997a: 150). The American writer sees this as "the return of the repressed" – the resurrected Author coming back from the dead to make the reader feel his presence for a moment, to capture and hold that which is transitory in "monuments of unageing intellect" "...when readers read as if the words on the page were only fleeting visual events, soon to be gone like flies, and not signs to be sung inside themselves – so that the author's voice is stilled – the author's hand must reach out into the space of the page and put a print upon it that will be unmistakable, uneradicable" (151). This is also why Johnson's eponymous House Mother steps beyond the 21 pages allocated to each character in the novel, and on her extra 22nd page confesses to be "the puppet or concoction of the writer (you always knew there was a writer behind it all? Ah, there is no fooling you readers!)" (B.S. Johnson 2004d [1971]: 204). The direct address is intended to break the barrier between fictional and real worlds, making the presence of the author felt as the voice embodied in the book. Yet, paradoxically, this may be read as a gesture sharply reinstating the division between them, and between the creator and his creation. Despite such doubts, authors keep resorting to similar devices, playing out Magritte's gesture again and again. In fact,

see also "Wśród przeczytanych łąk, asonansów… O literaturze totalnej trochę innym głosem" [Reading about Meadows and Assonances… A Slightly Different Voice on Total Literature] (2016).

House of Leaves opens with a provocative warning that serves the same purpose: "This is not for you" (Gibbons 2011: 17–30). In addition, one of Gass's heroines performs a similar gesture, something that is rendered all the more uncanny when it becomes clear that she is a personified book, inviting the reader to recognise her as the incarnated Word.

Book is a body[58]

Reaching for Gass's novella *Willie Masters' Lonesome Wife*, we reach for a body. A photograph of a naked female torso is displayed on the front cover, the title printed on the picture as if the letters were glued to her breasts.[59] The back cover shows a photo of her back and buttocks. After opening the book, we see a hand reminiscent of God's gesture of creation on the ceiling of the Sistine Chapel, the title issuing from the tips of the fingers. In the beginning is the word; in our hands this word is turning into flesh.

This is the flesh of Babs, the eponymous lonely wife, naked as the first woman at the moment of creation. In a large nude photograph she is opening her mouth, as if to bite the wooden block, carved with the letter "S," that she holds in her hands – the temptress with the forbidden fruit of knowledge. The initial 'S,' reminiscent of a snake, merges with the opening line, which contains the promise that "[s]he'd love him even if his head weren't shiny."[60] Here is Babs, parting her lips to suck in the text, to absorb it into her body. Or perhaps it is Babs issuing the text from her inside, "that spider goddess and thread-spinning muse" (*WMLW*). She/it promises to be "a little mouse of a woman, blond and skinny, and there'll be rings on [her/its] belly where men have set down drinks," "just as much a woman, gauzy muse and hot-pants goddess quite the same" (*WMLW*). She will be "busty, passive, hairy, and will serve" (*WMLW*). She will be a docile object in the hands of "Jim or George or Frank or Harry" as if she were the embodiment of male dreams (*WMLW*). She will show them all they have

[58] This subchapter is a revised version of an article that previously appeared in *Ways of Looking at a Blackbird* (ed. by Grażyna and Andrzej Branny, Kraków: Instytut Filologii Angielskiej, the Jagiellonian University, 2004, pp. 253–261).

[59] The photos were printed on the covers of the first edition (published as supplement no. 2 to the *Tri-Quarterly Magazine*, Evanston: Northwestern UP, 1968); some later reprints have not preserved that authorial, intentional design.

[60] All the quotes come from Gass *Willie Masters' Lonesome Wife* (Normal, Il.: Dalkey Archive Press, 1989); since the book is not paginated further quotes are identified only by the acronym of the title: *WMLW*.

ever wished to see: her breasts as round as rounded letters, pages swaying this way and that; the text reflected as if in a mirror, as if to reflect Bab's swaying "smart ass" (*WMLW*). She will display all her beauties: lying on her side, lying on her back, pressed down by the heavy words of reproach: **"OO-OOO-OO my Mister Handsome how could you?"**. Or tipping over a large, initial "T" with her bare foot (*WMLW*). Here is Babs inextricably linked with the book, built out of letters and narrated with photographs, "prick-tick-ily" turning phrases in her mouth (*WMLW*), wondering why there are no decent words for her, why she has to spin this vulgar story, why she has to give herself shamelessly to the reader. Taking the book in our hands, picking up Willie Masters' lonesome wife, we become – through this gesture – one of her numerous readers-lovers.

The pages of the book are unnumbered, as if paginating them would be somewhat akin to the act of tattooing digits on the body of an actual human being, like the Nazis did to prisoners in concentration camps. In fact, in one of the footnotes a narrator tells a vicious Holocaust 'joke' "about a very obese Jew whose smoke was so greasy it stuck in the flue. The Germans had slav the stack out with a bulgar serb of a croat they had hungarian a pole – back and forth, up and down, round and round, over and over – until there wasn't a bit of greece roumanian" (*WMLW*). As Michael Kaufman remarks, "Hitler's perversion of language (exemplified in phrases such as 'The Final Solution' or 'Work Makes You Free') turned Jews into things, into natural resources to be exploited for their hair, their fat, their skin" (1994: 92). By a similar, perverse process, in this joke a Pole becomes a pole, and by a reverse process *Lonely Wife* becomes a lonely wife.

Resorting to the material metaphor, Gass teases us into reading his novella in a shockingly literal way, balancing on the thin edge between philosophy and pornography as if the alliteration of the two pointed beyond a verbal similarity to some metaphysical reality. He teases us by promising an exciting story, whereas in fact he offers an embodied, experimental, philosophical treatise on the nature of language and literature. As H.L. Hix notes, Gass plays with typical readerly assumptions (Hix 2002: 63–64), encouraging his readers to look beyond them and to form other generic expectations. If the reader glides over the narrative surface, he will find only Babs' buttocks and her "Sweet Buttery," her dirty word games, and a penis in a breakfast bun. But if he delves beneath, into the footnotes, he will realize, with a little help from John Locke, that:

The use of words, then, being to stand as outward marks of our internal ideas, mark and those ideas being taken from particular things, mark, if every particular idea that we take in, masticate, and swallow down, should have a distinct name, names must be endless, names must be endless, names must be endless, names must be endless; and we must be endless to contain them. Mark – to prevent this, the mind makes the particular ideas, received from particular objects to become general like the spread of a disease, a blight of generals, brassed and belted, over half the earth, poisoning the ground, destroying the trees; which is done by considering them, as they are in the mind already such appearances, separate from all other things, naked, solitary, and apart from every circumstance of real existence, such as time, place or any other concomitant ideas, just as I am, in the spot, amidst my music, when I am parting from my clothing on the stage. This is called abstraction, sometimes love, and always the art of writing... (*WMLW*)

The material rhetoric of the work may alert the reader to the fact that, by calling different parts of her body by different female names, Babs makes a desperate attempt at simultaneously embodying the idea of the female and of the fictional. If in the act of reading the reader is supposed to get closest to the Platonic world, what better metaphor could one employ to express this? *Willie Masters' Lonesome Wife* is a material metaphor in which the tenor is the bare idea, and its vehicle a representation of a naked body. Gass-the-Arranger literally confronts the reader with a concept of the idea embodied in a submissive woman inscribed in the book.

According to Gass, it is ideas that are the true building material for the writer; these are expressed in words. These ideas – elusive, impalpable entities – manifest themselves to us as thoughts that we translate into words that we translate into sounds that we translate into graphic signs (Gass 1970: 29). Although words in the *Lonesome Wife* skillfully pretend to be "a string of noises, after all – nothing more really – an arrangement, a column of air moving up and down," "imagination imagining itself imagine" (*WMLW*), pure sound and pure music, to the reader they are presented – first and foremost – as graphic images. They "**pop**" out of the page, shine with the glossy "**brilliantine**" of the bold type, sparkle with "𝕽ecognition" or sudden "star*s" in the middle of a word, drawing the reader's attention to their shape, their material presence, the text's texture (*WMLW*). They imitate movement. Running in ascending and descending lines, they crumble into a constellation of asterisks, condense into a comic bubble, and issue a sentimental, intertextual sigh from *Tess of the d'Urbervilles*.[61] They speak in different typefaces as if in different voices,

---

[61] The speech bubble, which appears at the top of a page in the middle of WMLW, joins in a polyphony of voices playing out sexual innuendoes. It contains an unreferenced

pretending to tell us a story. In their obscenity, they are neither arousing nor indecent because they are merely black marks in a white space; it is only the reader that makes them either. They are naked, at the mercy of readers who will abuse them for their own purposes.

Hix claims that these typographic devices (such as coffee rings supposedly left on the body of the heroine/the book by previous lovers/readers) are not intended to persuade the reader of the authenticity of the events depicted in the work. Rather they remind us that we are constantly dealing with fiction (Hix 2002: 64). As Hix further remarks, events that are supposed to form the storyline "happen primarily to the reader, in the form of 'highly visual intrusions that systematically disrupt the textual givens of the moment'" (ibid.). So *Lonesome Wife*/lonesome wife only pretends to be a narrative. The reader has been led up the garden path all the way through and, accordingly, is openly challenged at the end of the book:

You've been had,

haven't you, joko? you sour stew-faced sonofabitch. Really, did you read this far? puzzle your head? turn the pages this and that, around about? Was it racy enough to suit? There wasn't too much plot? I thought the countess something fab. For the nonce. Nothing lasts. But, honestly, you skipped a lot. Is that any way to make love to a lady, a lonely one at that, used formerly to having put the choicest portions of her privates flowered out in pots and vases; and would you complain at having to caress a breast first, then a knee, to sink so suddenly from soft to bony, or to kiss an ear if followed by the belly, even slowly?

quote from Hardy's novel, in which Tess takes the momentous decision to marry Angel Clare: "'**I shall give way** – I shall say **Yes!** – I shall let myself marry him – I cannot help it!' she suddenly whispered [jealously panted], with her **hot** face to the pillow that night, on hearing one of the other girls **sigh** his name in her sleep. 'I can't bear to let **anybody** have him but **me**! Yet it is a wrong to him, and may kill him when he knows! O my heart – O – O – O – O!'" (Hardy 1992: 175; the italicised phrases differ from those in the original, which are given in the square brackets; the words in bold appear so in WMLW).

Only a literalist at loving would expect to plug ahead like the highway people's line machine, straight over hill and dale, unwavering and ready, in a single stripe of kiss and covering, steady on

from
start
to
finish

(WMLW)

At this point we cannot claim that we have not been warned, that we have not been shown that the lady we have been making love to is only "some flesh-like copy, some sexy pix and rubber lover, a substitute in plastigoop or blanket-cloth" (WMLW). She/it has been trying to make the reader see she/it as only a book – bound pages covered with signs, nothing more and nothing less. They have danced before our eyes, acted out the shapes we wanted to see, worn the costumes of different typefaces like actors who dress up for a play.

Gass theatricalises the text in several ways. Firstly, he arranges words on the page as if placing actors on the stage. Secondly, he makes Babs a stripper, hence a performer. Moreover, he even includes in the book a short drama with a hero called Ivan. Ivan discovers, to his shock and surprise, his own penis in a breakfast bun. The situation in which Ivan finds himself is theatrical, affected, implausible, absurd. It is surreal and real at the same time because it can only happen in theatre (or fiction). The man and his penis enter into a spatial relationship: he is here – it is there. Just as words are exchanged in a meaningful space on the stage. Moreover, the spatialisation of the textual situation is emphasised by the page layout. The theatrical insert is encased in a series of footnotes, which produces a Chinese-box effect. The footnotes force the reader to move back and forth through the space of the book and experience it as multi-layered and multi-dimensional. Thus the author-arranger encourages a performative, haptic reading. Indeed, in *Habitations of the Word* he reminds us that reading can be a sensual experience; books, just like wine bottles, should be opened in an appropriate way, smelled, tasted, felt, hefted and thumbed (Gass 1997c: 227–228). So the reader is invited to perform the text, to lend it his voice, to give it his own body, to invest it with life. Accordingly, he who can be *Lonely Wife's* best friend can also turn out to be its/her worst enemy:

Of the enemies of art (and what is war without enemies?), perhaps the worst are those who will not read, sense, see hear, sing, the word. For them it is not even a note. They look down upon a passage of Beckett, for example, as though it were a false trail in the snow; they will not step into such tracks. Yet if the inscription is skimped, *what* is real?

A novel is a mind aware of a world, but if the novel is not performed; if it is not moved as it ought to be through the space of the spirit, the notation notes not; because our metaphors, our theories, our histories, do not merely fall upon their page like pictures sent in black pricks over a wire; they must be enacted, entered into; they must be rolled like drums; they must be marched in columns, formed in hollow squares; they must be sometimes quietly hummed, or possibly panted. (Gass 1997e: 111–112)

In short, as Tadeusz Sławek suggests (2003: 16), they must be experienced as bodies, in their fleshness, or as "readable bodies" – something that may come as a surprise to the writer when he attempts to engage with pure ideas. Fajfer comments on this as follows: "while I was writing the invisible text, I came to appreciate the material significance of its physical medium, that is, the visible text. The visible text became a body; I could no longer treat it as a transparent medium" (2010k: 106).

In his insistence on the significance of inscription, the necessity to read or sing the work aloud, Gass's concept of the book is reminiscent of the ideas of Mallarmé and Joyce, expressed in *A Throw of the Dice* and *Finnegans Wake* respectively. Both considered their works as a kind of musical score, yet paradoxically their books cannot be perceived only in aural terms as they are intrinsically associated with the medium of print. Kaufman draws a contrast between Gass and Mallarmé all the same. As he puts it, unlike Mallarmé, who "figured books, with their uncut pages, virginal; Gass makes his twentieth-century novel, by contrast, with its machine-cut pages, of easy virtue" (88). In this it resembles Joyce's Molly, the modern, unfaithful Penelope whose textual body is also carefully designed (cf. Bazarnik 2011: 150–153).

Gass's book is also a practical lesson in feminine fiction, something that Joyce describes in *Finnegans Wake*. When speaking of the *Wake*'s mysterious manuscript, an anonymous commentator mentions that the elusive document inseparably unites the body of the letter and its envelope, or clothing. As depicted therein, the material document is "full of local colour and personal perfume and suggestive, too, of so very much more and capable of being stretched, filled out, if need or whish were" (Joyce 1989: 109). An impatient, insensitive, "captious critic" tends to ignore this, to rip off this "outer husk" as if he were stripping a woman in haste. But it is "hurtful to sound sense" to ignore the "husk," and to "concentrate solely on the literal sense," because "its face, in all its featureful perfection of imperfection" constitutes "the feminine fiction, stranger than the facts" (ibid.). In *Willie Masters' Lonesome Wife*, the impatient reader is offered photographs that spare him the effort of slow, gradual unveiling of the elaborate tissues of words. Paradoxically, however, the nude images, and other kinds of graphic "excess," serve to disguise the "feminine fiction" that is enveloped in "some definite articles of evolutionary clothing" (Joyce 1989: 109). It is only the "attentive, thoughtful, warm and kind" reader who attends to Gass's "lady language" in all her complexity and fleshiness – to the text (and its manifold verbal and nonverbal intertexts), typography, images, and the compositional space of the book – who will be able to achieve gratification in such a multimodal "intercourse."

Poetics of presence

Presentification

In liberatic works, the metatextual and material devices create an impression of actuality. They attempt to make the reader aware of himself or herself as the reading self, and to suggest the author's "presence." It is as if this is an attempt to fight back against the absence connoted by writing, which Derrida has pointed out. In other words, such devices may be understood as "presentification," a term I borrow from Hans Ulrich Gumbrecht to describe a set of strategies intended to produce this effect. Reflecting on contemporary culture, Gumbrecht notes a drive towards experiencing artefacts in a palpable, multisensory way. For example, with regard to history, he points to the desire to simulate or create an experience of historical events, an urge that has recently intensified and that is achieved through:

> the *presentification* of past worlds – that is, techniques that produce the impression (or, rather, the illusion) that worlds of the past can become tangible again – [it] is an activity without any explanatory power in relation to the relative values of different forms of aesthetic experience (providing such explanations is what we used to think of as the function of historical knowledge in relation to aesthetics). (Gumbrecht 2004: 93–94)

As Gumbrecht explains, it is an activity that stimulates an affective response. He claims that its value lies precisely in the experiential potential, which facilitates *feeling* rather than *understanding* of the past. As he stresses, "presentification" is concerned with experiencing "moments of intensity," and not necessarily with generating meanings that can be captured in words (hence, the subtitle of his book – "What Meaning Cannot Convey"). Even if meaningful sense is generated, this cannot be grasped in terms of precise, easily verbalised concepts. It is closer to deeply felt impressions, associations, and evocations.

With its emphasis on the affective response, this activity is related to *catharsis*. However, unlike Aristotle's concept, presentification is not limited to emotions with negative connotations. According to Gumbrecht, the intensity of the aesthetic experience connects with enchantment, rapture, elation, and the sense of being deeply moved. In my view, this may be related to the "immersion," "absorption," or "identification" experienced in literary reading. While recognising that these feelings are a facet of the encounter with art works, and constitute an important aspect of the aesthetic experience, Gumbrecht does not simply equate the feelings with the experience. Rather he stresses the phenomenological nature of aesthetic "moments of intensity." Following on from physical perception, they are bound up with decoding, understanding (sense making), and interpretation, but reach beyond these acts to feelings that can hardly be communicated in words. As we express it in *Oka-leczenie*, "it is elusive, between the tear and the breath / it is that which cannot be expressed" (Fajfer and Bazarnik 2009: lxvi).

Interestingly, Gumbrecht hints that the material rhetoric (which is essential to liberature) also plays a part in this process. As he argues, "the meaning-dimension will always be dominant when we are reading a text – but literary texts have ways of also bringing the presence-dimension of the typography, of the rhythm of language, and even of the smell of paper into play" (Gumbrecht 2004: 109). For him, material rhetoric facilitates the felt intensity of the aesthetic object. This is enhanced by various defamiliarising devices, including ones that are grounded in haptic experience, and that require readers-users to handle embodied literature in ways other than mere sequential page turning. In this way, their material concreteness becomes evident. Thanks to this, literary works can be experienced as tangible things, thereby enhancing the reader's sense of being physically present in the act (activity) of reading, and heightening his or her awareness of reading as an embodied and situated practice. Such observations are suggestive of the manner in which a liberatic book can be perceived as an index of the author's presence, something that is analogous to a handwritten letter. Although it may be nothing more than a simulacrum of an intimate, material piece of evidence for communication in "real life," the liberatic work still has the power of presentification effected through its aesthetic dimension.

Gumbrecht also argues that the intensity of presence is better experienced in a state of "insularity," when the beholder is able to temporarily isolate himself from the surrounding world. This occurs when "the sudden appearance of certain objects of perception diverts our attention from ongoing everyday routines and indeed temporarily separates us from them" (Gumbrecht 2004: 103, this is probably what Joyce poeticised as the epiphany). Artistic style can produce this effect when it evokes a fictional world so vivid that it absorbs the reader, causing them to experience a moment of "mental isolation." The nontransparent bibliographical code and material rhetoric can serve this purpose too. Both can take readers by surprise, and focus their attention on the material form of the work, inviting further questions: Why this shape? Why employ this device in the first place? Such features are subject to the customary protocols of interpretation as practiced in the visual arts, but they simultaneously challenge readers' expectations when it comes to literature. Since they stimulate several sensory channels (sight, touch, perhaps hearing, too), they simultaneously activate different cognitive operations, which demands heightened concentration and attention to the (multimodal) work that is being regarded; something that may facilitate the effect of isolation.[62] And when the linguistic and non-verbal codes begin to cohere in the beholder's eye, a moment of epiphany can occur. By stimulating the readers' cognitive and affective faculties through embodied reading, such works imply that they may be experienced more intensely than conventional works, functioning as dynamically developing events.

It is, however, important to recognise the literary nature of such works. Whenever we encounter a work of art, we draw upon our preconceptions and prior knowledge in a manner that streamlines the way in which we engage with the art object. To some extent our preconceptions shape what we take from a work, and whether we experience the work as verbal, visual, or some other type of art. According to Text World Theory, these silent assumptions have considerable "impact upon the world-building process as we make use of our previous experiences of other discourse-worlds every time we enter a new communicative situation" (Gavins 2007: 38). As Joanna Gavins explains, such preconceptions are also bound up with

[62] This is a hypothesis that requires further, empirical investigation. Alison Gibbons recognises the same necessity with regard to cognitive analysis of multimodal literature, and in the conclusion to her book mentions some studies of readers' affective response, and attention (involving eye tracking of page spreads) (2012: 219–220, 224). Another, more sociologically oriented, artistic study with a strong empirical component is described in de Tollernaere and Eerdekens "The Hybrid Book Genre of Word&Image Narratives" (2014), and de Tollenaere, Eerdekens, Lefèvre and Vandoninck, *Woord&Beeld verhalen. Transitionaliteit tussen woord en beeld in fictieverhalen voor volwassenen* (2010).

our familiarity with generic conventions since "[w]e have differing expectations, for example, of the textual structure of a novel (written text, a title, an author, page numbers, chapters, and so on) compared with that of the performance of a stand-up comedian (spoken text, limited interaction, comic content, and so on). These expectations often form an important part of the world-building process before a book has even been opened or the first joke has been told" (ibid.). Thus to postulate a distinct genre for literary texts bound to the book (i.e. the text's material foundation expressive of a material metaphor) means that we must first acknowledge certain regularities in the phenomenological perception of such works. We must concede that there are sufficient commonalities so as to form the basis of such a categorisation. This recognition will consequently have an impact on future readings; readings that will be then shaped by the overtly formulated conventions of the newly identified genre. To call it *liberature* is to direct the reader's attention to "the presence-dimension" of texts embodied in the book. I develop these considerations in the final part of this monograph. But before I do so, it will be useful to briefly remark upon the affinities between liberature and other, especially performative, arts.

Literary work is an event

The processual, relational, and dynamic nature of the literary work has been extensively discussed by many scholars before. Suffice it to mention at this juncture Bakhtin, Ingarden, Iser, or Fish. Recently, Derek Attridge and Johanna Drucker have returned to a discussion of the literary work as event.[63] Both scholars emphasise the active role of the reader, but they focus on different aspects of the reading process. Attridge stresses the uniqueness of the work, its eponymous singularity, as revealed by the dynamic act of reading. He attributes this to hybridizing forces that contribute to the effect of defamiliarisation, producing the impression of singularity:

> To succeed in writing a work that is genuinely original, and does more than extend existing norms, is to introduce into the cultural matrix a germ, a foreign body, that cannot be accounted for by its existing codes and practices. This is

[63] See also Terry Eagleton's *The Event of Literature* (2012), in which he likewise emphasises the sense of singularity entailed in the experience of reading a literary work. Besides, N. Katherine Hayles discusses this in "The Time of Digital Poetry: From Object to Event."

achieved not just by fashioning into a new shape the materials at hand – in literature these materials include the rules and regularities that govern its forms and its operation as well as its sonic, rhythmic, and graphic properties; in philosophy these are ideas – but, more importantly, by destabilizing them, heightening their internal inconsistencies and ambiguities, exaggerating their proclivities, and exploiting their gaps and tensions, in such a way as to allow the otherness implicit in these materials – the otherness they exclude in order to be what they are – to make itself explicit. (Attridge 2004: 55–56)

The otherness of literature, highlighted by Attridge as a source of uniqueness, consists *inter alia* in its relation to spatial arts.[64] This is something that liberature highlights when it resorts to literature's graphic properties, and refashions said properties so as to activate additional codes. These codes might be more typical of the visual arts, design, and architecture, and they are blended with the linguistic code. In other words, the singularity of liberature is related to its polymedial or intermedial aspects, which I address in the following chapter.

But the singularity of literature, suggested in Gumbrecht's notion of presentification, also hints at an affinity with theatre. After all, every performance is a unique, temporal experience; an experience that is particularly prone to evoking the feeling the Stanford scholar describes (he even mentions how he experienced such a feeling while watching a Noh play in Japan; Gumbrecht 2004: 151). Drucker makes this connection explicit when she notes that "any text or image [...] is performed when it is read, looked at, experienced" offering possibilities that are, all the same, neither "fixed or self-evident" (2009: 13). The American scholar-artist demonstrates this in her aptly titled article "Entity to Event: From Literal, Mechanistic Materiality to Probabilistic Materiality" (Drucker 2009), in which she discusses the aesthetic experience of the literary work along the lines of cognitive science. In contrast to Gumbrecht, who emphasises feelings, Drucker stresses the intellectual, epistemic aspect of reading. She focuses on how the unconventional materiality of a literary text can challenge readers' cognitive mechanisms, opening their minds to novel ways of thinking, understanding, and sense making. Inspired by cognitive neuroscience, she argues that such reading even affects neural processes, literally training readers' brains to think differently. Since her reasoning is most persuasive in its original form, I quote it below maintaining its shape:

[64]   This is widely discussed by W.J.T. Mitchell, for example in *Picture Theory: Essays on Verbal and Visual Representation* (1994).

In conclusion, I invoke aesthetics in order to suggest that the force of materiality supports provocations to knowing. Art is the practice of form-giving, aesthetics the field of philosophy concerned with knowledge that arises from perception. So if the task of art is form-giving, and form-giving is the expression of knowledge, then the possibility of envisioning reinvention of our understanding of our own processes relies upon a recognition that they are indeed at work. The sensible page is only the appearance of a provocation to perception – it is not a literal template transferred to the mind.

No exhaustive description, however thick, of the type, page, paper, print, style, conventions, mode and matter of this production will be sufficient to guarantee that it is read the same way twice. By definition, it can't be. Aesthetic expressions do not exist in a condition of self-identity any more than other objects. Look and think, be provoked, into a reading and response, a creation of the text, page, image, as an event. The cognitive mind, unaccustomed, reprograms, running its synaptic patterns through a habitual response it finds inadequate to the new task, so new tracks and trails are scribed

and inscribed, made to fashion a world of concept anew in the autopoetic mind. There, where the world is what we perceive it to be (paraphrasing Heinz von Foerster), the force of aesthetic propositions has its way, making it possible to imagine the world as it is, has been, may be.[35] Form is idea, but not in fixed form. The cognitive process is p e r f o r m a t i v e, not procedural, probabilistic, not mechanistic. Texts, images, experiences are not entities but e

v

e

n

t

s.

(Drucker 2009: 15).

Drucker's argument, shaped as it is by material rhetoric, resembles Fajfer's equally performative definition of his newly proposed genre in "~~lyric, epic, dramatic,~~ liberature."[65] He closes his essay with a statement

[65] See page 44 in the present book.

by Mallarmé about the mobility of the book, its potential for generating "some nameless system of relations which will embrace and strengthen fiction" (Mallarmé in "~~lyric, epic, dramatic,~~ liberature," Fajfer 2010d: 48). Drucker explicitly names the nodes of such a system: the reader, an aesthetic object (an embodied text), *and* interpretation; Fajfer would add the writer and emotions, too (see, for example, 2010b: 38).

Gumbrecht's account of reading also accommodates such an expanded model, but the emphasis is reversed. He concludes his enquiry into the aesthetic experience by referencing Jean-Luc Nancy's observation about contemporary readers who are overburdened with the obligation to come up with increasingly nuanced *meanings* (Gumbrecht on Nancy's *The Birth to Presence*, 106). This occurs in a world that is determinedly focused on sense making, on gathering and processing information via the increasingly disembodied consciousness—something that is (again) identified as the Cartesian heritage. With this in mind, the scholar wonders:

> And are we not precisely longing for presence, is our desire for tangibility not so intense – because our own everyday environment is so almost insuperably consciousness-centered? Rather than having to think, always and endlessly, what else there could be, we sometimes seem to connect with a layer in our existence that simply wants the things of the world close to our skin. (Gumbrecht 2004: 106)

Literary works that employ the rhetoric of materiality perhaps, then, respond to this desire. This is, after all, the diagnosis suggested by N. Katherine Hayles in *How We Became Posthuman*, and later developed in *Writing Machines*. The fantasy of disembodied information brings about the return of repressed corporeality, as seen in technotexts, which parade their materiality (Hayles 2002: 25). And when Fajfer speaks about liberature in which "[t]he physical and the spiritual aspects of the literary work (...) complement each other to create a harmonious effect"[66] (Fajfer 2010b: 25) he responds to this as well.

Again, I want to qualify Fajfer's vision, or recify his wording (probably inspired by common criticism usually expressed as "excess of form over content" and indicating the lack of balance between them). In the liberatic work the relation between the verbal content, the compositional space of the book, and other features of its bibliographical code may generate the impression of imbalance, disharmony or tension. What is

---

[66] Przybyszewska offers a comment to that effect in "Close Reading of the Liberatic Canon" (2014a: 79).

more, such a whole can sometimes be fragile, tentative and provisional, with fuzzy material boundaries (a book-in-a-box, or a book with several "chapters" to be hunted on-line or in other editions,which I discuss in further parts of this book). But this deliberately evoked impression is important to an overall meaning to be read from the work. I suppose Fajfer used "harmonious effect" to refer to the sense of illumination experienced by the reader when she grasps this interplay of elements that initially appeared incongruous, but ultimately "make sense." Hybrid works of this kind are especially fit for the task, being both interpretable texts and material objects whose physicality cannot be ignored. They are conspicuously stretched between what Gumbrecht calls "presence effects" and "meaning effects," achieved through linguistic and extralinguistic modes and means. So while reading a liberatic work, Gumbrecht would probably savour the moment of provocation, and the ever changing mobility of the book. In this sense he would keep interpretations at bay, as he did watching the Noh performance, because as he puts it: once you let yourself feel composure in the face of an aesthetic object radically different from your habits and expectations, "perhaps you cease to ask what these things mean" – they appear to you "just present and meaningful" (2004: 151). Or shouldn't we rather say "meaningFOOL"?[67] Because such works question, in quite radical ways, accepted, familiar, transparent conventions of meaning production.

These reflections resonate uncannily with Henri Chopin's passionate attack on "the all-powerful Word" that "creates the inaccurate SIGNIFICATION" (1971: 80) and call for a different art that could bring about the sense of the present: "...we are slaves of rhetoric, prisoners of explanation that explains nothing. Nothing is yet explainable. That is why a suggestive art which leaves the body, that resonator and that receptacle, animated, breathed and acted, that + and – , that is why a suggestive art was made; it had to come, and nourish, and in no way affirm" (81). Unlike Fajfer, Chopin is highly suspicious of the controlling, reductive, colonising position of the Word, and flatly reject the belief in its existential or redeeming worth. Yet what they share is the belief in the value of embodied art, only they choose a different media to work with. The French sound poet used his own body, while Fajfer resorts mainly to the body of the book. However, it needs to be mentioned that, in point of fact, theatre has always featured large in his creative biography.

---

[67] I owe this observation, and the p(f)un, to Tadeusz Sławek.

Book is a performative space

So the aforementioned parallels between liberature and the performing arts are not accidental. In several of his essays, Fajfer brings up theatrical metaphors and analogies, at one point comparing liberature to opera (2010k: 94). Reflecting on the significance of the book as a vehicle or channel for literary communication he notes that the book evokes, through its own physicality, a different experience of space for the reader:

> (...) the first, elementary space one deals with, even before one starts reading a work, is (...) an actual book – a material object. The outward appearance of the book, the number and arrangement of its pages (if there need to be pages), the kind of cover (if there need to be a cover) – this is the space of the literary work that includes all its other spaces. And, unlike those other spaces, this space is very real. (Fajfer 2010b: 26)

He further relates this to the experience of the audience in alternative theatre, and compares the job of the writer to that of the director in autonomous theatre[68] (having worked in it himself[69]). So the director begins his work by reflecting on the space where a play is to be staged, and shaping it in such a way as to turn it into a sign of its own. Such space, including the positioning of the audience, becomes integrated with all other components of the performance. Fajfer "expect[s] a comparable treatment of space from writers," envisaging a literary work to be a similarly integrated piece (2010b: 26). He postulates that writers should no longer approach the material space of the book without reflection but, as in Kantor's or Grotowski's theatre, they should consider it part of the setting that is on a par with other components of the fictional world created through language.

Thereby Fajfer hints at the performative potential of literature. Since this potential is usually latent, it can be understood as literature's hidden affordance (Gaver 1991: 80). For this potential to be actualised demands unconventional thinking about the writing space, but when this happens, the book becomes a performative space. Kalaga also alludes to this by calling liberatic texts "spectacular" insofar as they engage more than just the sense of sight

---

[68] According to Tadeusz Kantor, "[t]he theatre that [he calls] autonomous is the theatre which is not a reproductive mechanism, i.e., a mechanism whose aim is to present an interpretation of a piece of literature on stage, but a mechanism which has its own *independent existence*. (...) [A]ll the theatrical elements must be integrated to a degree and create a composite unit" (1993: 42–43).

[69] Fajfer's play *Madam Eva , Ave Madam* was devised according to these principles.

during the act of reading, and multiply the functions of compositional elements such as the letter, page, textimage, and volume (2010b: 78). Such works require a kind of performative reading from the reader-spectator, like that described by Drucker in "Entity to Event" (2009: 15). Whereas Gibbons, following Wolfgang Hallet, points out that the reader of multimodal literature turns into a user insofar as she interacts with the text in an engaging and performative way (2015: 421). This is in tune with Kalaga's observations regarding how liberature effectively generates a new type of literary reader-user, or to use Drucker's term, the reader-producer.

It is worth adding that, as far back as the 1980s, Jerzy Kutnik discussed certain, potentially liberatic, postmodern American novels as "performances." Emphasising the affinity of such works with other arts – music, dance, theatre, the happening, painting and sculpture – he listed three characteristics of performative literary works: their "indeterminate and playful character"; their focus on "the physical properties of the medium," "on the materials used or on physical aspects of production"; as well as the audience's involvement and "collaboration in making the work complete."[70] The features responsible for performative potential depend as much on stylistic choices as on the overall design of the material book, experienced in its spatiality and objecthood. Thus, Kutnik concludes, "a work of art can be an open-form event or process in which the medium of a given art form is employed not for the sake of transmitting some prearranged meaning but in order to produce a meaning which could not otherwise be generated and experienced" (Kutnik 1986: 229). It seems that the latter type of meaning is akin to Gumbrecht's experience of moments of intensity that defy or shun verbalisation. This is also related to Drucker's model of reading as an "intervention," constituting the work as an event by giving it a "determinate form from its potential" (2009: 13). Just like the audience in the autonomous, authorial theatre, the readers-users of liberature turn into participants in the spectacle in which the book becomes an interactive stage; an essential constituent of the literary work understood as an embodied reading event.

[70] These are also the features that Kalaga attributes to liberature, and Drucker to electronic literature.

Liberature and multimodality

The Intermedia

As suggested above, affinities with theatre, performance, and the visual arts, including sculpture, imply that liberature could be described as a kind of discourse in which the author intentionally blends the linguistic and non-linguistic codes,[71] and uses different materials as the space of inscription. This resort to mixed verbal, visual, and spatial resources inspired Wojciech Kalaga to describe liberature as "a hybrid transgenre" (2010a: 8; see also 2010b: 76–77). The Polish semiotician focuses on the ontological hybridity of works in which the physical shape of the text, or to use the Ingardenian term – its material foundation – is combined with the work's intentionality thereby creating a hybrid carrier of multiple senses. As he explains, the "materiality of text does not do away with its function as the intentional object, but it calls for concretising it along with its entire extraverbal, semiotic load," hence "a hybrid text is one that integrates senses emerging out of a collaboration of the semantics of language and the structure of the matter" (2010b: 76, 78, translation mine).[72] Consequently, non-linguistic aspects of materialised language contribute to the architecture of the book, which is no longer seen as a transparent container for words, but a legitimate constituent of the literary text. As we have seen, Fajfer envisaged the organic, unified fusion of the semantic and material dimensions of literary texts in generic terms, although such ontic hybrids have also been described as the intermedia, or as multimodal literature.

[71] Here I use "code" following Eco's broad understanding of the term.
[72] Kalaga deliberately resorts to the Ingardenian conception of the literary work in order to foreground the ontological complexity of liberature and other similarly hybrid works.

This invites a comparison of liberature with Dick Higgins' concept of the intermedia. This seems necessary given that some works mentioned as proto-liberatic in "A Brief History of Liberature" combine texts with drawings, or photographs (Bazarnik and Fajfer 2005a: 17–21), and hence fulfill Higgins' criteria for defining them in this way. In the mid 1960s, the American scholar-painter revived Coleridge's coinage in order to describe pieces that are conceptually and materially situated between different types of art. In his view, such works "fall between media"; they should therefore be understood as new art forms emerging when different media are conceptually fused in one piece (Higgins 2001: 49). The con-fusion is vividly demonstrated in a chart added to the revised version of his essay, in which different arts, media, and even genres are represented by overlapping circles. The chart also visualises the author's statement that "the use of intermedia is more or less universal throughout the fine arts, since continuity rather than categorization is the hallmark of our new mentality" (50).

Unlike Fajfer, Higgins did not consider his to be a classificatory term, but rather a useful analytic tool. As he explained in a 1981 expansion of his original article, intermediality "allows for an ingress to a work which otherwise seems opaque and impenetrable, but once that ingress has been made it is no longer useful to harp upon the intermediality of a work." Nevertheless, he hints that his term is involved in a kind of classificatory operation as it can help the audience see a work's "sometimes obscure pedigree" or its "historical trajectory" (ibid.). So it can become a useful tool for investigating a work's genealogical lineage and its generic set-up. Besides, some intermedial blends may result in artistic phenomena so unique and inspirational that this may consequently lead to new typological categories.

Thereby Higgins opens an interesting vista into the link between intermediality and genre. He suggests that exploring the intermediality of a particular piece may be useful in tracing its origin in a range of different arts, techniques, styles and genres. As a critical prerequisite, he postulates a mode of analysis that must account for both the distinctive features of the medium, and the formal organisation of the art piece, which includes the identification of its constituent genres. Such a criticial mode will also constitute an important stage in the work's reception. The media and genre-oriented analysis Higgins proposes should be carried out in order to facilitate an understanding of the piece that is almost hermeneutic. Indeed, he stresses how an understanding of the work's constituent parts fosters a sense of the whole (53), even if this is sometimes achieved through a somewhat apophatic procedure. For example, as far as the happening is concerned, Higgins notes that "[t]he concept itself is better understood by what it is not, rather than what it is" (50). Yet, as cognitive scholars suggest, in order to negate a concept one must first evoke it mentally in order to erase it.[73] So the "absent" genres that are present here function as a shadowy foil to the new, hybrid genre implied by the analysed work. Pointedly, Higgins openly states that by hybridising media and techniques, intermediality has the potential to stimulate the emergence of new typological categories:

> Some works will become landmarks and will define their genre, while the others will be forgotten. At best the intermediality was needed to suggest their historical trajectory, to see their sometimes obscure pedigree [...]. But if the work is ever to become truly important to large numbers of people, it will be because the new medium allows for great significance, not simply because its formal nature assures it of relevance. (53)

So Higgins' and Fajfer's perspectives converge insofar as both of them recognise that formal explorations may lead to the emergence of new genres, more in tune with the sensibilities of (new) audiences. However, in his reflections on liberature, Fajfer is not so much interested in cases where literature comes into creative interplay with other arts, but rather in situations where literature recognises the physicality of its own linguistic medium, the characteristics of its inscription technologies. He draws our attention to the complex ontological and phenomenological status of language as the embodied, physical articulation of meaning. Embodied in written and printed forms,[74] it has an important aesthetic dimension. He is convinced that liberatic writing does not always entail mixing different media, as it can focus on exploring and exploiting the latent potential of one medium.[75] Admittedly, such explorations may trigger tendencies

---

[73] See Lakoff's *Don't Think of an Elephant* (2004: 3), and Gibbons's "This is not for you" (2011: 20–21).

[74] For the sake of brevity, I use the word "writing" to cover all kinds of texts inscribed permanently on some surface, including print and (hand)writing. When necessary for my discussion, I do, however, make distinctions between them.

[75] Though initially he seems to concentrate on the graphic aspect of language evident in writing and print, in his later artistic practice Fajfer also explores the sonic form of language and non-verbal sounds, incorporating them into his multimodal works (see his electronic poem "Primum Mobile," included as a DVD in his liberatic poetry volume *ten letters*, and *Powieki* [Eyelids], a hybrid work combining the printed book and an electronic hypertext that is available on CD and online).

that bring literature closer to the other arts. Print moves closer to graphic art: a drawing, a picture, or a design. And this has not only invited critical comparisons between liberature and the intermedia, but also comparisons with shape or concrete poetry, and artists' books (something that is discussed above). But even if works associated with these various categories share common traits, and even if the outcome of such a convergence of art forms is indeed intermediality, Fajfer claims that intermediality is not a necessary or indispensable feature of liberature. He insists that the primary matter with which the liberatic writer works is language, even if this language aspires to the concreteness of an object.

Liberature and concrete poetry

What, then, is the relation of liberature to concrete poetry? First of all, "concrete poetry" seems to be a historical term, referring to aesthetic practices widespread in the 1950s in various parts of the globe (Brasil, Switzerland, Germany, Scandinavia, Central Europe, the UK, the United States) involving a host of artists who often worked in international environments.[76] In Emmett Williams' words, that "international movement" was "blessed with a disunity that unshackles it from the aims and aesthetic principles of the many manifestos it engendered" (quoted in Bray 2015: 299; see also Sławek 1989: 28–29), and its wide geographical and cultural scope has resulted in about as many definitions and descriptions of concrete poetry as there were practitioners. What concretists did share was a preoccupation with "the word as totality [...] reaching out to semantic, syntactic and pragmatic possibilities – an intelligible object treated with concrete intentions as a useful thing" (Gomringer 1970b: 68). In concrete texts, syntax is realised as a "constellation" or juxtaposition of elements in "qualified space" rather than a linear progression (Gomringer 1970a: 67; de Campos, Pignatari, and de Campos 1970: 71). Therein words or word-images function as discrete units proliferating, dispersing, and destabilising senses (Bense 1971: 73; Sławek 1989: 13). Sometimes the poetics of concreteness can be executed only locally, in part of a work, appearing as an "interlay" in an otherwise more traditionally shaped text. This is why Tadeusz Sławek suggested that it may be more useful to speak about spots of concreteness – or places

[76] For a selection of poems and manifestos see Williams *An Anthology of Concrete Poetry* (2013 [1967]), and Solt *Concrete Poetry: A World View* (1971). For an overview of the genre see Bray "Concrete Poetry and Prose" (2015).

in which concreteness discloses itself – rather than lay out the norms and rules of an alleged genre (Sławek 1989: 41).[77] This approach may be especially helpful when considering prose, as concrete features might be (re) discovered when we look as far back as the eighteenth century English novel, *Tristram Shandy* being the prime example (cf. Bray 2015: 305). Sterne's much discussed work uses several material metaphors. The notorious black page appears at the moment of Pastor Yorick's death, symbolising the darkness of the grave, but also the black curtain falling over the stage when the performance is over.[78] The marble page, "a motley emblem" of the author's work, with its chaos of colourful lines and patches is a humours, visual representation of the chaos of narrative threads tangled in the book, and the irregular, doodling line is supposed to reflect meaders of the plotless plot. Finally, there is "a chasm of ten pages made in the book" by a ripped-off chapter, allegedly too perfect to fit in the (w)hole (Sterne 1990: 250).[79] However, it is likely that the motivations of early novelists like Sterne were more mimetic than aimed at a philosophical critique of language implied by the 20th century concrete poets.

According to Joe Bray, the concreteness of a text is basically effected through specific formatting; formatting that utilises the white space so that it functions as a compositional element alongside linguistic elements. Again Sterne's *Tristram Shandy* provides us with an excellent example. The carefully planned double spacing[80] between lines of dialogue carried out by Mr. and Mrs. Shandy establishes "a rhythm and a pace" to their unsuccessful communication. As Christopher Fanning affirms, "the very physical space on the page increases the impact of the satire, offering not just a score of a performance but a performance in itself, more subtle than the obvious typographical ploys for attention that force the presence upon the reader, because it acts by means of absence, empty space" (2002: 196). Discussing the origins of concrete prose, Bray stresses that the literary innovations of *Joseph Andrews* are fundamentally connected

---

[77] "Chodzi o to, by normatywność konkretu zastąpić jego operatywnością, tzn. by nie mówić o poezji konkretnej jako o odrębnym rodzaju literackim, lecz aby poszukiwać miejsc ujawniania się konkretności, realizacji konkretu w każdym tekście" (Sławek 1989: 41). In a similar spirit, Przybyszewska suggests that it would be more useful to speak about "liberariness" as a local or global feature of literary texts rather than liberature as a genre (2015: 62).

[78] Allusions to *Hamlet* cannot be missed, of course.

[79] Cf. Bazarnik "Popsuta przestrzeń" (Ruined Space) (2006) on a more detailed discussion of Sterne's material metaphors, and the unfortunate impact of removing them from modern Polish editions on the reading of the novel.

[80] Sterne supervised the printing of the novel himself (Fanning 2002: 179–180).

to modifications in the layout and a highly self-conscious use of spacing that is modelled on poetic conventions. Fielding himself described his novel as an "Epic-Poem in Prose," which, as Bray explains, is "a blend of techniques and styles associated with verse and prose" (Bray 2015: 304). This is something that might account for "the text's systematic use of graphic design and its concern with the visual layout" (ibid.). Incidentally, this corroborates Higgins' point about such blends giving rise to new generic forms. Such an understanding of Fielding provides another argument to support the thesis that the physical form of presentation (the layout) is related to genre.[81]

In Bray's further description of concrete prose, however, there is little analogy (beside typographic experimentation and the use of white space) with the objectives and principles of the concrete poets. Bray lists James Joyce, Raymond Federman, Ronald Sukenick, B.S. Johnson, Christine Brooke-Rose, Alasdair Gray, and last but not least Mark Z. Danielewski, as authors who can qualifiy as concrete writers. All of whom – arguably – were driven by motivations contrary to those of the concrete (Kostelanetz 2000: 131). Effectively, Bray concludes that both concrete poetry and prose are fundamentally characterised by the poetics of the blank: a deliberate employment of white space in dialogue with units of text (words, lines and blocks of text; 298). Limiting the specificity of concrete literature to the flat surface, the British scholar implies that, even in the case of fiction, concreteness does not have to be book-bound. Rather it is page-bound, and can be executed likewise on a paper sheet and on the screen.

Concrete poetics was indeed mostly realised in short forms, i.e. poems, whereas liberature concerns longer texts, the spatial organisation of which is bound to the book.[82] While embracing the opportunities offered by the graphic surface of the page, liberature foregrounds the book as "the qualified space" (to borrow the Noigandres's term), or compositional space, which functions as a sign of its own within literary discourse. And even if we juxtapose liberature with the concrete literature expounded

---

[81] As Finn Fordham informed me Samuel Richardson also used iconic typography to represent Pamels's distress after she has been harrased, but I have had no chance to verify this so far. However, I am convinced that our knowledge of the 18th century novel would benefit from more in-depth re-reading from the perspective of multimodality (admittedly, scholars such as Ian Watt or Maurice Couturier were well aware of the material rhetoric employed in it.)

[82] Though Henri Chopin's *Le dernier roman du monde* (1961) s o u n d s as a concrete novel, it is described as an artist's book in many sources. It consists of 256 upaginnated pages printed in different inks, and a vinyl record, and is the first book of Chopin's trilogy about the end of dictature, followed by *Le homard cosmographique* and *La crevette amoureuse*.

by Ulises Carrión, his reflections on the book as a self-reflexive, "autonomous reality" only illuminate the difference. Although Fajfer and Carrión agree that the book is not to be seen as a mere container for words, they fundamentally differ when it comes to the status of the text within the book, and ultimately the status of the book itself. For the Mexican artist, as it was for the concrete poets, the text can be "any (written) language, not only literary language, or even any other system of signs," preferably freed from any obligation to "bear a message," to communicate images, feelings, ideas, experiences, to encode the author's intention, to serve his or her rhetorical purposes. Carrión asserts that such a work "neglects intentions and utility, and it returns to itself, it investigates itself, looking for forms, for series of forms that give birth to, couple with, unfold into, space-time sequences" (Carrión 1985: 4). This is in tune with Bense's account of concrete poetry as "a kind of literature which considers its linguistic means [...] primarily as representation of a linguistic world which is independent of and not representative of an object extrinsic to language or of a world of events" (Bense 1971: 73). So if concrete poetry neglects or rejects the mimetic function of language, and instead turns to exploring itself as a kind of metacode, liberature still retains interest in the former, though it is open to formal experimentation.

Besides, for concretists and conceptualists language does not seem to be connected to an individual author. Consequently, a text can be non-literary, found or even plagiarised, minimal, reduced to a single character, a punctuation mark, or even its incomplete part, as in Solt's "Moonshot Sonnet." The ideal book is then a book filled with blank pages that communicates only with its structure (Carrión 1985: 4). By contrast, for the liberatic writer language is a necessary component, an instrument for individual expression that is enhanced by its embodied features. Even if the language is minimal, in liberature it cannot be reduced to a purely visual sign. Its visuality always oscillates between the semantic and the abstract, as in Fajfer's series of poems "Actaeon" and "Act-Aeon" in which the isomorphic (or tautological) phrases "7 letters" and "ten letters," alongside groupings of Arabic numerals, form a simple narrative sequence about the transgressive, fatal act of the mythical hunter (see Fig. 6). Likewise, when Danielewski leaves a single, large, black dot in the centre of (the otherwise totally blank) page 312 of *House of Leaves*, the mark in fact functions as a full stop; the punctuation mark that closes both a sentence informing us that Navidson's film "runs out here," and chapter XII of the novel. So, in these liberatic works, such "concrete" moments also function at the syntactic (grammatical) level, and at the level of plot.

[Act-Aeon]

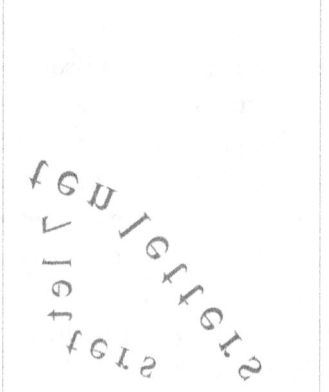

Fig. 6.
Zenon Fajfer
"Act-Aeon"
(excerpt from
ten letters, 2010)
By courtesy of
the author

Another point of divergence concerns certain affinities espoused by the Polish and the Mexican artists. Although Carrión hints at the possibility of a new literary genre located in the book,[83] for him the creative direction of concrete writing shifts from literature towards "a new art," and beyond: towards concrete poetry, bookmaking, artist's books, conceptual art, installation, and perhaps performance. Ultimately, he claims that:

> In order to understand and to appreciate a book of the old art, it is necessary to read it thoroughly.
> In the new art you often do NOT need to read the whole book.
> The reading may stop at the very moment you have understood the total structure of the book. (Carrión 1985: 6)

For Fajfer creativity runs in the opposite direction: towards literature. In liberature the work should be read in its entirety because all of the literary aspects of the text are important, and open to the established protocols of interpretation. But these interpretations need to be expanded by a medium-specific analysis that could also account for the physicality of the book, and it is crucial to grasp and interpret the interrelation between literary and physical qualities. By no means do liberatic artists reject or deny their literary affiliations. They take responsibility for words, for their concreteness and representational potential, authoring them in concrete shapes. Considering themselves writers and poets they do *write books* which they expect to be read even more thoroughly than "the old" literary books Carrión mentions. Agnieszka Przybyszewska, who critically juxtaposes the Mexican and Polish manifestos, also notes that liberature calls for a kind of "expanded reading." And she concedes that any apparent similarities between Carrión and Fajfer are misleading. The artist's book and liberature do, for Carrión and Fajfer, require different interpretive approaches. The former relies more on the codes of the visual arts, whereas the latter relies on the literary code enriched by the visual code (Przybyszewska 2015: 282–283).

[83]   As he notes in his manifesto, "Books, regarded as autonomous space-time sequences offer an alternative to all existent literary genres" (Carrión 1985: 3). This in turn chimes with Maurice Blanchot's ideas in "The Book to Come."

It follows that Fajfer seems to see liberature as a fundamentally mono-medial genre. This genre is located within literature, although he admits that some liberatic works mix media and modes, for example when they include images or photographs alongside the text. His stress on mono-mediality is based on the silent presupposition that literary language is always already an embodied medium *and* a complex semiotic mode. Language so understood is not only a linguistic system (*langue*), but a materially grounded writing (a mass of *parole*), rich in visual texture and evocative materiality, including its (latent) phonetic dimension (signalled by the specificities of the coding system[84] that are actualised by the reader). It is a culturally and socially contextualised phenomenon.[85] In this sense it can be better described as situated discourse.

Nevertheless, the rich potential for stratified semiosis that is possible with discourse thus conceived is often described in terms of multimodality. Or as the editors of *Perspectives on Multimodality* define it, "the interdependence of semiotic resources in text [...], particularly in written/visual communication. Indeed, the kind of text where the 'language' can be excised as an independent unit is, in many areas, fast becoming the exception rather than the norm" (Ventola, Charles, and Kaltenbacher 2004: 2). This description does not clarify whether language should be understood as a medium or a mode, perhaps because there is as yet no uniform terminology, nor methodology, to successfully deal with this distinction in the vigorous field of multimodal studies (Ventola, Charles, and Kaltenbacher 2004: 1–6; Machin 2013: 349–350; Maziarczyk 2013: 23–27). For example, Gunther Kress and Theo Van Leeuwen, authors of seminal studies on the subject, imply that language is a mode realised in different media. As they state, this mode[86] is a semiotic resource through

---

[84] For example, non-standard spellings can reflect dialect pronunciations, and different typefaces can code phonetic features. Commonly, CAPITALS STAND FOR SHOUTING, whereas in B.S. Johnson's *House Mother Normal italics stand for vocalised speech*, and Roman type codes interior monologue. In *Oka-leczenie* different fonts are iconically related to the characters' voice and appearance.

[85] For example, Fajfer hints at a culturally and historically determined perception of typeface when he describes a mental experiment in which the Polish national anthem is printed in Gothic type and the Cyrillic alphabet (Fajfer 2010c: 31–32).

[86] This meaning of mode is of course different from the grammatical mode, expressing a degree of probability, certainty, necessity, or ability, and the mode as part of network of literary genres and modes, in which the latter implies a general tone, mood, and often the topic of a work (see Fowler 1982: 106–107). In fact, Fajfer's proposal to treat

which meaning is expressed in culturally acceptable ways via material vehicles, i.e. media (Kress and van Leeuwen 2001: 21–23, 125). An interesting variant of this definition, and one that is relevant to our discussion
of liberatic discourse, is offered by Helmut Stöckl. The German scholar
describes language as "a mode in its own right"; a mode, however, that
"can be medially realised in either speech or writing. Both are governed
by the grammar of language, but being different medial or material vari-
eties of one mode they entail a number of concomitant, additional submodes."[87] In this formulation, writing – characterised by attributes that
"contribute to its meaning beyond the linguistic" – is a medial variant of
the linguistic mode (Stöckl 2004: 11). Moreover, due to its materiality,
this medial variant activates sub-modes and shares the material channel of communication with other major modes, such as the image. Next,
Stöckl defines typography and layout as peripheral modes of language,
while fonts and typefaces (including colour, shading, spacing, and para-
graphing) are considered its submodes. These can be further characterised by features such as saturation, contrast, tension, etc. (12). Such features are typical for visual communication, but can also be semantically
relevant in a (verbal) text. Stöckl's networked model of mode-medium
interrelations embraces dimensions of discourse which Fajfer addressed
in a more poetic way when he spoke about the appearance of the word
in "~~lyric, epic, dramatic~~, liberature" (Fajfer 2010d: 43). At the same time
Stöckl, like other multimodality researchers, stresses the fact that,

> the purely mono-modal text has always been an exception while the core prac-
> tice in communication has essentially been multimodal all along.[2] The domi-
> nance of linguistics, however, and the concentration on language as the central
> mode, paired with a lack of adequate models for the analysis of other modes,

---

██
    liberature as *rodzaj* (as expressed in his original 1999 manifesto) was perhaps closer
    to the meaning of mode or kind, and not genre (pol. *gatunek*). The distinction between
    the two categories is hierarchical and much strictly delineated in the Polish than in the
    Anglophone genre studies, and much of the ensuing controversy has been related to
    this difference. I discuss this in the following part of the book.

[87] In *The Work of Art. Immanence and Transcendence* Gerard Genette discusses the dis-
    tinction between works of verbal art based on speech and writing. He refers to them
    as "autographic" and "allographic" objects of immanence respectively. Perhaps at this
    point it is also worth mentioning "orature, literature and liberature," terms used by
    Radosław Nowakowski, another important figure in the Polish liberature movement
    (*Traktat kartkograficzny* 2002). Nowakowski distinguishes these three different types
    of creative verbal art on the basis of their mediality. His ideas have obvious parallels
    to Ong's distinction between orality and literacy.

made verbal mono-modality appear to be the standard and dominant form of communication. (Stöckl 2004: 10)

Incidentally, this corroborates the initial diagnoses of Fajfer and Hayles regarding the prevailing critical and writerly neglect of the material features of literary discourse. In fact, my postulation of the genericity of liberature is based on the premise that authors who are acutely aware of the multimodal and multimedial potential of literature foreground it and use it to enhance their work's thematic dimensions. This awareness is then reflected in literary works which utilise ways of making meaning that rely both on the linguistic mode and its peripheral semantic resources. In this sense, liberature could be described as multimodal literature. Moreover, it is evident that at least some liberatic works are multimodal in a broader sense. They combine language (print, handwriting), images, and architectural structures, as indicated by Kalaga in his description of liberature as a hybrid transgenre. This is why we now need to ask whether liberature and multimodal literature are not merely two different terms that refer to the same category of texts.

According to Alison Gibbons, the latter term entered literary studies fairly recently, its use on the increase since roughly the turn of the millennium. She associates this fact with the development and influence of digital technologies on creative writing (2008: 107).[88] Gibbons defines multimodal literature as "a body of literary texts that feature a multitude of semiotic modes in the communication and progression of their narratives. Such works are composed not only of words, type-set on the page in block fashion as has become publishing convention" but also include images, other graphic elements, non-standard typography, page layouts, etc. (2015: 420). Although Gibbons focuses on printed forms, multimodal literature is by no means limited to this medium, as she makes clear in the introduction to her monograph *Multimodality, Cognition, and Experimental Literature*. Multimodality is easily realised in the digital media, in the form of an electronic file activated by software, as an app accessible through computer hardware, an e-book, or another mobile device. Therefore, multimodal literature appears to be an umbrella term for a range of

■
[88] She mentions the following studies: Gunther Kress and Theo van Leeuwen's *Reading Images: The Grammar of Visual Design* (1996) and their *Multimodal Discourse: The Modes and Media of Contemporary Communication* (2001); Anthony Baldry and Paul J. Thibault's *Multimodal Transcription and Text Analysis: A Multimedia Toolkit and Coursebook* (2006); and *New Directions in the Analysis of Multimodal Discourse* ed. by Terry D. Royce and Wendy L. Bowcher (2007).

texts realised in different media and distributed through different platforms. By contrast, liberature (though sometimes hybridising print and digital media as in Fajfer's *ten letters* and *Powieki* [89]) is fundamentally bound to the book understood as a printed text that constitutes a conceptual whole with its specific material embodiment. Beside serving as the material support for the text, the architecture of the book, i.e. its compositional space, functions as another important semantic mode operating along with the linguistic mode. Only reading the work in its two modalities (linguistic and material/architectural) enables the reader to engage in ways of sense making that embrace the whole piece.

Interestingly, in her monograph Gibbons decides to limit her discussion to multimodal printed literature, or in fact the multimodal printed novel. The latter has a great deal in common with liberature, as it "experiment[s] with the possibilities of book form, playing with the graphic dimensions of text, incorporating images, and testing the limits of the book as a physical and tactile object" (2012: 6). Other features of this category are: the use of colour in typefaces and images, varied typography, unusual textual layouts and page design, "concrete realisation of text to create images, as in concrete poetry," flipbook sections, and "devices that draw attention to the text's materiality, including metafictive writing," as well as footnotes, and the deployment of a self-interrogative critical voice. Such works also mix genres, "both in literary terms, such as horror, and in terms of visual effect, such as newspaper clippings and play dialogue" (2).

Gibbons' list overlaps to a large extent with the list of properties offered in my discussion of liberature as a prototype-based kind of fuzzy genre (Bazarnik 2010b: 159–161).[90] But a closer, nuanced look at the differences between the two indicates how liberature and multimodal literature can be distinguished as related, but not identical, categories. First of all, Gibbons

[89] Fajfer's work consists of an intricate cycle of poems printed in a codex and recorded on a CD to be displayed with Flash software on a computer screen. Meanings arise from the interplay between the two media and the textual forms specific to each. Though its dual setup could suggest that it is "digital-born print literature," its digital component would be better described as print-born electronic poetry since all of the animated poems began life as (hand)written texts. We might even imagine that transitions between the two parts (indicated by hyperlinks in the electronic part) could be marked typographically on the printed page and "activated" in the minds of attentive reader-users. What would be missing from such a monomedial version, though, would be the sound, movement, and opalescent colours accompanying selected poems on screen. These medium-specific features indicate that the digital part cannot be seen as a mere digitalisation of the printed content.

[90] The overlap is noted by Grzegorz Maziarczyk in his discussion of textual materiality (2013: 35–36).

considers images to be a default component of multimodal literature. By contrast, in liberature they are not obligatory, though myself and Gibbons both note that the use of varied typography, colour, and what she terms "concrete realisation of text to create images as in concrete poetry" are frequent features in both types of texts. Moreover, when images appear in a liberatic work, they do not illustrate or complement a text, but usually enter into syntactic-semantic relations with it, as in the flipbook section of Steven Hall's *Raw Shark Texts*, which visually narrates the approach of the eponymous predator. Due to its narrative-mimetic function in the overall structure of Hall's novel, this "concrete," mobile section of the book co-shapes the compositional space, foregrounding the sequentiality and materiality of the printed codex. In other words, thanks to this section Hall's narrative draws attention to its own bookhood, or to use Pressman's term, its bookishness (2009: 477).

Though Gibbons distinguishes flipbook sections as a separate feature of the genre, she does not offer any general term that would account for the compositional space, an aspect of the liberatic work that I subsume under the spatial structure of the text, and consider essential to liberature. I see it as related to the diagrammatic iconicity of the work,[91] understood as "isomorphisms between structural relations in language and [the] relational patterns of its referents" (Nöth 1995: 126). It can be extrapolated that in liberature this can be seen in isomorphisms between the work's linguistic component (text) and the architecture of its material support (Bazarnik 2005a: 26, 36; Bazarnik 2010b: 160).[92] Perhaps Gibbons covers a similar idea when she speaks of "unusual textual layouts and page design." This, however, could be limited to only part of the work, and Gibbons does not explicitly name any feature that could account for the compositional space of the *whole* work. This is understandable insofar as she does not specifically focus on the printed book as a distinct sign.

The compositional space, an essential aspect of the liberatic work, can be seen as part of the "navigating mechanism" that directs the progress of reading, and is responsible for the work's ergodic potential. This feature is not specified in Gibbons's list, but in her later discussion she refers to the "enactive" response or "performative engagement of the

---

[91] The other type of iconicity, called pictorial, refers to a resemblance between the form of the sign and its denotation (Nöth 1995: 126).

[92] Hence, I find it hard to take Przybyszewska's criticism that I limited my application of iconicity in liberature only to its pictorial type (cf. Przybyszewska 2015: 48–49).

reader" (2012: 210) as aspects of multimodal literature. As regards other "navigating devices," the British scholar mentions footnotes, along with "self-interrogative critical voices," which she lists separately from "metafictive" elements and "devices that draw attention to the text's materiality" (2). These elements correspond to self-reflexivity or metatextuality, and materiality in my list. When the use of such devices involves a "reflexive loop" in which the work "interrogates" the technological conditions of its own creation, the work fulfills Hayles's criteria for technotexts; that is texts that "strengthen, foreground, and thematise the connections between themselves as material artifacts and the imaginative realm of verbal/semiotic signifiers" (2002: 25).[93] As such all these categories of texts overlap with metafiction, or to use Federman's term, surfiction – the kind of writing that foregrounds its own linguistic and extraverbal constructedness. In my view, this indicates how all these terms constitute a constellation of non-hierarchically related categories, differentiated by slight varitations in their defining features. As regards metatextuality or self-reflexivity, I would locate these concepts at the crosssection of the rhetorical and thematic dimensions of liberature and multimodal literature, thus providing an important clue regarding the shared thematic scope of the genres, namely a preoccupation with writing as an embodied, technologically determined practice. That being said, liberatic works seem to favour a few other themes, which I discuss in the following chapter. It remains unclear if Gibbons envisions a specific thematic scope for the multimodal print novel or for multimodal literature more generally.

Another subtle difference between multimodal literature and liberature lies in their prioritisation of certain literary (sub)genres. Within the broad field of "multimodal printed literature" Gibbons places special

---

[93] Gibbons admits that the aforementioned features (including "varied typography," "use of colour in both type and imagistic content," "concrete realisation of text to create images as in concrete poetry") can be found in literary works from other periods. Nonetheless, she claims that the post 9/11 period has brought a wave of creative writing markedly different from that of the past. It is informed by new, digital technologies, and characterised by an extensive use of varied media and modes. In this she shares Hayles and Jessica Pressman's conviction that this is "an emergent literary strategy that speaks to our cultural moment," namely the rise of digital technologies and their influence on creative writing (Pressman 2009: 465). Undoubtedly, this kind of materially-conscious writing has been on the ascent in recent decades. But (allegedly exceptional) historical examples of this practice suggest that such a writerly strategy has always been available, albeit as a marginalised practice that has frequently been dismissed as eccentric and experimental (see Bazarnik 2005b: 9–10).

emphasis on the novel. She believes that "multimodal printed literary fiction" should be treated as "a genre in itself" (which comes very close to my understanding of liberature, and echoes Couturier's treatment of the novel as a print-based genre). She admits that this genre also includes graphic novels and children's picture books, and that it is related to "other creative multimodalities," such as figural texts and concrete poetry (Gibbons 2012: 2). This emphasis on the novel is perhaps not so strong with liberature. Liberatic works might rely on a narrative component, navigated by the reader through the work's material form, so that the work consequently resembles an open ended novel or hypertext. Equally, liberatic works might embrace lyrical, poetic texts, arranging these in a compositional whole as they are printed/inscribed in carefully designed material volumes. Arguably, examples include Fajfer's *ten letters* and *SPOD*, Andrzej Bednarczyk's *The Temple of Stone*, Jen Bervin's *Nets*, Herta Müller's *Der Wächter nimmt seinen Kamm*, and Philip Meersman's *This is Belgian Chocolate*. Of course, the hybrid nature of all these texts raises the weighty question of their generic status and, related to this, the question of genre itself.

What is nevertheless evident is the fact that, just like Fajfer and myself, Gibbons does not neglect to speak of genre. What's more, in the introduction to her monograph she explicitly announces a double goal in this regard: "to expand the perception of what multimodality is and what it can be, as well as develop a *genre*-specific understanding of literary multimodal word-image unions" (Gibbons 2012: 2, emphasis mine). Unfortunately, Gibbons seems to leave the latter issue undeveloped. She does, however, reject John Bateman's "Genre and Multimodality model" (his GeM Model, in which genre features as one of several constitutive layers of a multimodal document). For Gibbons, this model is too static and author-oriented, and therefore less capable of accounting for the reader's experience, which is of central interest to her (18). Indeed, in Bateman's model, genre is a conceptual frame that informs the manner in which writers shape their discourse in order to fulfill a specific function in a particular social context. Therefore he places emphasis on text production, not reception. Besides, Bateman limits the application of his model to non-literary multimodal documents, which is also why Gibbons finds it of little use in her discussions of literary fiction.[94] Nevertheless, it is discernible that hers, like mine, is a prototypical model, and she notes that "[m]ultimodal literature as a genre is

---

[94] This may be useful because, as we shall see, authors often treat genre as an important point of reference in their creative work.

not uniform, but rather exists on a spectrum, from minimal to extensive in the level of incorporation of multimodality" (Gibbons 2015: 420), "within which there are more and/or less prototypical examples" (2012: 3). Our lists indicate that we share the conviction that genres are essentially scalar phenomena, which means that a particular work is more or less saturated with the enumerated features, but no one feature is considered to be "the obligatory" one, nor hierarchically related to another. Only taken together, they account for the work's specificity, and consequently, its generic identity (Gibbons 2012: 3; Bazarnik 2010b: 159).

Agnieszka Przybyszewska is another scholar who makes the point about the gradability of liberatic features (2015: 15). The Polish scholar authored the entry on liberature in the Polish Scholarly Press's updated dictionary of literary genres and modes,[95] and recently published *Liberackość dzieła literackiego* [Liberariness of the literary work], an extensive, critical monograph on the development of the concept. For her, the fuzziness of the category (initially postulated by Fajfer and further explored in my aforementioned article) invalidates its potential generic status (61–63). Having revised her initial position, she recently proposed that, rather than speak about liberature, it would be more reasonable to talk about *liberariness* as a more or less pronounced trait in certain works. That is, to use the term in its adjectival form rather than conceptualise it as a noun and claim an "existence" for the genre. Ironically, she defines "liberariness"[96] as "literature in the form of the book" (160), a kind of literary writing inextricably connected with the material mechanics of the book, which echoes Fajfer's definitions and betrays a similar classificatory drive. She concludes that the term (in all its variants: liberatura, liberary, liberariness) is a useful addition to the toolkit of literary terms as it highlights a heretofore unnamed dimension of literature: its semantically loaded visuality and the material features of the medium. As she notes, the term might come in handy not only for analysing contemporary writing, but also for research on historical works with such material facets. As a consequence,

---

[95] *Słownik rodzajów i gatunków literackich* [A Dictionary of Literary Kinds and Genres], ed. by G. Gazda (Warszawa: Wydawnictwo Naukowe PWN, 2012).

[96] In fact, she tentatively suggests the coinage "liberacy" (Przybyszewska 2015: 335), probably inspired by the Polish version of the noun. She later uses her new coinage in English abstracts of her Polish articles (cf. abstract and keywords of "Toward Playable Literature," 2014b: 127). This is unfortunate as English speakers are more likely to see or hear an echo of "literacy." While this aptly communicates the combination of traditional alphabetic, visual/spatial, and media literacy demanded by liberatic works, it does not direct attention to the properties of texts, as Przybyszewska desires, but rather to the skills readers must possess.

the recognition of these additional, non-verbal codes brings about a modified understanding of literary communication:

> Creating liberature means a thoughtful reflection on all elements of the process [of literary communication], a potential exploration of those that are conventionally mute. So the concept is very broad, and one of the major attributes of works classified as liberatic is the fact that they evade predictable forms, they take one by surprise, since they reject conventionalised techniques of literary communication. They embody, in the form of the book, the adage "medium is the message." And the usefulness of the term, especially in its proposed, adjectival form, comes to light through the fact that this lets us underline a continuity in the tradition of this kind of communication which uses the written word. (Przybyszewska 2015: 385, trans. by KB)[97]

While Przybyszewska has her reservations, I believe that this does not prevent her from slipping into a generic usage of the term as, for example, when she discusses the *generic* differences between concrete poetry and liberature (Przybyszewska 2015: 125, emphasis mine), or when she juxtaposes liberature with electronic literature, comics, and artists' books. Admittedly, she does not treat these categories as literary genres *per se*, but it is clear that she understands these terms as a means of classification. After all, she analyses their features in order to draw distinctions between similar, yet non-identical, phenomena, and to outline how they might be grouped together within and across such broader conceptual domains as art, book, literature (e.g. 293). And this is very close to how Ib Ulbæk construes genre: as an element occupying a specific position in a hierarchically ordered conceptual system, interrelated to other similar hierarchies (Ulbæk 2015: 428–429, 434–440). So it seems that – while ostensibly rejecting Fajfer's supposedly limiting, classificatory term – Przybyszewska in fact constructs her own system of classification for literary texts without overtly admitting this.

---

[97] "Kreowanie liberatury oznacza uważny namysł nad wszystkimi elementami tego procesu, potencjalne eksplorowanie tych z nich, które konwencjonalnie pozostają nieme. Pojęcie jest więc szerokie, zaś jednym z głównych atrybutów dzieł zaliczanych do liberackich jest to, że wymykają się przewidywalności formy, zaskakują, gdyż odrzucają skonwencjonalizowane metody literackiej komunikacji. Ucieleśniają w formie książki formułę 'środek przekazu jest przekazem'. A użyteczność terminu, zwłaszcza w proponowanej tu przymiotnikowej formie, przejawia się również w tym, że pozwala on podkreślić ciągłość tradycji takiego podejścia do komunikowania się przez słowo pisane" (Przybyszewska 2015: 385).

In a similar vein, Grzegorz Maziarczyk, the author of a study of textual materiality in contemporary English fiction, wonders if my postulated list of characteristic features for liberature forms a sufficient basis for a fully-fledged genre, especially given that "they can be found in a variety of more established genres and they cannot obviously be exclusively correlated with just one of them" (Maziarczyk 2013: 36). As I have mentioned, he compares my list with Gibbons's, but does not go so far as to conflate liberature with multimodal literature, noting the differences discussed immediately above. Ultimately, while Maziarczyk seems to have adopted Gibbons' hierarchy of multimodal literature, he leaves the question of the generic distinctness of liberature unresolved (ibid). Yet, unlike Przybyszewska, he does not question the validity of the genre itself. In his discussion of a subgenre of the novel *as the book* he resorts to the concept without any qualms, evidently considering this to be a staple in his theoretical toolkit.

Despite their objections, neither Maziarczyk nor Przybyszewska substantially explain how they understand the concept of literary genre. Both, however, resort to it. And this is something that is evident, for example, in the title of Maziarczyk's study devoted to "the novel as book," or Przybyszewska's discussions of concrete poems, graphic novels, and comics. It seems that both scholars assume that literary genre is a dated, historical notion; one that is rather irrelevant and inadequate as a tool for discussing contemporary, experimental works. Przybyszewska in particular shares this conviction. She addresses the question in passing when she addresses Fajfer's (in her opinion ineffective) criticism of the division of literature into the lyric, epic, and dramatic kinds. Referring to Romulad Cudak, the co-editor of three volumes of essays on 20th century Polish genre studies, she contends that this tripartite model, deeply rooted in the European tradition, has generally survived "the poststructuralist revolt" and still retains its validity (probably for historical studies; Przybyszewska 2015: 33–34). The fact that both Gibbons and Fajfer continue to find genre useful as a tool for discussing works that share some common characteristics, creating a "family resemblance," does however suggest that the concept has more uses than merely historical classifications. With this in mind, in the following part I address this problem further, and argue that it still makes sense to invoke genre in relation to embodied, experimental, book-bound literature of the present, and the past.

PART THREE

The question of genre

Genre trouble

A "venerable error"

The word 'genre' derives from the Greek *genos* and Latin *genus*, i.e. 'race' or 'kind.' It entered the English language via French in the early nineteenth century (White 2003: 376), therefore coming into the language quite late. The same is true of "literature" – in the modern sense of imaginative works that possess an aesthetic quality, and which form a canon of texts important to a given culture – and the two words share a comparable vagueness. The etymology of 'genre' further imposes an analogy with biological taxonomy. With a long-lasting tradition going back to Aristotle, this analogy is responsible for the first, and still fairly common, understanding of genre as a tool for classifying texts and evaluating them against some prescribed criteria (Fowler 1982: 37; Fishelov 1993: 19–53; Miller 1994: 20; Rosmarin 1985: 23; Swales 1990: 34, Frow 2006: 26–7, 55–69).

But for Alastair Fowler "this is a venerable error" (Fowler 1982: 37). The narrow, taxonomical perspective has not proved viable since many, if not most, literary works trespass upon, blur, or explode prescribed boundaries and often, if not always, blend several genres (Fowler 1982: 45–46, 171–190; Genette 1992; Beebee 1994; Frow 2015: 43–54). This is what must have led Croce to declare the "impossibility of such systematizations," and to formulate his radical proposition that "[a]ll the books dealing with classifications and systems of the arts could be burned without any loss whatever" (1995: 114–115). Another essential factor that contributed to his view was the historical reconceptualisation of literature, rooted in German romanticism. In the wake of this reconceptualisation, "[t]he literary work came to be considered as an autonomous process, self-instituting and self-reflexive, entailing the laws of its own production and of its own theory. Hence, genre, in the sense of the literary genre, became the genre of self-generation... in its generalised and self-generating movement, literature seems to imply its own specification" (Chartin *et al.* 1980: 236, qtd. in Dowd 2006: 12). Convinced of this position, some literary critics have questioned the utility of genres for the classification of literature, if not the utility of the category *per se*, especially where this relates to twentieth and twenty-first century literature that supposedly defies generic labels[98] (cf. Cohn 1989: 11). Such critics either limit the application of generic categories to historical texts (e.g. Przybyszewska 2015: 53), or reject them altogether because of their unsatisfactory and supposedly constricting nature.[99]

That being said, genres are, all the same, commonly used in a classificatory capacity, be it in schools, libraries, bookshops, supermarket stalls, or online where one routinely finds labels like "classics," "historical fiction," "adventure," "poetry," "drama," "graphic novels," "thrillers," "non-fiction," "literary criticism," and many more. By no means is this limited to contexts that call for a simplified system of labelling. In fact, as Dowd and Rulyova remark, recently,

> [t]hrough technological change, engagement with 'genre' in both its theoretical guises and its more vernacular usages, the term has become ubiquitous in academia and among the general public, the latter encouraged by internet search engines, online retail and new platforms for the dissemination of film to think in patterns, types and categories. (Dowd and Rulyova 2015: 3)

Likewise, despite repeated claims that it is an outdated tool for literary studies, genre constitutes a frame of reference in many recent scholarly articles and monographs. Suffice it to recall *The Novel as Book* and *Multimodality, Cognition and Experimental Literature*, mentioned above. Scholar of Victorianist literature Bożena Kucała outlines why this kind of taxonomy is practiced in literary research. As she notes, in the "highly heterogeneous" category of texts whose sole common denominator seems to be their "dialogic relation with the Victorian age," "[s]everal attempts have been made to devise a classification scheme with a view to a systematic analysis of the genre" (2012: 45). In her use of intertextuality to map this diverse field, genre comes to function as an important analytical instrument. Evidently, for researchers, taxonomy has some explanatory value

■

[98] This would be true of so called "high" literature. But genre thrives in popular fiction. This kind of writing benefits from a normative-formulaic concept of genre; a set of guidelines that determines what makes a "good" horror, fantasy, or love story. For readers, in turn, this provides the comfort of finding what they want in a text.

[99] Barthes' concept of Text, or Blanchot's "the book to come" may serve as examples.

too, and this is especially true in chapter two of Kucała's study where she uses the Victorian realist novel as a foil against which she interprets selected neo-Victorian works.

This should not be surprising because genre is a kind of categorisation, and categorisation is one of the fundamental cognitive activities essential for organising, storing, retrieving and operationalising knowledge. It entails making sense of experiential data, and relating what we perceive to previously acquired knowledge (Rosch 1978; Medin and Aguilar 1999; Miller 1994: 24–25; Auken 2015; Ulbæk 2015; Gabora, Rosch, and Aerts 2008). First of all, categorisation enables us to deal efficiently with the richness of the world, making it manageable and comprehensible. Eleanor Rosch notes that one of its primary aims is "to reduce the infinite differences among stimuli to behaviorally and cognitively usable proportions" (1978: 29). It therefore consists in grouping objects and phenomena according to some perceived similarities, which are then abstracted into concepts, models and schemata (Rosch 1978). Thanks to these conceptualisations, we are able to "interpret situations in terms of previous situations that we judge as similar to the present" (Gabora, Rosch, and Aerts 2008: 85). It then follows that genre is "necessary to [both] language and learning" (Miller 1994: 20) because it facilitates the organisation of, and access to, "a mental database of texts" in an efficient way. In literary studies, genres emerge as a consequence of similar cognitive operations, and perform a similar function. David Fishelov asserts that they serve "to group different texts into a limited number of recognisable generic categories" (1999: 53). The aim of this is to deepen knowledge about the literary field, from both a synchronic and diachronic perspective. This is possible since the various ways of gathering texts into hierarchies, or networks of relations, underlie theoretical models that aim to explain literature in general (1993: 1–19, 155–160). Evident disappointment with genre as an (arguably inadequate) tool for exploring the complexities of contemporary literature must, however, be responsible for its poor reputation among literary scholars. This includes those who have expressed reservations about conceptualising liberature as another genre of literature.

A demise or regeneration of the (literary) species?

The skepticism of some literary critics has been counterbalanced by vigorous research carried out in the fields of rhetoric, discourse studies, sociolinguistics, applied linguistics, pragmatics, education, and cultural anthropology.[100] The focus has shifted from literary to non-literary genres, illuminating aspects arguably overlooked or downplayed by literary studies. In Aviva Freedman and Peter Medway's *Genre and The New Rhetoric*, a volume collecting vital articles in the field from the end of the 20th century, the editors explain how this reorientation helped to refine the traditional, classificatory function of genre, foregrounding its other variables and functions:

> Current genre studies (which incidentally tend to concentrate on non-literary texts) probe further; without abandoning earlier conceptions of genres as 'types' or 'kinds' of discourse, characterized by similarities in content and form, recent analyses focus on tying these linguistic and substantive similarities to regularities in human spheres of activity. In other words, the new term 'genre' has been able to connect a recognition of regularities in discourse types with a broader social and cultural understanding of language in use.
>
> [...]
>
> [The work done in the field] forces us all to reanalyse and rethink the social, cultural, political purposes of previously taken-for-granted genres, and leads to an archeological unearthing of tacit assumptions, goals and purposes as well as the revealing of unseen players and the unmasking of others. (Freedman and Medway 1994: 2)

Such inquiries have continued in the new millennium, inspired by dynamic research in the related disciplines. Alastair Fowler, in an outline of genre theory over the past century that appears in the *Encyclopedia of Literature and Criticism* (1990, reissued 2000), persuasively demonstrates how literary scholars have considerably developed an understanding of the concept of genre, and flags how this could be further refined, for example by taking account of modern theories of meaning such as the theory of relevance (Fowler 1990: 151–163). David Duff's *Modern Genre Theory* (2000), a selection of essential readings in the field of 20th century literary genre theory, inspired a whole series of new publications on the subject. In 2003, *New Literary History* published an issue on theorising genres and the relevance for interpretation. In 2007, *PMLA* followed suit. Both publications bear witness to the unwavering validity of the concept, while essays collected therein offer new insights from eminent scholars in the field. 2006

---

[100] For an overview of their influence on genre studies see chapter 1 "Locating Genre Studies: antecedents and Prospects" in Freedman and Medway (1994: 1–13), and Giltrow and Stein "Genres in the Internet: Innovation, evolution, and genre theory " (2009).

brought two more important publications. *Genre Matters: Essays in Theory and Criticism* was edited by Dowd, Strong, and Stevenson, and includes Brian G. Caraher's illuminating discussion on how cultural and historical motives engender literary genres. John Frow's *Genre*, is a succinct, comprehensive study of the subject that appears in Routledge's New Critical Idiom series (its second, revised edition came out in 2015). And the trend is on the rise. Most recently, Garin Dowd and Natalia Rulyova edited *Genre Trajectories: Identifying, Mapping, Projecting* (2015). This volume (covering genres in literature, film, and teaching practice) was the product of several interdisciplinary workshops held from 2012 to 2013 as part of the Genre Studies Network at the Universities of Birmingham and Leeds, and University College London. Natasha Artemeva and Aviva Freedman's recent collection *Genre Studies around the Globe: Beyond the Three Traditions* (2016) focuses on non-literary genres but widens the scope of the discussion by bringing together, and negotiating between, Anglophone, European and Latin American approaches.

As for Poland, in 2000 the Institute for Literary Studies of the Polish Academy of Science published a post-conference volume entitled *Genologia dzisiaj*, i.e. "Genre Studies Today," which was edited by two leading scholars in the field, Włodzimierz Bolecki and Ireneusz Opacki. *Teksty Drugie*, a major journal for literary studies, also devoted a special issue to "Genres and Monsters." In the wake of the alleged demise of "literary species,"[101] and the debates that followed, Danuta Ostaszewska and Romulad Cudak at the University of Silesia edited three complementary volumes collecting the most important Polish writings on genre in linguistics (2007), literary studies (2008), and contemporary literature (Cudak 2009), and organised further conferences on the matter. As if to top it all off, in 2012 the prestigious academic publisher PWN issued a thoroughly revised edition of *Słownik rodzajów i gatunków literackich* [A Dictionary of Literary Kinds and Genres]. The project was supervised by Grzegorz Gazda, the editor-in-chief of the long-running journal *The Problems of Literary Genres*.[102] Incidentally, in a Bourdieusian gesture of legitimisation, it

---

[101] Stanisław Balbus gave his essay the provocative title "Zagłada gatunków," i.e. "the demise of species." He argues that genres are indelible historical and pragmatic categories that continue to govern expectations of the possible *types* of meaning to be found in a specific text (2007).

[102] Its publication apparently inspired the launch of *Genre: Forms of Discourse and Culture* in the United States (cf. the journal website: http://www.ltn.lodz.pl/index.php?option =com_content&view=article&id=95&Itemid=63, access: 7 June 2015).

features an entry on *liberatura* as a recent type of creative writing (Przybyszewska 2012: 521–26).

In Scandinavia, a research group for genre studies based at the University of Copenhagen has prioritised the investigation of literary writing. They specify that their aim is "to establish a cohesive connection between aesthetic and functional theories of genre, in order to reinvigorate the study of genre in aesthetic research fields, and the inclusion of aesthetic subjects in Genre Studies" (http://genre.ku.dk/genre-studies/). Further useful information related to literary forms can be found at the GXB ("Genre across Borders") portal, which "aims to offer a comprehensive overview of the multiple strands of genre scholarship and their relationships, in order to catalyze intellectual exchange and pedagogical innovation and to help us understand the processes and motivations of genre development, evolution, and circulation" (http://genreacrossborders.org/). This resource also deals with contemporary literature.

Online, vigorous, grass roots discussions of generic matters have stimulated intensive research into genres in the digital environment (see, for example, Giltrow and Stein *Genres in the Internet: Issues in the Theory of Genre*, 2009). Some new types of discourse in Computer Mediated Communication have a conspicuously aesthetic dimension – it's no wonder that this is referred to as electronic *literature*. The classificatory drive is present here too, as illustrated by the keywords used to index the contents of the three anthologies that make up the *Electronic Literature Collection*.[103] Genre can serve as a means of defining and binding together contemporary interpretive communities, and it seems that users and producers of digital content feel the urge to mark out the identity of their work by attaching generic names to what they experience and create on-line. As Dowd and Rulyova observe, genres, and their modified forms, are "tacitly and explicitly involved in engaging political discourses of expression, representation and the production of subjectivity in the context of the societies and cultures in which they emerge" (2015: 4).

Incidentally, genre-oriented activities in cyberspace affirm the culture-bound nature of the conceptualisation of genre. Likewise, studies of genre are culture-related, taking place within particular ethno-cultural traditions. It was the hierarchical framework of the three classical kinds (Pol. *rodzaje*): the epic, the lyric and the dramatic, and genres (Pol. *gatunki*) as specific categories suborinate to them, that has been

---

[103] Cf. *ELC 1*, http://collection.eliterature.org/1/aux/keywords.html; *ELC 2*, http://collection.eliterature.org/2/; *ELC 3*, http://collection.eliterature.org/3/.

a source of controversies related to the alleged generic status of liberature. The Anglophone genre studies approach these categories in a more pragmatic, or functional, way. This has helped me to understand how liberature could be conceptualised as a genre after all and it is within this tradition that I offer my discussion here. Moreover, today it is evident that genre studies need to take sociological factors into account in a more explicit way.[104] They investigate diverse "cultural forms that arise in human interaction, the patterns and forms of culture, and the role they play in our production and interpretation of cultural utterances" (Auken, Lauridsen and Rasmussen 2015: vii). Auken, Lauridsen, and Rasmussen (all members of the aforementioned research group, and editors of the recently launched series *Copenhagen Studies in Genre*), explain that these "utterances" can be a wide range of linguistic and cultural texts, "in a very broad sense, including TV programs, the genres of everyday conversation, juridical documents, sculptures, school essays, etc., etc. Genres are everywhere in culture, and the concept of genre follows close behind" (vii).

This chimes with Bakhtin, who drew attention to the generic dimension of every enunciation. He noted that "each sphere in which language is used develops its own relatively stable types of [...] utterances," shaped by norms and conventions that regulate relations among the content, "linguistic style," "compositional structure," context of use and parties involved in a communicative act. "These utterances reflect the specific conditions and goals of each such area [...] and are equally determined by the specific nature of the particular sphere of communication" (Bakhtin 1996: 60). In other words, genre analysis should not be divorced from the context of use, a claim that takes us closer to Fowler's suggestion that the theory of relevance may be helpful in taking account of readers' and authors' "cognitive environments" and "interests" (Fowler 1990: 161–162). Todorov extended this thinking to the diachronic relations of genre forms. He described these forms as "institutions" that "function as 'horizon's of expectations' for readers and as 'models of writing' for writers." They can therefore be understood and investigated as formal codifications of socially intelligible and acceptable meanings (1990: 18–19; see also Jauss 2001).

Bakhtin went so far as to say that all typified utterances may be understood as "speech genres," which are seen as either simple or complex

---

[104] I sketch this kind of reading of liberature in "Liberatura w polu produkcji kulturowej" [Sociological Contexts of Liberature] (2015a).

depending on their form and function.[105] He describes the latter as generic hybrids since they arise from combinations of simple forms of "unmediated speech communion." Their status changes insofar as they "lose their immediate relation to actual reality and to the real utterances of others. For example, rejoinders of everyday dialogue or letters found in a novel retain their form and their everyday significance only on the plane of the novel's content. They enter into actual reality only via the novel as a whole, that is, as a literary-artistic event..." (Bakhtin 1996: 60). This is an important moment in thinking about genre. The Russian scholar accentuates the essentially heterogeneous nature not only of actual texts,[106] but of the more abstract category of genre. He also highlights the entanglement of ideology and worldview with style (62–63), which has a bearing on the rhetorical, organisational and thematic dimensions of genre that is related to implication and relevance (Frow 2015: 79–100). In Bakhtin's view, only some literary genres are considered complex, but scholars inspired by his thoughts have pointed out that perhaps all literary genres are complex in the Bakhtinian sense. For example, Fowler indicates the manner in which non-aesthetic factors are an important force in the emergence of new genres (2003: 186–187). So genre comes to be understood as an amalgam of variables; variables that are dynamically modified under the pressure of aesthetic and extra-aesthetic concerns.

Such thinking anticipates conceptualisations of genre as "a typified rhetorical action" that is grounded in its social context (Miller 1994: 20). As Carolyn Miller argues, we can speak of genre if we can distinguish a category of discourse "interpretable by means of rules," the meaning of which is inferred from the situation in which it is used, from the social context. In order to formulate a genre-claim, we must consider the linguistic specificity of texts (style, register, medium), the forms in which texts are presented and delivered in relation to their purpose, the authors and other agents instrumental in text production, the audience, and other exigencies of a situation. Miller notes that the rules specifying the dimensions

---

[105] Some constructive criticism of this distinction has been offered, inter alia, by Susanne Günthner (qtd. in Wysłouch 2007), and Seweryna Wysłouch. Frow offers a subtle, critical resume of Bakhtin's simple and complex forms; by relating this to the inherent dialogism of any utterance he argues that in some specific situations any seemingly simple form can aspire to complexity, i.e. a form of heteroglossia (Frow 2015: 45–46). This is another argument in favour of considering the intention of the speaker/writer, and the context of use, as important variables for genre. I stress this because these parameters are essential for the concept of liberature.

[106] Even those that could be considered "pure" examples of a genre.

of genre are fairly general because genre occupies a mid-position in the hierarchy of categories describing language in use; it is higher than discourse and lower than form: "Genre serves as the substance of forms at higher levels; as recurrent patterns of language use, genres help constitute the substance of our cultural life" (31).

Consequently, genre is redefined. It is not simply a set of rules or laws regulating the formal and thematic features of texts. Rather, genre comes to be understood as the "typified rhetorical ways communicants come to recognize and act in all kinds of situations, literary and nonliterary. As such, genres do not simply help us define and organize kinds of texts; they also help us define and organize kinds of social actions, social actions that these texts rhetorically make possible" (Bawarshi 2000: 335). So it is more useful to think about them in terms of the conventions that discipline or regulate "textual behaviours." With regard to artistic texts, genres employed in this capacity indicate what is perceived as "creative writing," or "literature," or "poetry," or "the novel," or "the graphic novel," etc. at a specific moment in time, and how this differs from other aesthetic uses of text in design, advertising, graphic arts, film, etc.

Thinking about the emergence of a new genre, such as liberature, we can see this as an action that aims to modify regulatory conventions in the literary field (Bazarnik 2015a; 2016). While the chances of success for such an action might be marginal, success can be achieved if it is "rhetorically possible." In other words, a modification can happen when the author activates some hidden potential of the medium, actualising this in a creative act in a manner that is recognisable to their audience. Readers, in turn, "whether they know it or not, (...) are also continually guided by relevance to what they assume to be the writer's intentions" (Fowler 1990: 161). These intentions can be inferred from the very departures from conventions. It is these intentions, as Fowler notes, that "promise, after all, the pleasure of recognizing intended harmonies" (ibid.). What has "existed in potential" at a given cultural moment can, therefore, be brought out by works created according to thus modified conventions. Scrutinised with a view to categorising them, such works either bring about the reconceptualisation of an existing genre to which they are related, or serve as a springboard for a new generic category.

This is close to Aristotle's idea of entelechy, and it is related to the idea of emergence. Cognitive scholar Andy Clark suggests that "a phenomenon is emergent if it is *best understood* by attention to the changing values of a *collective* variable" – a collective variable being "a variable that tracks a pattern resulting from the interactions among multiple elements in a system," which may include aspects of the environment (Clark 1997: 112, qtd. in O'Connor and Wong 2015; emphasis mine). "Emergence will come in degrees as a function of the complexity of interactions subsumed by the collective variable" (ibid.). Clark's description indicates how a literary genre may emerge out of the interplay between the author's treatment of aesthetic conventions, audience expectations, and technological and economic determinants (see Miller qtd. in Dowd and Rulyova 2015: 1). This broader model of genre "forces us all to reanalyse and rethink the social, cultural, political purposes of previously taken-for-granted genres, and leads to an archeological unearthing of tacit assumptions, goals and purposes as well as the revealing of unseen players and the unmasking of others" (Freedman and Medway 1994: 2).

One such discovery is writers' serious engagement with material forms of presentation, usually combined with their more or less overtly expressed intuition that their "material," book-bound writing gives rise to an emergent new genre. Consider only a handful of examples spanning over three hundred years: commentaries by the self-conscious narrators of Sterne and Thirwell, and Mallarmé's preface to *The Throw of the Dice*:

> Tell me, ye learned, shall we for ever
> be adding so much to the bulk—so little
> to the stock?
> Shall we for ever make new books, as
> apothecaries make new mixtures, by
> pouring only out of one vessel into
> another?
> Are we for ever to be twisting, and
> untwisting the same rope? for ever in
> the same track -- for ever at the same
> pace?
>
> (Sterne, *Tristram Shandy*, V. 3)

Aujourd'hui ou sans présumer de l'avenir qui sortira d'ici, rien ou presque un art, reconnaissons aisément que la tentative participe, avec imprévu, de poursuites particulières et chères à notre temps, le vers libre et le poème en prose. Leur réunion s'accomplit sous une influence, je sais, étrangère, celle de la Musique entendue au concert; on en retrouve plusieurs moyens m'ayant semblé appartenir aux Lettres, je les reprends. Le genre, que c'en devienne un comme la symphonie, peu a peu, à côté du chant personnel, laisse intact l'antique vers, auquel je garde un culte et attribue l'empire de la passion et des rêveries; tandis que ce serait le cas de traiter, de préférence (ainsi qu'il suit) tels sujets d'imagination pure et complexe ou intellect: que ne reste aucune raison d'exclure de la Poésie – unique source.

(Mallarmé, "Preface" and "Préface", 122–123)

And I suppose it was just possible that I just wanted to insert a pause in my usual love stories, my usual bonanzas of the private life, but I'm not so sure. [...] I didn't want to be *topical*. I think instead it had just something to do with this new mania for connections, my idea of integrity that meant you had to follow every thought as far as you could, into all the sad dead ends. And to present this new way of thinking I began to imagine new forms, like pull-out sentences, and multiple high-speed changes in direction. I imagined concertina pages of stories, pasted pictures. And why not? [...]

I wanted to make reading an experience that aged you.

(Thirwell, *Kapow!*, 18–19)

The "trick," as it were, lies in one's ability to see that this is possible, and realise the possibility; to add, by a slight "twist of the rope," not only "to the bulk" but also to "the stock." The three writers, coming from different ages and working in different media ecologies, were able to spot the opportunity to go beyond the conventions of materially transparent literature and turn their books into material metaphors. Likewise, Fajfer reflected on his own writing in relation to what he considered innovative in the literary tradition. By coining "liberature" he simply gave a name to a concept that emerges from authorial practices of material rhetoric that have always been with us but which have been thrown into a stark relief by the writing technologies of the new media (Fajfer 2010b: 28; 2010e). As Jessica Pressman remarks, today "the aesthetic of bookishness" is becoming "an emergent literary strategy." It is probably more widely used because it "speaks to our cultural moment" (2009: 465) in a more profound way than was previously possible. Now the writer has access to tools that enable him or her to physically shape their material in a way that is almost as individual as the material of a painter or sculptor. He or she can write, design and print a book all by him/herself with less expense than was possible in the days of the Hogarth Press.

Yet, somewhat ironically, "printed artifacts" do become akin to paintings and sculptures when it comes to their *re*-production. They might defy the demands of automatised production, being too costly and time-consuming to bring out in a trade edition. Major publishers are unwilling to take risks and depart from editorial routines, even with established authors. I suppose it is no coincidence, then, that Jonathan Safran Foer produced his liberatic *Tree of Codes*[107] with Visual Editions, just as Adam Thirlwell did with *Kapow!*. Independent, fringe or small publishers are more open to material writing, but they are often associated with artists' books. Consequently, the writer may redefine him or her self as an artist, deliberately refusing to reproduce a work in multiple copies or limiting the print run. If, on the other hand, he or she decides to make the work available on the web, a number of issues related to authorship, accessibility and indeed economy arise. Such sociological factors are in fact fundamental in differentiating between the artist's book, liberature, and electronic literature (and "books powered by the magic of the Internet"[108]) as aesthetic entities. Sociological and economic forces exert an influence on the way authors position themselves in a creative network (as writers, or as artists, or game desigers), and the type of implied audience their works project, which has a bearing on the formal, rhetorical and thematic properties of their works.

So, as Bawarshi stresses, it is essential that we need to consider genres, including those relating to literary texts, in their specific ecology: the broadly understood conditions under which they are created and disseminated (2001). This is suggestive of the ways in which the material forms of actual texts (utterances) are produced and distributed, and the purposes they serve, because they can be instrumental in understanding genre. This is in turn closely connected with the impact of media and technology on linguistic norms and conventions, readers' habits and expectations, and authors' practices, including the degree of authorial agency (Bazerman 1994). Bawarshi even goes so far as to propose that "genre theory and analysis as a method of inquiry [...] might very well help us synthesize the multiple and often factionalized strands of English Studies, including literature, cultural studies, creative writing, rhetoric and composition, and applied linguistics" (2000: 336). (We might add to his list all other disciplines investigating areas of communication and creativity.) Not only does he find genre useful in categorising texts, but also essential for cross-disciplinary research into culture, "because genres, ultimately, are the rhetorical environments within which we recognize, enact, and

[107] See Kris van Heuckelom (2012) and Ariko Kato (2012) on the liberatic character of Foer's book.

[108] This is the name invented for the digital-born kind of creative writing showcased by Editions at Play, the digital twin of Visual Editions, an innovative publishing house based in London (see https://editionsatplay.withgoogle.com/#/ and http://visual-editions.com/ respectively).

consequently reproduce various situations, practices, relations, and identities" (ibid.). In other words, to use Dowd and Rulyova's apt phrase, genre emerges as "the coordinating concept" for different disciplines in the humanities (2015: 1), appealing because it is used to capture a "snaphot" of the inherently fluid and dynamic reality of culture. Given the number of works that have amassed that employ material poetics, it is no wonder that this has stimulated the need to name these emergent phenomena; hence Fajfer's *liberature* and Hayles' *technotexts*, Pressman's *bookishness* and Emerson's *readingwriting*. All are ways of categorising and conceptualising hazy constellations that have called for a name. All work (often silently) on the presupposition of genre, but only liberature seems to be explicit about this.

Categorising and (re)conceptualising

Ideas and shadows

As signalled above, the categorisation of texts into genres can be carried out according to different criteria related to knowledge, purpose, and even the philosophical stance, worldview or ideology motivating the categorising agent (Ulbæk 2015: 428–429, 435). This raises the question of the inescapable subjectivity of classification. The problem of subjectivity may be partly alleviated by resorting to the concept of the interpretive (discourse) community; a community that sustains and perpetuates particular ways of creating texts, and inferring meanings from them, in accordance with what is considered relevant by *both* readers and writers. Hence, Frow defines genres as "frames that establish appropriate ways of reading or viewing or listening to texts [...] made up of material and formal features, a particular thematic structure, a situation of address which mobilises a set of rhetorical purposes, and a more general structure of implications" (2006: 31). A common feature of literary genre theories is that prime importance is attached to stylistic variables; that is, choices in linguistic form that are motivated by aesthetic, thematic and rhetorical concerns (which can be seen as the modern expression of decorum). It is this factor that seems to play an instrumental role in distinguishing among literary forms. But Frow draws our attention to the fact that the organisational (or else compositional) and rhetorical variables of literary genres may also be related to the non-linguistic submodes of language. As I have noted, these submodes are crucial for setting liberature apart from other types of literary texts. The concept of liberature enables us to distinguish between works whose authors make use of them and deliberately hybridise the linguistic and bibliographical codes treating the form of the book as a sign in its own right, and those who leave such decisions to others, judging them to be semantically and aesthetically irrelevant. This is a valuable nuance since some authors choose to utilise only the typographic submode, or use non-verbal codes in parts of their works,[109] which makes their texts akin to, but not identical with, liberature.

Frow defines genres as frames that structure the conditions of comprehension and interpretation. In his discussion of this he focuses on recipients who act as genre verifiers. However, it is evident that authors play a comparably significant role, both in terms of the formation of genres and their ongoing function. After all, an author's approach to generic conventions constitutes a fundamental force in the shaping of a literary work. Even if an author claims to disregard "all conventions," and deeply believes in the singularity of literature, they are more or less aware of current categorisations that exist in the discourse communities they address. This knowledge is then reflected in their work because, after all, "no man is a lonely island." As Derrida argued, genre always leaves a trace, a mark or "re-mark," on a text, and "this re-mark – ever possible for every text, for every corpus of traces – is absolutely necessary for and constitutive of what we call art, poetry or literature" (1992: 229). As he saw it, individual works do not belong to a genre but rather "participate" in genres due to "the [generic] trait" on which they "re-mark" (227–228).[110] In other words, one cannot shun a concept without first evoking it, if only for it to be erased.[111] The generic dimension is thus a precondition of art because, while striving for originality, for singularity, for uniqueness, authors inevitably conjure the shadowy presence of the generic norms they defy. As the philosopher poetically put it:

[A generic designation] tolls the knell of genealogy or of genericity, which it however also brings forth to the light of day. Putting to death the very thing that it engenders, it cuts a strange figure; a formless form, it remains nearly invisible, it neither sees the day nor brings itself to light. Without it, neither genre nor literature come to light, but as soon as there is this blinking of an eye [...], at

---

[109] See Sławek's 'spots of concreteness,' which I mention in the subchapter "Liberature and Concrete Poetry."

[110] I return to this point below. In the mean time, let me stress that Derrida also notes that this dynamic is responsible for innovation in poetics, the "arts and crafts" of writing (which, remember, is also a technology). The generic "re-mark" "underwrites the eruption of *technē*, which is never long in coming. I submit this axiomatic question for your consideration: can one identify a work of art, of whatever sort, but especially a work of discursive art, if it does not bear the mark of a genre, if it does not signal or mention it or make it remarkable in any way?" (1992: 229).

[111] See footnote 73. The title of "~~lyric, epic, dramatic,~~ liberature" seems to be a practical demonstration of this claim.

the very moment that a genre or a literature is broached, at that very moment, degenerescence has begun, the end begins. (Derrida 1992: 231)

So there is no genre in literature, Derrida suggests, but there is no literature without a genre, too. Ultimately, both rely on "a principle of [generic] contamination," which is their fundamental "trait." Incidentally, Thomas O. Beebee makes a similar claim from a phenomenologically informed Marxist-historicist position (1994: 265). For contemporary genre scholars it is evident that actual literary works always realise more than one genre convention. Such hybridity is especially evident in texts that oscillate between fact and fiction, the increasingly popular realm of "faction," (auto)biography and autobiografiction, narratives of memory and trauma (cf. Dowd and Rulyova 2015: 4–5).

Although Brian Caraher rightly chastises the French philosopher for "promulgat[ing] and prosecut[ing] an outmoded, distinctly neoclassical sense of 'genre' and its quasi-metaphysical regime of discursive laws and orders" (2006: 38),[112] I believe that Derrida managed to capture something important from the perspective of poets and writers – those "naif alphabetters"[113] who, unversed in literary theories but versed in literature, creatively misread writerly norms and conventions. Also, I cannot resist the temptation to relate Derrida's words to *Oka-leczenie*. While tackling death in its physical, spiritual, and symbolic dimensions, the work rang the death knell of the literary genre as we, its authors, knew it. Writing our book, we were certain that we were working *within* the literary tradition. What happened during the writing process can be described as "degenerescing," or perhaps "de-genre-ating." The book became contaminated with its Other.[114] Consequently, the "mute-I-lated" *Oka-leczenie* engendered – materially and conceptually – a "third space." It thereby brought to life "a new entity," "a formless form." At that time, it (both the space and the form) remained "nearly invisible" because there was no "eye" to see it.[115] Or else,

---

112 The "sin" Fajfer was also "guilty" of.

113 The phrase comes from page 107, line 10 of *Finnegans Wake*, from a passage which, in an even more obscure and poetical-satirical way, addresses creative and uncreative misreadings, illusions or dreams of individual authorship, and the materiality of writing (cf. Bazarnik 2011: 70–96).

114 Compare W.J.T Mitchell's remark that with writing it is not only voice that throws it into relief, but also the image, and its visual dimensions; elements that our alphabetic culture has so effectively suppressed (1994: 113–114).

115 But we felt it, as if it were a palpable object. This brought into play another sense, the sense of touch that furnished the work with a haptic dimension.

the "mute-eye-lated" "I" needed a "conceptual instrument" with which to identify the blurry figure emerging in sight.

The idea of liberature or what is a concept?

As Kant famously said, "intuitions without concepts are blind" (A 51/B 75; Kant 1998: 193–194). Without conceptualising a shadowy entity and imbuing it with a name, it remains just a vague impression. This act of imbuing a shadowy entity with a name is precisely what Fajfer did when he coined a term that hybridised literature and the book, via a Latinised noun, to describe a kind of writing that we had intuited from our own creative practice, and from our readerly experiences. Proceeding from intuition to conceptualisation, he merged two cognitive domains: that of literature (that is, creative writing invested with aesthetic, expressive qualities) and of the book (as its space of inscription). This kind of cognitive operation has been called "ception" (Talmy in Tabakowska 2016: 13). According to Leonard Talmy,[116] ception is "a cognitive domain" that encompasses "all the cognitive phenomena, conscious and unconscious, understood by the conjunction of *perception* and *conception*. While perhaps best limited to the phenomena of current processing, *ception* would include the processing of sensory stimulation, mental imagery and currently experienced thought and affect" (Talmy in Tabakowska 2016: 13, emphasis E.T.). Ception finds its expression in linguistic forms that capture the dynamic relation between perceptions, or Kantian intuitions, and an attempt at understanding *what* they are. As Tabakowska explains, the "cepting" mind searches through familiar categories in order to match a perceived phenomenon with one or more of them (ibid.). Following Talmy, she enumerates as many as thirteen parameters that condition the process. Thus a "cepted" mental object is evaluated, in various degrees, by palpability, clarity, ostension, localizability, identifiability, objectivity, intensity, content/structure, type-of-geometry (or else size and shape), accessibility to consciousness (related to the amount of attention it engages), certainty, actionability (i.e. how easy it is to examine or manipulate it) and stimulus dependence (14–15). Depending on their prominence,

---

[116] It needs to be noted that Talmy's notion of ception was developed on the basis of Stephen Palmer and Eleanor Rosch's unpublished paper "Ception: Per- and Con-" (after Tabakowska 2016: 13). For details of his theory see Talmy "Fictive Motion in Language and – Ception" (1996) and Talmy *Toward a Cognitive Semantics* (2000).

the object may appear as more or less accessible through sensual perception, more or less vivid, autonomous, distinct and distinguishable from other similar phenomena; thus, the resultant mental image may be felt to be more like an object (a thing), or a concept (an idea). As Tabakowska stresses, the parameters do not pertain to the features of the object as such (or in Kantian terms, a noumenon), but to the way it is perceived or experienced; hence they are "phenomenological in nature" (ibid.). Also, as Talmy notes, they partly overlap, forming an interrelated, open set, so their number can be reduced or extended (21).

Related to this is the developing ecological theory of concepts. Writing about this theory, Gabora, Rosch and Aerts (two cognitive psychologists and a mathematician) propose that "[c]oncepts and categories do not represent the world in the mind, as is generally assumed, but are a participating part of the mind-world whole. Therefore, they only occur as part of a web of meaning provided both by other concepts and by interrelated life activities. This means that concepts and categories exist only in concrete complex situations" (Gabora, Rosch and Aerts 2008: 95). That is, they emerge as semi-stable models abstracted from a dynamic set of phenomena perceived as similar in a given situation. They are based on prior experiences and already acquired knowledge, which have already been conceptualised, so that new concepts are built out of previously formulated ones. Only then are they,

> charged with the potential to dynamically interact in myriad ways with conceptions of other objects as well as with the goals, plans, schemas, desires, attitudes, fantasies, and so forth, that constitute human mental life. And it is through these interactions that their relations are discerned, and together they thereby come to function as an integrated internal model of the world, or worldview. Thus it is when stimuli in the world come to be understood in conceptual terms that they acquire the weblike structure and self-organizing dynamics characteristic of an ecology. (Gabora, Rosch and Aerts 2008: 95)

The scholars also draw our attention to the fact that even concepts that are well established and seemingly fixed are ever so slightly modified under the pressure of the context in which they are applied, slightly coloured by the subjective perspective of "interrelated life activities," which is close to the linguists' description of "ception" (Tabakowska 2016: 21, cf. also Chuderski and Bremer 2011: 38). They further note that,

> If categories ultimately arise from life activities, basic level categories could provide an entry to the events and processes that produce them. And as a worldview

builds up from basic level categories to include more detailed as well as more abstract levels of conceptualizing, it becomes more interconnected, more of an ecology, that comes increasingly to reflect what is unique about the circumstances and idiosyncrasies of the individual. (Gabora, Rosch and Aerts 2008: 96)

These cognitive theories explain how new notions emerge when a perceived object cannot be easily located within the aforementioned web, or if it can only be located at the margins of the parameter scales of ception, or when it fits none of the familiar categories. Then "[a]ttempts at understanding – or ceiving – such an entity lead to novel conceptualisations, neologisms, metonymies or metaphors. These are all cases of a creative mind trying to come to terms – in both literal and metaphorical sense – with novel experience" (Tabakowska 2016: 20). According to the ecological model, such linguistic creativity is informed by the "goals, plans, schemas, desires, attitudes, fantasies" of the per/con/ceptualiser. This description resembles Dowd and Rublyova's account of genres as "fundamentally unstable models" that "scholars, artists, scientists, poets, musicians, writers and linguists" use to articulate "their models of the world" (2015: 2). This view of genre casts light on how Fajfer's "idea of liberature" arose in idiosyncratic circumstances, yet managed to address questions relevant to other agents in the cultural field. It emerged as a blend of the "lower level categories" of BOOK and WRITING, and its "weblike structure" of meaning was determined by Fajfer's own creative practice, reading, work in theatre, and curatorial activities. Working on *Oka-leczenie*, Fajfer explored the representational and pictorial potential of alphabetic writing and its submodes (print and handwriting) and its relation to other, ideographic systems of language notation. The readerly experience indicated to both of us that other writers practiced literature as a material activity. Theatre provided us with an enhanced sense of space as a potentially aesthetic dimension of the literary work, and our prior experience with performing arts prompted us to look at the book as a staging of a story or lyrical situation. Consequently, we came to see the publishing process as an opportunity for a textual performance by both the author(s) and their reader(s). Moreover, the performance was designed to be interactive from the start, in tune with the audience involvement we had practiced in theatre, and in line with the Shandean tradition of dialogue with "Dear Reader," who is encouraged to doodle in the book. Finally, it is important that Fajfer's seminal article, in which he "cepted" the idea, accompanied an exhibition of unconventional and artists' books. Since the emerging concept did not match any familiar category, he resorted to a neologism that fused the most essential aspects of a *type* of creative writing; hence, his resort to genre as a concept used to categorise literary works. So liberature was (con)cepted because that allowed us to grasp what a literary work might *also* be, and how it might be read in its totality (or should I say (w)holeness?) as a textual object and material artefact. And the ception of bookbound writing took the nominal (rather than adjectival or verbal) form because he felt liberature was "an idea,"[117] akin to "a thing" rather than "a quality" or "an activity."

A term may be invented as a consequence of ception, but it will not be ac-cepted unless it brings with it some epistemic "profit" to other language users. As Ulbæk remarks, a category that comes into use addresses not only the question of *what* a phenomenon is but also *what knowledge* it brings out (2015: 422–423). Liberature must have brought about some advantage since it has been in use for over a decade, welcomed by both authors[118] and scholars.[119] As I have argued, its major epistemic payoff consists in foregrounding material aspects of literary texts as semantic resources, the architecture of the book as the device navigating reading, and the interpretive benefits that follow from these recognitions. Przybyszewska, who has voiced reservations regarding its generic status, concedes that liberature is a valuable attempt to "grasp theoretically" the kind of writing that does not downplay its materiality, in which "the book as the interface, is not neutral and, being an integral component of the work, [...] should be subject to reading and interpretation as well" (2014a: 104; cf. 2015: 55 and 62). However, while praising liberature for "demonstrating that such works remain in continuity with the past literary tradition," she strongly objects to conceptualising it as a genre. In her view, this entails the unnecessary labelling of literary works, which "leads to aggressive arguments about sharp boundaries between concepts" (or else genres), "eliminates border areas" of

[117] See, for example, the following reflection in "(Non) Description of liberature": "It was an analysis of some basic entries in the dictionary (material, form, literary work, book, time and space, layout) that led me to formulating the *idea* of liberature in response to the "Platonic" attitude of critics towards writing and the book" (Fajfer 2010f: 60; emphasis K.B.).

[118] Examples can be found in authors who have published their books with the "Liberatura" imprint of Ha!art, including Polish writers like Robert Szczerbowski and Dariusz Orszulewski, as well as foreign ones like Raymond Federman and Herta Müller. Radosław Nowakowski, who changed the name of his small independent press from Książkarnia "Ogon Słonia" (Bookmaking Workshop "Elephant's Tail") to Liberatorium, is another prime example.

[119] See Przybyszewska *Liberackość dzieła literackiego* (2015), and her other publications mentioned in the bibliography of her monograph; see also Kalaga (2010a, 2010b), Kato (2012, 2014), Heuckelom (2012), Ranocchi (2012, 2013, 2014).

arts, and excludes hybridisation, which in the case of a hybrid term seems "somewhat absurd" (Przybyszewska 2015: 15). So "instead of speaking of liberature as a class of works," she proposes to "use a gradable and more practical category of *liberatic quality* or *liberatic dimension* of the literary work" (2014a: 104, emphasis A.P.; cf. also 2015: 383). She is convinced that the adjectival form allows us to better underline the continuity of materially grounded literary communication (2015: 385). All the same, as she explains, she does not refrain from using liberature in its nominal form for convenience's sake (15), and admits that the Polish concept allows us to highlight "transmedial and trashistorical" tendencies in the literary tradition more efficiently than *technotexts* or *bookishness* (62).

This brings me to a crucial nuance as regards ways of conceptualising liberature as genre, which will hopefully throw light on the controversy about its ontological status. In thinking about genre (also about specific genres) as a concept – that is, as a mental representation of a class of entities – we tend to understand it as a definition. In other words, as Mieke Boon observes, we tend to equate a concept with an accurate, exhaustive description of the properties possessed by an actual specimen, in line with the prevalent empirical tradition: "striving at an account of concepts as definitions that are strictly faithful to what is empirically given" (Boon 2012: 233). Hence, genre appears as a "reflection" or "representation" of an objectively existing class of texts. Such a conceptualisation does not reflect many of the actual ways in which genres are used, though it definitely underlies its taxonomic function. Attempts at describing genre in terms of a prototype, or a fuzzy set, are aimed at reconciling its actual, heuristic use with this conceptualisation.

Reflecting on how concepts are construed, Boon also mentions that concepts are felt to be like *objects* or *properties* or *processes* (230).[120] The first is reflected in nominal forms, in our case: liberature, technotext, multimodal literature, electronic literature, readingwriting; the second is expressed through adjectives and nouns derived from them, such as bookish and bookishness, liberary or liberatic and liberariness, multimodal and multimodality. These grammatical forms express the preconceptions associated with the two types of conceptualisations, which according to cognitive linguists are gounded in experiences of objects and properties in real life (Tabakowska 2016: 17–21). In other words, the way one understands

---

[120] She discusses the formation of concepts in the sciences but her analyses are also relevant to other contexts as she describes more general, abstracted mechanisms that can be easily applied to other conceptual domains.

a concept already implies its practical application. Fajfer's nominal form directed him to use the term as a category of literary texts, hence a genre. Przybyszewska thinks about liberature in terms of qualities or features possessed by some texts; hence her preference for liberariness. Her objection to conceptualising liberature as a genre is thus connected with thinking about genre in terms of a specific understanding of definition.

Understanding genre simply in these terms pushes us to imagine it as a mirror that just reflects a phenomenon "as it is" (which immediately exposes the inadequacy of such an approach), or a list of features to be ticked off (which takes us back to an outdated, prescriptive notion of genre). It suggests that actual things, i.e. texts, should be "exactly like the model." It follows that genre comes to be understood as a kind of filing cabinet, a storage box, or a pigeonhole. This allows for a more flexible sorting of phenomena. Still the aim is to check what is and what is not like the model. It is, however, clear that understanding liberature in particular, and genre in general, as only a sorting device is not a fully adequate approach. That is why Przybyszewska rejects this conceptualisation, and is inclined to see liberature as a gradable property. This then prompts us to conceive of liberature in terms of the prototype theory, but Przybyszewska discards this also on the grounds of its subjectivity. Without going into details, let me only remark that Gabora, Rosch and Aerts address criticism of this nature. They recount arguments in favour of such an approach, including the culturally grounded processes ivolved in the formation of concepts, and the essential role of context-dependent relevance, something that is also evident in their ecological model of a network of concepts.

Boon, in turn, proposes that we reconsider the concept as an *epistemic tool* (2012: 229–233). As she argues, this brings about a considerable epistemic payoff, enabling us to ask a wider variety of questions about the phenomena we investigate. Reconceptualising genre in this way is indicative of the ways in which we can handle texts, look into them, and operate on them. This way of looking at the concept (in our case the genre) foregrounds its actionability, that is the "possibility to manipulate it" (Tabakowska 2016: 15). So genre can, for example, be compared to an optical device like a microscope. Such a device enables us to look into the complexity of a work in greater detail, to discern its different "tissues" (i.e. styles, registers, conventions), and even to investigate its genetic (i.e. intertextual) structure, as is done with the electronic microscope. It also allows us to notice a complex relation between the author's agency – as reflected in rhetorical structures and material forms of presentation – and the reading protocols this prompts. Following the optical metaphor, genre can also be used as a telescope, enabling us to look into spatially and temporally distant textual bodies and learn about the socio-cultural circumstances of their production. As Bawarshi remarks, the "container view of genre [...] overlooks the sociorhetorical function of genres – the extent to which genres shape and help us recognize our communicative goals, including why these goals exist, what and whose purposes they serve, and how best to achieve them" (2000: 339). The telescope analogy illuminates the fact that literature is a universe of texts in which genres can function as constellations held together by socio-cultural forces (akin to formalists' description of literature as a system). Finally, the genre of liberature re-emphasises once more the necessity and value for literary studies of historicised, textual and genetic research. Functioning as a spotlight, it helps to bring into focus the role of editors, publishers, typesetters, book designers, and printers, whose voices are embodied in the materiality of literary artefacts. Crucially, it helps to identify works in which authors had a major say, and helps us to understand that editions of print-bound literature requires more medium and genre conscious editorial and publishing practices that respect authors' intentions. Finally, from readers it requires multimodal literacy.[121]

A theory of liberature

Fajfer has sometimes remarked that for him liberature is "a theory." So it is worth mentioning that concepts have also been understood as "theories." This is yet another way of avoiding the trap of the "definition approach" and addressing the relevance of context, which can be used for "context dependent" categorisation (Gabora, Rosch, and Aerts 2008: 92–93). This approach consists in developing a kind of "practical theory" of how a concept is understood in different contexts. Gabora, Rosch, and Aerts explain it by showing how GREY CLOUDS are conceptually closer to BLACK CLOUDS, but GREY HAIR is more similar to WHITE HAIR; something that is related to different "theories" people have about HAIR and CLOUDS (2008: 93). Likewise, we can infer that Fajfer's liberature was understood in relation to his "theory" of literature and of "the book," and perhaps also "the artist's book," with liberature considered to be more similar to the former than the latter. Vague as it certainly is, this way of contextualising liberature throws into relief its intermediate position between traditionally

[121] This is what Przybyszewska finds especially valuable about liberature (2015: 385–386; 2014a: 104).

viewed writing as "pure content" independent of its embodiment, and "pure form" symbolised by Carrión's totally blank book. Resorting to this approach as a heuristic tool, we may also notice that liberature partly overlaps with multimodal literature (i.e. Steven Hall's *Raw Shark Texts*, Danielewski's *House of Leaves*, Fajfer and Bazarnik's *Oka-leczenie*, Thirlwell's *Kapow!*, Meersman's *This is Belgian Chocolate*, Fajfer's *ten letters/dwadzieścia jeden liter*, etc.). By contrast, however, liberature is limited to printed material forms, even if it sometimes includes a digital component (e.g. Steven Hall's *Raw Shark Texts*, Robert Szczerbowski's *Antologia*, Fajfer's *ten letters/dwadzieścia jeden liter* and *Powieki*). It is produced in multiple copies (an edition), whereas multimodal literature embraces digital multimodal texts (with no printed support), and one-of-a-kind artists' books with a considerable textual component. Liberature is, nevertheless, wider than the "multimodal print novel" discussed by Gibbons, as it also includes lyrical, poetic texts (Meersman's *This is Belgian Chocolate*, Fajfer's *ten letters/dwadzieścia jeden liter*, Bervin's *Nets*). It is akin to techotexts, but differs from them insofar as it is limited to printed matter, while techotexts can be exclusively digital. This comparative heuristic approach can be linked to what Fowler says about the use of genre:

> If it is true that readers do not so much decode as select the most accessible relevant inferences, then those of them who are familiar with appropriate genres will access the topics and formal conventions of these first, and so form assumptions of intended meaning more easily. Organization according to genre offers a rich encyclopedia of mutually related words, formal patterns, ideas, emotions and shared assumptions, on which readers automatically draw for relevant items. Subsequently, of course, good readers further enrich this relatively crude communication of meaning with many inferences—doubtless including some based on the individual writer's relation to his generic group, or on his known eccentricities, originality and the like. Thus, the idea that genres constitute horizons of meaning may not be wrong, so much as lacking in explanatory detail. (Fowler 1990: 161–162)

Let us now investigate how these "horizons of meaning" are established with regard to the specific properties of texts, as inferred from the book's architecture, compositional and rhetorical structure, and thematic content.

Dimensions of genre

Structural, rhetorical and thematic dimensions

Frow distinguishes three "structural dimensions" of genre that, taken as a cluster, determine the scope of *what* can be expressed and *how*. These are "the formal organization of genre," "the rhetorical structure," and "the thematic content" (Frow 2015: 81–83). The first dimension refers to ways of "shaping the material medium," starting from such an elementary decision as the choice between oral or written language, i.e. the semantic medium and its submodes. Other formal choices include text length, its layout, and all that can be called the physical setting. Though he does not consider these last parameters as generic components *per se*, nevertheless Frow acknowledges that they function as "framing conditions which govern and may signal generic structure" (80). They shape the medium in a physical sense, but this is also related to ways of generating sense in the linguistic layer. An example is structuring a poem into stanzas, and using enjambment, which is a spatial-visual way of adding meaning to the syntactically generated sense. This means that the choice of the printed book as form may be comparable, as a generic signal, to graphic properties of poetry regulated by punctuation marks.[122] It is a meaningful way of segmenting textual space, "and it stipulates certain kinds of textual cohesion" (81) related to the book's architecture: a codex, a leporello, a "shuffle" book, a scroll, etc. This is, in turn, related to the other aspects of the formal organisation of the work, which embrace "the 'immaterial' categories of time, space and enunciative position" (ibid.). In liberature these categories cross-sect the book form in ways that produce the effect of blending

---

[122] As I have mentioned above the form of the book can be treated as a punctuation mark (cf. "Book is a navigating device").

the fictional space and time with the actual space of the book interface and the reading time (cf. Bazarnik 2010a). The fusion may be reinforced through metatextual, narratorial comments, or by covert, ambiguous passages that may be metaphorically related to the architecture of the book. This happens, for example, when the unnamed narator of *The Unfortunates* thinks about his friend's physical disintegration. The word "degeneration" is the last of the section, separated from the preceding text by an extremely long blank.

These formal aspects of genre are interconnected with the rhetorical dimension, which pertains to relations between senders and receivers, "organised in a structured situation of address" (Frow 2015: 82). In the case of the literary work, the situation includes the choice of material interface: a printed book, an e-book, a hypertext, an app, an audiobook, etc., which has a bearing on the implied audience as well as on the implied speaker or speakers. This is related to a kind of agreement as to the truth status of the represented world (fictional but realist, fictional and fantastic, non-fictional with fictionalised elements, as in a biographical novel), and modality (language as print, print and images, as speech recording, etc.). In the case of liberature, the choice of the printed book (in all its architectural forms) in combination with metatextual elements – especially those that draw the readers' attention to the bookishness of the work – contribute to the presence effect, and meaning effects, too (Bazarnik 2006; 2007a; also 2010a: 122–123 and 129–130).

Finally, the thematic content is defined as "the shaped human experience that a genre invests with significance and interest" (Frow 2015:83). It is worth noting that Frow recognises a thematic content even in music, which can only be spoken about in metaphorical terms. Such content might be identified with the emotional tone of a piece that is characteristic of a given genre, for example, the meditative tone of the nocturne or the triumphalism of the military march (ibid.). Some genres can have a fairly narrow and specific repertoire of topics or themes, or forms of argument, or settings and character types, or organisations of time and space, which Bakhtin termed the chronotope (1981: 84–258). This is connected with the work's modality and degree of verisimilitude, that is the aforementioned aspects of the rhetorical dimension of genre, which in turn shape and are shaped by the formal organisation.

Scholars are inclined to agree that thematic content is an indispensable dimension of genre. That is to say, every genre can be characterised by a repertoire of favoured or "more or less obligatory topics" (Fowler 2003: 190). Admittedly, these may be fairly general, as in the case of narrative genres where the thematic content concerns "kinds of action, the kinds of actors who perform them, and the significance that accrues to actions and actors" (Frow 2015: 83). In other cases, the theme must be derived from the formal and rhetorical dimensions of the work, as, for example, with the sonnet, where the thematic scope has transformed from the specific subject of idealised, courtly love to a lyrical, philosophical, satirical or humourous reflection on any subject, possibly with a surprising twist in its presentation (the volta or punch line).[123] But for Frow the thematic dimension of the sonnet remains somewhat unspecified, and he considers the structural organisation to be the dominant generic trait (84). So paradoxically, a form that is considered to be a fairly strong example of a literary genre exhibits a striking lack of an "essential" generic dimension.

Does liberature have a thematic dimension?

Fajfer has always insisted that for liberature one cannot determine any set of themes, however generally described. He is of the opinion that authors are at absolute liberty to choose a topic and shape it in a liberatic way.[124] Likewise, Przybyszewska condones unlimited thematic freedom in liberatic works. Simultaneously, she notes that it is partly due to this lack of a specific topical focus that liberature cannot aspire to a generic status (2015: 30). So the thematic aspects seem to be lacking over all.

If I agreed with the outspoken assertion that liberature does not have any thematic content, I would be inclined to agree with Przybyszewska that liberature should not be conceived of as a genre. It would rather fit the category of mode, in the sense proposed by Fowler and corroborated by Frow. That is in the adjectival sense of a kind of general textual colouring; a "qualification" or "modification" of a text whose "leading"

---

[123] It seems that even Queneau's radically experimental, nonsense sonnets in *One Hundred Thousand Billion Poems* and comparably experimental, collaborative *Sonnet of Sonnets* (Bazarnik and Fajfer 2012) fit into this frame.

[124] Although he never explicitly expressed this in any of his articles, I deduced this from "Liberum Veto?" (2010i: 111) and the conversations that we held when I was writing the present book.

genre would be more specific. It would give the text a specific tone or style,[125] without the sense of a fully realised set of generic markers. Hence, there would be a *liberatic* novel (Danielewski, Hall, Bartnicki), a *liberatic* thriller (Danielewski, Orszulewski), a *liberatic* cycle of poems (Fajfer, Meersman, Queneau), a *liberatic* essay (Nowakowski's *Traktat Kartkograficzny*; Derrida's *Glas*). In this sense an analogy could be established with a "*gothic* thriller, *pastoral* elegy, *satirical* sitcom," or *dramatic* lyric, *lyrical* drama, *epic* drama" (Frow 2015: 71–72). However, following Fowler, Frow derives modes from genres that "over time take on a more general force which is detached from particular structural embodiments." This suggests that before we coin an adjective, we should have a noun referring to "a more specific organization of texts with thematic, rhetorical, and formal dimensions" (73). Let us then consider if it were possible after all to describe the thematic scope of liberature in a way analogous to the novel, the short story, or the sonnet.

Liberature may constitute a comparable case because its formal dimension is realised through the compositional space, the semantification of the material artefact in relation to the text inscribed in it, and the frequent employment of semantic submodes of language as well as non-linguistic codes. Like the sonnet, its generic dominant is the formal organisation and rhetorical structure of its linguistic material. As Frow notes in connection with the sonnet, haiku, the Latin elegy, letters and blogs "*formal and rhetorical structures always convey meaning.*" This he considers "central to [his] argument about genre" (2015: 84; original emphasis). Somewhat paradoxically, Fajfer and Przybyszewska would most likely agree with Frow's statement. After all, the semantic dimension of form is crucial to their varying accounts of liberature, regardless of their larger differences. Drawing on this, I would like to show how the choice of the signifying material form *is* related to subject matter. What's more, I am inclined to think that it may often be the very choice of theme that predetermines whether a work will take the liberatic shape. In other words, I suggest that liberature as a specific form of literary expression may be thematically motivated.

Considering its dominant formal concerns, liberature can be seen as a genre preoccupied with the expressive potential of "the word" (Fajfer 2010d). That is why it goes beyond the exploitation of the purely linguistic

[125] In fact, the liberatic style has been distinguished as one of the artistic, literary styles of contemporary Polish (Dąbrowska 2013).

potential of writing, and further concerns itself with exploring writing's visual and material submodes. This is bound up with an exploration of what has for a long time been the major site of writing; namely, the book. The self-centred interest of the genre is, moreover, reflected in its name. The polysemy of the Latin component suggests that the book is to be "liberated" from its practical, utilitarian duties in order to serve only the autonomous, aesthetic purposes of literature. And since this involves defamiliarisation, originality, and newness, the liberation is extended to the material form of the book as well. Hence, the various, surprising shapes liberatic works are known by: an accordion book, a multiple codex, a bottle-book.

Investigating the expressive power of "the word," liberature also strives to reproduce, imitate or simulate non-verbal aspects of the oral performance of language: gestures, pitch and tone of voice, facial expressions, and the like. In writing these are reflected in devices that aim to reconstruct the aura of the "situation of spoken communication," which Jan Assman identified in ancient Egyptian writing. His comparative analyses of oral, written, and inscriptional communication suggest that features of scripts (print), which are typically "neutralized and minimized in everyday, utilitarian writing," can serve this purpose (Assman 1994: 26). The scholar argues that a monumental architectural structure (such as a temple or a tomb) replaces the absent body of the speaker, recreating a physical site of communication that is grounded in space and time, while the aestheticised script corresponds to the loud, elevated tone of voice used by priests in religious ceremonies. Likewise, a book that utilises unconventional structure, layout, and typography aspires to evoke these oral aspects of communication. That is why book-bound works rely so heavily on material and conceptual metaphors of embodiment and performance.

In his discussion of the formation of genres, Fowler notes that in "the process of conceptualisation of a genre, an important part was played by metaphors" or synecdoches. Related to these are the "metaphoric attributes of genres" (2003: 189–191). So for example, for pastoral poetry the metaphor might be a reed or pipe, taken as a conventional attribute of the genre. "But," Fowler wonders:

> ...weren't early pastoral idyls and eclogues, for Theocritus if not for Virgil, accompanied on actual reed pipes? And, if so, should we not think of the *avena* [reed] as a part of the external situation, the *context of utterance*? Genres are coming to be understood as virtual contexts: as providing for the individual

work a context equivalent to the pragmatic context of speech. Abandoning the notion of genres as fixed classes, criticism moved on in the 1980s and 1990s to discussing them as coded structures or matrices for composition and interpretation. Perhaps now it is time to move on again, and to think of genres as fields of association like those in actual situations of utterance. (2003: 190; emphasis mine)

For liberature, the staple metaphor *and* context is the book, something that Robert Grudin most self-reflexively demonstrates in his liberatic *Book: A Novel* (1992). His work opens with two epigraphs indicative of two important synecdoches associated with the genre. The first is the Latin adage: "*Liber fons libertatis*" (i.e. the book is the source of liberty/liberation"), and it is as if he here anticipates Fajfer's fusion of "liber" and "liberty." The other is an excerpt from the *Odyssey*, which points to a key topos of liberature:

> Stretch'd on the downy fleece, no rest he knows,
> And in his raptur'd soul the vision glows.
> Homer, *Odyssey*, Book 1, trans. Alexander Pope

In this image, the teller's "soul" constitutes the setting of the "visions." In other words, the events are in fact set in the teller's mind, which draws upon memory, or activates the imagination, to generate his tales. Hence, the book with its material content functions as a material metaphor for the head or the skull in which the mind or brain is locked. The homodiegetic narrator of *Tristram Shandy* makes this explicit when he comments humorously on Locke's essay on human understanding, but in fact on his own writing as well:

> I will tell you in three words what the book is. – It is a history. – A history! of who? what? where? when? Don't hurry yourself. – It is a historybook, Sir, (which may possibly recommend it to the world) of what passes in a man's own mind"
>
> Sterne, *Tristram Shandy*, vol. II, ch. II.

It is no coincidence that B.S. Johnson uses this very line as an epigraph that he places along with others on the inside wall of the box of *The Unfortunates*. The British writer draws on Sterne in his introduction to *Aren't You Rather Young to Be Writing Your Memoirs?* and therein claims that the novel is the literary form best suited to representing the human psyche (Johnson 1973: 11; 26). Accordingly, all his novels experiment with the material presentation of their literary content, and the material structure of the books themselves. The topic that then emerges from this cluster of works displaying liberatic properties concerns representations of the mind, mental processes, and various, often altered states of consciousness.

Related to this is the theme of mental or epistemological crisis or trauma; hence, liberature frequently deals with a traumatic event or experience, usually the loss or death of a person close to the narrator. It seems that this emotional intensity calls for a *dramatic* expression. A dramatic experience cannot be spoken about, but it can possibly be shown, acted out, if not re-enacted (behaviour so characteristic for posttraumatic disorders). In a sense, the form becomes a way of harnessing an emotional excess that cannot be expressed in words alone. Practically all Johnson's liberatic novels are directly concerned with this topic: the trauma of "absurd" death from cancer, uncontrolled violence, abuse, or simply aging. In Federman's *The Voice in the Closet* and *Double or Nothing* the narrator is the sole member of his family who survives the Holocaust. Hall's *The Raw Shark Texts* is a (post)modern version of the Orphic myth, and so is Fajfer's *Powieki*. *Oka-leczenie* and *(O)patrzenie* are narratives of dying.[126] Anne Carson's *Nox* is a modern liberatic elegy, mourning the death of the author's brother. Likewise, Herta Müller's collage poetry *Der Wächter nimmt seinen Kamm* (1993) elegises the friends she has lost through her exile, or those driven to suicide or murdered by the Securitate. In one of her poems "the king bows and kills"[127], while the eponymous guard picks up his comb in order to use it as a deathly instrument. In fact, the subject is so vast that it requires a separate study, therefore I can only gesture towards it here. Danielewski's *House of Leaves* and Orszulewski's *Jezus nigdy nie był aż tak blady* are psychological horrors or thrillers in which the main characters are hunted and killed by human or non-human monsters. After all, even Sterne's satirical, jocular, cock-and-bull story is also his "turtle and hare" race with Death:

[126] Przybyszewska writes about "spaces of death" in *The Unfortunates* and *Oka-leczenie* in "W pudełku i na wadze – o przestrzeni śmierci i przestrzeni tekstu w utworach Brayana [sic!] S. Johnsona oraz Zenona Fajfera i Katarzyny Bazarnik" (2007c).

[127] The phrase was later used by Müller as the title of a collection of essays *Der König verneigt sich und tötet* (2003).

Alas, poor YORICK!

But liberature can also be a narrative of rebirth, as our *Oka-leczenie* suggests. The potential of posttraumatic growth, regeneration, and, as we have seen, re-genrification, seems to be inscribed in these works. They can "be both," as Ali Smith ingenuously demonstrates in her recent novel that considers this thematic, or "moral conundrum" (2015: [George] 3[128]). In its opening she brings in Hannah Arendt who, commenting on Benjamin's power to think poetically, said,

> ...although the living is the subject to the ruin of the time, the process of decay is at the same time a process of crystallization that in the depth of the sea, into which sinks and is dissolved what once was alive, some things "suffer a sea-change" and survive in new crystallized forms and shapes that remain immune to the elements, as though they waited only for the pearl diver who one day will come down to them and bring them up into the world of the living as "thought fragments," as something "rich and strange," and perhaps even as everlasting *Urphänomene*. (Arendt 1968: 51)

A similar hope informs liberature's traumatic-thanatic writing. After all, the young survivor of *Double or Nothing* manages to navigate the ruins of his past and reach the New World. Although his story is provisional, conditional and fragmentary, nevertheless, upon finishing the work, the reader is somewhat convinced that he has settled in Detroit, joined a jazz bad, and developed some relationships, and that the Author has managed to complete the *book*. In *Raw Shark Texts*, Eric Sanderson manages to evade the jaws of the memory devouring monster, and slips through the conceptual loop into another world where he hopes to live happily ever after. *House of Leaves* closes with Yggdrasil, the mythical tree of life, and *Oka-leczenie* with a semi-colon, promising a continuation of the sentence (and the story). This is because liberatic writers seem to believe "that language is a living growing changing organism" (Smith 2015: [George] 9). So perhaps, liberatic works also communicate that death is just a transformation. The demise of one form leads to the birth of another.

---

[128] This novel consists of two parts, one narrated by a British teenage girl called George, the other by Italian Renaissance painter del Cossa. It comes in two versions: one begins with George's story; the other with the painter's story. However, the split is not reflected in the pagination running continually throughout the whole book. The edition I am using begins with George's part, and the page number refers to this version. The readers in possession of the other version need to search for the correct page reference in George's part on their own.

Genre functions

Genre as a (proto)type

Institutions for storing and accessing knowledge (schools, libraries, dictionaries, encyclopedias, databases, etc.) are an important cultural environment in which genres perform their categorising function. In connection with teaching and cataloguing, John Swales remarks that "it is apparently common in classificatory work to consider genres as 'ideal types' rather than actual entities. Actual texts deviate from the ideal in various kinds of ways," but some simplification for the sake of practicality is unavoidable and does not invalidate the usefulness of genre as such (Swales 1990: 34). Likewise, drawing on the work of E.D. Hirsch, Alastair Fowler points to the advantages of construing genre in terms of the prototype (1982: 41–42). He notes that a type, unlike a class, may include only a singular specimen, which seems to partly alleviate the Crocean dilemma. Besides, not all specimens belonging to a type need to display the same characteristic (which, as he claims, is essential for a member of a class; Fowler 1982: 38). As a consequence, he suggests that genre is better understood as a framework within which works are compared synchronically and diachronically for shared characteristics in a heuristic way (see also Rosch 1978: 36–37; Ulbæk 2015: 432–433; Fishelov 1993: 53–84), rather than being tested for their purity, and eliminated if they do not fulfill specific criteria.

Stressing the practical or utilitarian aspect of genre use, Fowler calls this approach functional; a position shared by Dirk de Geest and Hendrik van Gorp, who discuss genre from the systemic-functional perspective. Taking their inspiration from cognitive psychology and linguistics,[129]

---

[129] They draw on Eleanor Rosch's research in human categorisation, Lakoff and Langacker's study of conceptual metaphor, as well as studies of semantics by George Kleiber, John R. Taylor and Dirk Geeraerts.

the Belgian scholars argue for genres to be understood as "prototypically structured categories" (de Geest and van Gorp 1999: 39–42). In their view, genre should be seen as a loose set within which some elements are located closer to the centre, while others hover on the edges, without forming any distinct borderline. The centre of such a set is determined by a prototypical work that contains the highest possible concentration of features associated with a genre. But we must bear in mind that the prototype does not need to be any actually existing text. It is rather a conceptual model against which actual works can be tested to determine their relation to the prototype. So it constitutes a "cognitive reference point," the conceptual centre of a fuzzy set[130] consisting of all texts akin to it. A literary work "participating in" a genre shares a greater or lesser number of features with the prototype; the more features it has in common with the model work, the closer to the centre of the conceptual space it is positioned. Liminal elements of the set may be located quite far from the centre, but due to some prominent feature they would still recognisably belong. This also implies that some works can be located in a shared fuzzy area between two or more genres, as generic spaces overlap due to some characteristics held in common. Finally, de Geest and van Gorp explain that:

> [i]t may even occur that two non-representative members have (virtually) no relevant common attributes at all yet still function as members of a single category because they both partially, but in a totally different way, bear family resemblances to the prototypical instances(s). On the other hand, it may also be the case that an instance is so similar to another category that the exact boundaries between the categories tend to get blurred or to disappear altogether. (1999: 42)[131]

[130] The concept of the fuzzy set was first applied to pattern classification by Lofti A. Zadeh, R. Bellaman and R. Kalaba in 1964. A year later, Zadeh published an article that discusses this in more detail, in which he defines this fuzzy set as "a class of objects with a continuum of grades of membership" ranging from one to zero (1965: 338–339). Analogous concepts can be found in genre criticism. For example, David Fishelov observes that Weitz's description of the genre of tragedy as a "loose set" suggests that it can be seen as "a disjunctive set of sufficient conditions" that ultimately lets us point to its elements that evidently qualify as its members and to some borderline cases (Fishelov 1993: 62). Fowler's *Kinds of Literature* is in fact grounded in understanding genres as a loosely hierarchised network of fuzzy sets with many overlapping areas among various combinations of sets.

[131] See also Rosch 1978; Ulbæk 2015; and Gabora, Rosch, and Aertz 2008.

I have followed their theoretical model in "Liberature or on the Origin or (Literary) Species", convinced that it has the advantage of being operational as a classificatory model, while also allowing us to deal with "undecidable instances and ambivalent borderline cases" (50).[132] Although the model has been criticised for endorsing potentially radically idiosyncratic categorisations, categories construed in this way are not as subjective or arbitrary as one might think.[133] They do not represent only or mainly one's "own private awareness of a genre" (Wysłouch 2007: 290; Przybyszewska 2015: 53-55). After all, any "private awareness" is based on culturally transmitted knowledge, and is therefore context-dependent (Gabora, Rosch and Aertz 2008). When one offers a subjective generic identification, the generic claim must respond to, and negotiate with, different generic claims offered by other readers. Besides, recent studies of the prototype indicate that this need not be narrowly understood as a more or less open set of features. As Gabora, Rosch and Aerts argue, its position among other related concepts, and the enunciative position of the agent using it, are also pertinent:

> Prototypes with their rich noncriterial information and imagery can indicate, on many different levels, possible ways of situating oneself and navigating complex situations. Basic level object research (Rosch, Mervis, Gray, & Boyes-Braem 1976) indicated that category formation is not arbitrary but takes place in such a way as to maximally map the informational structure of the world. [...] If categories ultimately arise from life activities, basic level categories could provide an entry to the events and processes that produce them. And as a worldview builds up from basic level categories to include more detailed as well as more abstract levels of conceptualizing, it becomes more interconnected, more of an ecology, that comes increasingly to reflect what is unique about the circumstances and idiosyncrasies of the individual. (2008: 95–96)

Thinking about liberature in terms of information navigation does, for example, make it possible to map more accurately the shadowy area between literature and the artist's book, or to see how liberature can be situated among various types of multimodal creative writing. Moreover, using the prototype approach to genre as a heuristic tool, and analysing actual works in this way, can help us to see them in all of their complexity, and to

Genre functions

---

[132] In "Genre and Categorization" Ulbæk offers a logical and formal analysis of genre as a prototypical concept.

[133] See Rosch "Categorization" for a response to the objection.

better perceive such works as performative challenges for the reader. Finally, as Higgins and others have suggested, a disagreement over the genre or identification of several overlapping genres in one work may lead to the proposal of a new generic category, which happened in Fajfer's "manifesto."

Literary soleras: sommeliers

To illustrate how the fuzzy prototype theory may account for the generic dimensions of "eccentric" works, and consequently lead to the formulation of a quasi or full generic category, let me mention a most radical example. *Finnegans Wake* is described as a borderline specimen of the novel. How does the radically undefinable text "fit" in with the category? Well, it does not. That is, not quite. But the novel can *also* be a way of seeing Joyce's book. Why? Because it demonstrates some typical features of the genre: it is a bulky text of continuous script, opening with a passage that describes a landscape in a manner that is somewhat in the vein of nineteenth century realist novels. In addition, some passages are narrated by a more or less identifiable narratorial voice, and the work is laid out and typographically structured like a novel: divided into untitled yet clearly distinguishable units that look like books and chapters. What's more, its author had previously written two novels that considerably expanded the boundaries of the genre, so *Finnegans Wake* can be perceived as a repeated instance of this artistic "action," performed in the literary field. In this respect, the work corroborates the arguments of Miller (1994), Bawarshi (2003; 2008), or Bazerman (1994) that genre can be an instrument of cultural intervention. If genres are "the sites in which communicants rhetorically reproduce the very environments to which they respond – the habits and habitats for acting in language" (Bawarshi 2001: 71), the novel is, almost by definition, a textual site for experimenting with language, for testing *novel* ways of telling stories, for mixing and blending forms, styles, and... genres, and for engendering *novel* subgenres (Bazarnik 2015a: 69–70). If we realise this, calling *Finnegans Wake* a novel seems almost obvious. We can see how some of its formal and rhetorical features, as well as the context of its appearance, invoke this particular generic frame for Joyce's obscure work; though of course the novel is not the only genre in play.[134]

---

[134] In *Joyce and Liberature* (2007a) I explain how *Finnegans Wake* can be read as as bookbound work. Since it is a complex and lengthy argument, I have decided not to summarise it here, and would instead like to refer the reader to my monograph.

My cursory analysis was inspired by A. Walton Litz's similar discussion of the generic complexity of *Ulysses*. He shows how investigating the book through the lens of the novel leads to specific readings, shedding light on some neglected or obscured aspects, as was achieved with S.L. Goldberg's interpretation of *Ulysses* as realist fiction (Litz 1974: 112–113). Beside being an analytical tool, this indicates that genre also operates as an interpretive code. While arguing for "the singularity of literature," Litz simultaneously hints at the reciprocity of generic expectations and our understanding of a particular text. This implies that genre is an essential part of hermeneutic reading. However, since Litz's understanding of genre appears to be fundamentally classificatory, he sees and highlights limitations to a generic approach; for example, important features that do not fit in with a preferred generic pattern might be overlooked, or interpreted as "flaws." Consequently, he diagnoses that the "problem" readers have with *Ulysses* (as with other experimental, hybrid, multimodal works) lies in the fact that the work blurs generic boundaries and defies generic pigeonholing. This is why the scholar ultimately questions the use of genre criticism, as this threatens to smooth out "the irregular achievements of Joyce's generation" (120).

Alberto Manguel, the author of the fascinating *A History of Reading*, raises the same objection with regard to the limiting effect of genre, which he considers rather detrimental to reading. According to the Argentinian writer, it curbs the reader's response, lulls his curiosity and attention, and blinds him to the richness of actual works:

> Rooms, corridors, bookcases, shelves, filing cards and computerized catalogues assume that the subjects on which our thoughts dwell are actual entities, and through this assumption a certain book may be lent a particular tone and value. Filed under Fiction, Jonathan Swift's *Gulliver's Travels* is a humorous novel of adventure; under Sociology, a satirical study of England in the eighteenth century; under Children's Literature, an entertaining fable about dwarfs and giants and talking horses; under Fantasy, a precursor of science fiction; under Travel, an imaginary voyage; under Classics, a part of the Western literary canon. Categories are exclusive, reading is not – or should not be. Whatever classifications have been chosen, every library tyrannizes the act of reading, and forces the reader – the curious reader, the alert reader – to *rescue* the book from the category to which it has been condemned. (Manguel 1996: 198)

I partly sympathise with such reservations, especially because a generic label (even if we treat genre as prototype) can draw excessive attention to features that corroborate the label, while suppressing those that would problematise the classification. But I am also convinced that – as is the case with Litz's article – Manguel's example suggests a way out of the "genre trouble." This is because he shows how the use of genre can and should open a work up to several different readings. Ultimately, while individual generic taxonomies might seem reductive, genres are necessary and useful insofar as they serve as intuitive, presupposed frames for approaching any text. They constitute an important entry point, a preliminary step into more nuanced interpretations. Due to this capacity, they can facilitate the reading of obscure works, allowing readers to quickly ascribe a familiar generic category to a text, rather than reject it as illegible precisely because it *is* illegible to them within their intuitive network of genres.

Encountering an initially confusing work (such as *Ulysses*, *Finnegans Wake* or *Gulliver's Travels*) one first wonders *what* it is. I haven't carried out any empirical studies, but I can testify from my experience of numerous workshops and presentations on liberature that this is the first question asked by audiences unfamiliar with the books, and even by those better versed in experimental writing (Cuber, Jankowicz). It is a legitimate question; and it begs for an answer in the nominative form. We are all familiar with heuristic procedures that help us formulate preliminary, tentative hypotheses in relation to genre: the title and size of a text, its opening lines, epigraphs, allusions and other intertextual elements, along with the layout, all provide initial hints (Fowler 1982: 88–105; Balbus 2007: 164). But as one reads on, things may become more and more complicated; if contradictory generic clues are encountered then the hypothesis needs to be constantly modified. Ultimately, the degree of formal hybridity can be so high that the reader may wonder about the identity of the work. Generic fuzziness or indeterminacy can be seen as the author's clever strategy of attracting the reader by offering a piece unlike any other; mysterious, enigmatic, inscrutable. Hence the work may be judged original, fascinating and attractive. On the other hand, such works can be perceived as hermetic, isolationist, elitist, conceited, obscure, unclear, lacking structure, purpose and sense. Hence they are viewed as poor, weak, provocative, a ruse or hoax, unworthy of attention. Still, it is evident that in both cases readers' responses are entangled with generic expectations, which are detectable in reviews, and in readers' choices.

Being interested in the history of the novel, would I have reached for *Ulysses* if I had seen it classified as a romance or porn rather than a classic of the genre? And would my local library have refused to lend me the book during my teenage years if the librarian had not judged it the former?

It was precisely this kind of mismatch between generic expectations and the generic schemata inscribed in Joyce's book that was responsible for the notorious response to the work. Indeed, some disappointed readers have repeated after Molly, "There's nothing smutty in it" (Joyce 1998: 62). However tentative, fuzzy or off-hand generic labels might be, they turn out to be a useful tool for orientating oneself when faced with the vast expanse of literary writing. As is the case with stereotypes, they may be wrong or have limited accuracy in relation to the complexity of individual works. Yet to do away with them would be to deny ourselves a handy (if imprecise) crutch that provides some preliminary understanding, and has pragmatic benefits, too.

Again, Fowler confirms that "[w]e identify the genre to interpret the exemplar" (1982: 38). This capacity of genre is grounded in preconceptions, followed then by the recognition of initial generic signals, anticipations and preliminary assumptions that are later corroborated or modified accordingly. That is all that Jauss subsumes under the term "horizon of expectation" (22). Genre forms an important part of this horizon, both for the author who (more or less) deliberately and self-consciously tunes his or her linguistic and extralinguistic codes to comply with, or defy, particular norms and conventions, and for the reader whose preliminary step is fundamentally genre-motivated. As Thomas Pavel emphasises,

> Genre is a crucial interpretive tool because it is a crucial artistic tool in the first place. Literary texts are neither natural phenomena subject to scientific dissection, nor miracles performed by gods and thus worthy of worship, but fruits of human talent and labor. To understand them, we need to appreciate the efforts that went into their production. Genre helps us figure out the nature of a literary work because the person who wrote it and the culture for which that person labored used genre as a guideline for literary creation. Considerations about genre are thus unavoidable and those who dispense with them do it at their own risk. (2003: 202)

So genres need not be viewed as reductive labels, but rather as hypotheses to be tested and verified by both readers and authors. In other words, they can be used as a tool for critical thinking. As Fowler stresses, genre "is an instrument not of classificiation or prescription, but of meaning," the most important code of literary *langue*, with its own syntactic and semantic aspects (1982: 22). In a similar vein, Gerard Genette thinks of genre as the architext, an overall frame delimiting possible senses or types of senses rather than specific meanings. It functions as a signpost to where and how sense can be sought (Genette 1992; Głowiński 2007; Balbus 2007: 165–170). So Fowler proposes that,

> One may usefully think of genres as domains of association specialized, literary equivalents of the fields of association whereby meaning is communicated in ordinary speech. As such, the genres adjust a reader's mental set and help in selecting the optimally relevant associations that amount to a meaning of the literary work. (2003: 190)

In liberature sense emerges from the interplay of text and its material form; writers, the architexters, fabricate their houses out of leaves. Most readers will intuit this from the architecture of liberatic books, but the lack of a category means that their reading remains at the level of an impression, intuition, or apprehension in this respect. As I have argued above, to give this feeling a name is to offer them an instrument with which they will be able to see these associations more easily.

The above examples strongly indicate that generic hybridity in literary works is not an exception, but a rule. As Fowler metaphorically puts it, "[t]he wines of Helicon are all soleras" (1982: 46). He is convinced that all literary works are generic hybrids defying easy, unequivocal classifications, which he connects with the fact that most writers tend to transgress generic regularities. Thomas O. Beebee makes the same point quite emphatically, stating that "most works not only can but *must* be analyzed in more than one generic way in order for their message to have any effective meaning or value" (1994: 265). This is because they always bear traces of different genres, sometimes fully fledged historical literary genres, sometimes closer to Bakhtinian single speech types. Occasionally a genre is incompletely realised; then it gives a text a specific overtone, hence, a comic novel, a lyrical drama, a gothic thriller. Fowler and Frow refer to this kind of incomplete generic pattern as a mode (Fowler 1982: 106–107; Frow 2015: 71–72). Genette sees this in a way that is essentially similar, but he reverses the terminology. He considers the lyric, epic and dramatic dimensions of a text to be archegenres, whereas he calls lower level forms modes (Genette 1992). The adjectival form indicates that a work is "flavoured" with some generic features on the stylistic or thematic level, whereas its compositional dominant is based on another genre or genres. "Concrete" is often used in this way when it constitutes the stylistic dominant, for example with reference to Federman's *Double or Nothing*. It is in the modal sense that Agnieszka Przybyszewska proposes to understand liberature, arguing that the adjectival use of the term is more adequate since it pertains to the material rhetoric, i.e. style or poetics of the work. This is because for her a system of genres seems to work like a set of Chinese boxes; these are essentially external to any actual work, and critics can make use of this system to sort out the messy reality of creative writing.

However, when genre is reconceptualised as an instrument or *device* for shaping the material of language, it enables us to see what a group of works share in common, and how these commonalities are realised. Used in this way, liberature functions as a lens through which we can see how some actual works are similar insofar as they investigate the meaning of writing within a material space, understood in relation to the literary tradition.[135] This tradition includes preconceptions about the literary work as a container for "the pure spirit of the human mind," as well as preconceptions about the alleged immateriality of language, writing as a purely intellectual activity and as a mere "shadow" of speech, and writing and reading as disembodied practices. Liberature embraces works that critically examine these issues, often playfully responding to the stereotypes; hence the satirical flavour evident in some liberatic works. Another shared feature is the manner in which liberatic works reflect on the status and function of the literary author, his or her identity, responsibility and role in the process of composing and producing the work. What appears to be such a solitary endeavour ultimately turns out to be a collaborative enterprise. In the face of the writer's disappearance among other agents on the writing scene, liberature argues for his or her *I-density*. This is an attempt to counteract the dissolution, or to materialise the ghost, or at least to crystallise its shadow in the form of a book.

In its preoccupation with "the death of the author" liberature turns out to be a death narrative, too. Many liberatic works are concerned with this theme, describing responses to loss or the process of dying. Liberature is a kind of thanatic literature, offering a way of speaking the unspeakable, expressing the inexpressible, a way of writing down trauma, crisis, and chaos. Admittedly, many literary texts deal with these topics in one way or another. But liberature deals with them in the Other way, coupling word and image, idea and matter, body and soul in the "marriage of heaven and hell." And simultaneously, in response to "the death of the author,"

---

[135] Alternatively, liberature may be understood as a literary Swiss army knife accompanying Fajfer's books. Once you use it – *Kapow!* – out of the magic bottle of the genre springs a constellation of bookbound writing, simultaneously similar and different because each work always takes the shape of the container selected for storing its spirit.

it also facilitates "the birth of the reader" since the liberatic work acts as a midwife bringing out his or her presence in an act of embodied reading.

Literary soleras: winemakers

Ironically, authors themselves are not free from the aforementioned generic dilemmas and apprehensions that perplex critics and scholars. Jeri Johnson quotes Joyce, who in his attempts to classify *Ulysses* "began by calling it a novel, soon abandoned this for 'epic', 'encyclopaedia', or even *maledettisimo romanzaccione* ['damnedest monstrously big novel,' (ed. note)], and finally settled simply for 'book'" (J. Johnson 1992: xiii). This terminological chain, culminating in "the book" as a quasi-generic term, opens up a vista for my argument. The "generic signals" (Fowler 1982: 92), or epitexts in Genette's wording,[136] suggest Joyce's possible 'horizons of expectations' while writing *Ulysses*. The work began as a potential short story for *Dubliners*, and continued as a kind of sequel to *A Portrait of the Artist as a Young Man*; so *Ulysses* must have been planned as yet another short, then long, narrative. When Joyce hit upon the idea of relating the work to the *Odyssey*, the epic must have provided another potentially useful context. The next label may have been suggested by the drive to map and catalogue the city, to paint its portrait. And the Italian epithet half-jokingly alludes to the monstrosity of the emerging textual-generic hybrid (let us only recall that *Ulysses* also incorporates a drama, a mock catechism, as well as stylistic pastiche and parody). Interestingly, the last label he offers draws attention to the work's material form, as if to suggest this also has some generic potential. Joyce's use of the word indicates that "book" has a semantically loaded frame of reference that could help readers understand his writing. What impact can this have on our reading?

If the author of *Ulysses* indeed treated the material shape of the work, its compositional space and its paratexts (in the editions he controlled[137]) as peripheral semantic modes (as McGann suggested in *The Textual Condi-*

---

[136] As Jeri Johnson explains, these "euphemisms" (xiii) come from Joyce's letter of 21 Sept 1920 to Carlo Linati, which according to Gerard Genette constitutes a private epitext, i.e. an authorial statement commenting on, and influencing an interpretation of his work (Genette 1997a: 371–372).

[137] For example, he was involved in choosing the colour and lettering of the cover, and introduced subtitles to the "Eolus" episode (for more details see Ellmann 1983, and Slote 2004).

tion and I argued in *Joyce and Liberature*) then his use of "the book" could be taken as a semi-generic category. It would refer to a type of literary work that syncretises several different styles, forms, and conventions, including an "obligatory" rule requiring text to be semantically tied to the form of its material presentation. In other words, Joyce might have intuitively suggested that *Ulysses* can be categorised as a book-bound work.

Many, if not all, of the authors whose works are mentioned here as liberature offer comparable comments. These can be found in various paratexts, as well as in metatextual passages included in the main body of their texts. A prime example of this is Fajfer himself, whose coinage of liberature foregrounds the book-bound nature of thus labelled works. In his articles, Fajfer discusses this with reference to his own writing and there the principle can be seen in action. Even the deliberately slanted trimming of his book of essays constitutes a non-verbal statement of the "cause." In another performative gesture, the authors of *(O)patrzenie* tear off a corner of the book cover so that readers immediately notice its material body.[138] Any modification of, or divergence from, standard formats and the familiar codex automatically foreground the book's materiality. Combining Genette's term with that of "material rhetoric," such modifications to standard book form could be called "the material paratext" (or perhaps, following McGann, "the material bibliographical code").

Some authors stick to the "material" convention but use the colophon to draw attention to the bookhood of their works. Suffice it to mention just a few examples. Federman's statement of "total authority" over his book in the final "Warning" of *Double or Nothing* is enhanced by typographic tension between the colophon and the title page, which is imbued with semantic significance.[139] In Krzysztof Bartnicki's *Prospekt emisyjny* this is taken to an extreme insofar as the layout of the work imitates a business prospectus, mimicking "a disclosure document that describes a financial security for potential buyers" and provides them with "material information" about a company's financial condition ("Prospectus (finance)"). The insipid, "unbookish" format subversively illuminates the significance of the book's material shape. By overloading the reader with technical information about the agents responsible for the content, printed on the book's cover, the book sets up an elaborate ruse. Because here the sole agent is, of course, its author. By providing in *House of Leaves*

Genre functions

---

[138] For an analysis and interpretation of the gesture see Ranocchi "Liberature and Person: An Anthropological Question" (2014).

[139] I discuss this in *Joyce and Liberature* (Bazarnik 2011: 14–19).

seemingly precise, yet highly confusing, information about the kind of edition, Danielewski makes the reader wonder which copy she owns, thereby enhancing her awareness of the actual, material object. Steven Hall's *Raw Shark Texts* uses a strategy similar to Danielewski's book, as its several editions, plus translations, include different, additional content. The inside of the box holding the text of *The Unfortunates* bears a note explaining the mechanics of reading a disbound book. Finally, there is Robert Grudin's somewhat forgotten but hilarious work simply called *Book*. A "metafictional novel," "avant-garde satire," and "burlesque of all bookishness,"[140] it constitutes a witty response to Magritte's provocatively honest "pipe." Well, in any event, *Book* is a book is a book. Or even *the* book if you happen to have it on your shelf.

In all these cases, the status of the colophon is ambiguously suspended between factuality and fictionality, questioning and blurring the boundary between the reader's world and the represented world. Alison Gibbons discusses how the provocative dedication "This is not for you" in Danielewski's *House of Leaves* generates the same effect (2012: 58–60). Thanks to such hybridity, the textual "thresholds" expand into the third space that stretches between the fictional discourse of the narrative and the factual discourse of the reader. In this capacity, liberatic "paratexts" contribute to the totality effect, in fact corroborating Genette's argument that their presence transforms "text" into "book" (1997a: 17). So in a liberatic work the usually unread[141] paratextual elements acquire a fully textual status and should be read like any other chapter or poem because they constitute a part of the whole.

---

[140] Cf. "real preoccupation is with language and the reflexive nature of literary forms; his novel is a burlesque of itself and of all bookishness" (Kelm 1992: 124).

[141] Unless the reader is a librarian or a scholar looking for bibliographical information.

Classifying and cataloguing

Patching the system

Finally, I want to return briefly to the classificatory function of genre to show how liberature may be of use. Swales claims that the classificatory value of genre "lies in [genre's] use as a research tool for categorizing and filing individual texts, that is, as an effective storage and retrieval system" (1990: 34). It is an aspect evident to librarians and information managers who treat classification as a complex analytical operation (which incidentally again suggests that genre is also a tool for interpretation). In order to be classified, a text must first be analysed with a view to identifying the features that are responsible for its specificity, and consequently for its generic setup. If it does not quite fit with any already existing category, two options are available: the category that comes closest can be modified so as to account for the outlying work, or a new category can be postulated[142] that modifies or fills a gap in the existing classification system. Once the adjusted or new category is accepted by a community of users,[143] it facilitates the retrieval of specific data involved in a given class of texts. It is worth mentioning that since 2007 the Library of Congress has been developing a system of genre/form headings motivated precisely by the important analytical potential of this type of metadata,

---

[142] As Higgins points out in "The Intermedia" (2001), see also Fowler 1982: 157–159; Fishelov 1999: 52.

[143] Such a discourse community may even be formalised as an institution that has the power to decree the "existence" or "disappearance" of categories. Examples might include the editorial team of a dictionary of terminology in a discipline, a terminological committee, or library cataloguing staff. This indicates the socio-political dimension of genre, prompting further questions about control of the cultural field, the right to (self-)identification, and even freedom of expression. This aspect of genre is openly addressed by the Sidney school of genre studies (cf. Freedman and Medway 1994: 8–10), and it was recently addressed also by North American scholars (e.g. Bawarshi 2003).

especially with regard to computerised data mining and user interfaces (Young 2009). As Janis Young, a senior cataloging specialist at the Library of Congress, explains, subject headings tend to conflate the distinction between "what the item is about," and how its content is expressed. In other words, a book *about* poems is not the same as a book *of* poems, but both types of publication would be catalogued under the same subject heading. Hence, genre seems to be a handy category which would let cataloguers and database users distinguish between such publications, that is between their content and form, and thus enable more efficient searches (Young 2009). So again it becomes evident that generic classification does not only serve to pigeonhole for pigeonholing's sake, but that it is helpful for a nuanced analysis of the complex of information encoded in a text. It enhances data findability, which in turn affects users' understanding of what texts are and how they function in culture.

Interestingly, it is in this context that the utility of liberature has been noticed, causing arguments to be made in its favour. At a conference on data management in library science, Alina Grochowska proposed that "liberature" should be introduced as a subject term in the electronic catalogue for the Polish National Library, alongside such terms as "poemix" and "concrete poetry" (both also missing from the list of officially approved keywords according to her).[144] She noted that works described in criticism using these terms had been catalogued under very broad subject headings, such as "Polish poetry of the 20th c." or "Art of the 20th c.," neglecting to reflect the idiosyncratic nature of such publications. Within such a system, only users already familiar with the material will be able to find what they are looking for, and they may be unable to retrieve other similar, potentially useful items. Many may well remain ignorant about the existence of materials potentially pertinent to their research. Or they will be misled about the specific features or categorisation of particular works because they are "hidden" under inaccurate tags.[145] A part of the information therefore remains latent, thus disfiguring, misrepresenting or

---

[144] Her presentation entitled "Does the language of subject terms of the National Library of Poland keep up to date with the development of academic fields and their terminology?" was given at a conference of the Polish Librarians Association "Pracuj lokalnie, myśl globalnie. Opracowanie i wyszukiwanie informacji w bibliotekach" [Work locally, think globally. Data management and research in libraries] held on 28–29 November 2007 in the National Library of Poland in Warsaw, and published on the PLA website www.ebib.info.

[145] This is exactly the kind of argument Janis Young used in her talk to justify the introduction of genre/form headings.

"trimming" the scope of a field. For example, if the metadata for works of concrete poetry labels it as "art" rather than "poetry," a search for "Polish poetry" will return results suggesting that this kind of creative writing was either not present in Poland, or that Polish poetry was narrower in its creative scope than was actually the case. That is why Grochowska proposed that liberature, concrete poetry, and poemix should be added to the list of officially approved subject terms, especially given that they had already come into critical use.

As it turns out, the Jagiellonian Library seems to have responded to her suggestion. A recent subject search using the term "liberatura" returned ten works labelled "Polish liberature." These were not published in the "Liberatura" series, yet were described so by the library cataloguers.[146] A comparable search in the National Library of Poland in Warsaw revealed that they do not use liberature as a subject term. Books published in the series are variously catalogued as "Polish prose – 21st c." (e.g. *Spoglądając przez ozonową dziurę* (sic!) and *(O)patrzenie*), "Polish artist's book" (*Oka-leczenie*), "English novel – 20th c." (Johnson's *The Unfortunates*), as well as under other broad generic labels.[147] As regards *Oka-leczenie*, its classification implies a misleading genetic affiliation with the visual arts, since the subject heading covers books created by visual artists as limited editions, or as one-of-a-kind works. Surprisingly, the same subject heading is not used for *(O)patrzenie*, which was issued as part of a set with *Oka-leczenie*; the former is labelled only as "Polish prose." Admittedly, this is a welcome modification to the 2007 subject heading classification, when the work was tagged as "album" (Grochowska 2007).

The subject headings are comparably confusing in the case of Herta Müller's collage poems. *Der Wächter nimmt seinen Kamm*, her first volume of poetry that appeared in a bilingual edition,[148] is tagged as "German artist's book" (and German poetry). However, a selection of her later poems, which were published in codex form under the title *Kolaże*, is classified as "German collage" (and German poetry").[149] These examples demon

---

[146] See the results of the search: https://chamo.bj.uj.edu.pl/uj/search/query?match_1 =PHRASE&field_1=s&term_1=Liberatura+polska+1990-.&theme=system (access: 7 March 2016).

[147] See the result of the search at: http://alpha.bn.org.pl/search~S5/?searchtype=X&searcharg=liberatura&searchscope=5&SORT=D&extended=0&SUBMIT=Search&searchlimits=&searchorigarg=dliberatura (access: 7 March 2016).

[148] A bilingual edition, published in the form of the book-in-a-box (trans. Artur Kożuch, Kraków: Korporacja Ha!art, 2010. Liberatura series, vol. 15).

[149] See the author/title search at http://alpha.bn.org.pl/search.

strate how a generic classification makes "available a set of knowledges on which the users of texts draw" while excluding others, and how this is related to "social practices" in "commercial and educational institutions" (Frow 2006: 31[150]). So even if a category is conceptually viable, it will not be accessible to users unless it is recognised by a discourse community influential enough to legitimise it.[151]

Forms of knowing

It is worth noting here that several liberatic works feature material and conceptual ways of organising knowledge as an important theme. Suffice it to mention Danielewski's *House of Leaves*, Federman's *Double or Nothing*, Szczerbowski's *Anthology*, and Nowakowski's *Nondescription of the World*. This can even be seen in poetic liberature, such as Mallarmé's *Un Coup de Des*, Fajfer's *ten letters*, or Paweł Dunajko's anepigraphic [   ], the work that problematises this by defying even classification through a title. In Steven Hall's *Raw Shark Texts* this theme is addressed via a tension between the database and the story; both ideas are, in turn, related to concepts of the self. The main protagonist, Eric Sanderson, represents a traditional, "narrative" idea of the self that comes to be attacked by conceptual monsters: a memory-devouring fantastic shark, and a multiple-bodied, networked creature called Mycroft Ward. The latter represents a database-related approach to identity, hybridising human bodies with computer hardware and software.

Ward was a nineteenth-century amateur scientist who invented a way of perpetuating his existence by transferring the content of his mind, that is all of the information stored in it, into another man's mind – and body, of course. Once reduced to an apparently disembodied, amorphous, "liquid" pool of information, he could be downloaded (that is, poured) into any "container," which he/it gradually did so that he/it finally took over hundreds of people. The obsessive search for more bodies was triggered

---

[150] See also the subchapter "Synchrony and diachrony" in the first edition of his monograph (pp. 128–131), which shows how the conceptualisation of genre is relevant to cataloguing and bookselling practices, readers' hermeneutic practices, and a systemic approach to literary history. It is substantially rewritten, omitting the reference to cataloguing, in the revised edition of 2015.

[151] This begs for a sociologically oriented analysis of the genre according to Bourdieu's theory of the literary field, which I undertake in "Liberatura w polu produkcji kulturowej" [Sociological Contexts of Liberature] (2015a).

by the fear of sudden death – the first "remediated" Ward took part in the Great War, which made him acutely aware of the body's precariousness and fragility. But his/its invasion of more and more bodies only accentuates the fact that in order to be preserved all information needs material support. In this respect, *Raw Shark Texts* seems almost to illustrate Katherine Hayles' reflection that opens her seminal book:

> Information viewed as pattern and not tied to a particular instantiation is information free to travel across time and space. [...] The great dream and promise of information is that it can be free from the material constraints that govern the mortal world. Marvin Minsky precisely expressed this dream when, in a recent lecture, he suggested it will soon be possible to extract human memories from the brain and import them, intact and unchanged, to computer disks.[23] The clear implication is that if we can become the information we have constructed, we can achieve effective immortality. In the face of such a powerful dream, it can be a shock to remember that for information to exist, it must *always* be instantiated in a medium, whether that medium is the page from the *Bell Laboratories Journal* on which Shannon's equations are printed, the computer-generated topological maps used by the Human Genome Project, or the cathode ray tube on which virtual worlds are imaged. (1999: 13)

Besides, what Ward did not realise is that the mere transference of data into another material support affects the content. Content inscribed in a different material foundation, not to mention a different material medium, is modified[152] because the form of presentation is also a piece of information: about knowledge structures and value systems. The original, all-too-human desire to prolong one's existence, when multiplied onto several identical copies that were regularly updated and synchronised,

> turned Ward's preservation command into a feedback loop. [...] Once it had begun, there was no way to stop the loop gathering momentum. As the weeks passed, Ward became a slave to his own machine. In the face of his ever growing all-devouring urge to survive, Ward made more and more amends to his

---

[152] Or simply lost. To quote a familiar adage from a related discipline, something's always lost in translation. This is evident in the Kindle edition of Hall's work, which is unable to "narrate" in a flipbook manner (mechanical animation) the emergence of the conceptual shark from the depths of the white pages. When the students of my MA seminar had the opportunity to hold the printed book in class they were amazed to discover this episode; the majority of them had read the work in digital form and had therefore missed the attack of the conceptual monster.

system and blindly stripped away his own humanity one piece at a time. (Hall 2007a: 205)

But Hall's novel is not a naïve and simple criticism of the database, juxtaposing the most modern way of organising and preserving knowledge with a more "natural" form of the story. Rather, it highlights the limitations of this method of organising data, something that is humorously symbolised by the "Undex (Incomplete UK)" that is added to some editions. The "Undex" definitely helps the reader navigate the story, and retrieve some information quickly, thus working as a seemingly efficient memory aid.[153] But then it indexes only the knowledge its author considers significant. Ironically, for example, it does not include "self," as if the concept (and the word) were absent from the story. It does, however, feature "signs of life" and even the actual author's name, which is mentioned on the colophon and title page (Hall 2007). Accordingly, page references to "Sanderson, Eric, The Other" and some of those to "Ward, Mycroft" are blanked with a black ■ (ibid.). Despite the fact that the index acknowledges their identities, its apparent defect denies the reader access to relevant textual locations. Or else, the blanks may be read as empty signifiers, which in a sense they are. Eric, suffering from memory loss, cannot relate himself to anything or anyone, cannot fill in his self with any meaning. His self can only gradually emerge from the story the other, old Eric constructed for him. In another sense, Eric acts as a player who enters a game and gradually discovers his self, building up his identity through playing it, solving puzzles, fighting monsters, dodging unexpected attacks, and so on. As for Ward, the conventions of the index allow us to infer that the black mark refers to the earliest information about him that should be included in the first pages of the book, but which is difficult to locate, encoded, or perhaps irreparably lost.

So we can see how the compositional space of the book along with its other (diagrammatically and pictorially) iconic dimensions highlights the theme of the search for knowledge (also self-knowledge), its accessibility, and its entanglement with material forms of presentation.[154] For Hall, the choice of the printed codex is a deliberate aesthetic and compo-

■

153 This is another telling detail as Eric suffers from amnesia and therefore relies heavily on all kinds of written reminders: sticky notes, letters he sends to himself, etc.

154 See also Hayles' "Material Entanglements: Steven Hall's *The Raw Shark Texts* as Slipstream Novel," in which she explores the tension between the database and the narrative. On the narrative versus the database see also Manovich 2001.

sitional gesture, as its material structure is directly related to the concept of the narrative self insofar as the bound volume embodies the sequential coherence of a story. But the inclusion of the "Undex," as well as the visual materials included in chapter 36, the final chapter, calls into question the notion that this is the sole, unitary form of organising knowledge. And consequently the notion of the self as a coherent, continuous whole is challenged. Moreover, the paratexts include information about three different editions: the UK, the Export, and the Unspace edition; and the key to the "Undex" suggests the existence of "Negatives," i.e. alternative or complementary versions of events presented in the story that are dispersed across digital and "real world" spaces. This is confirmed by the author's own admission on the on-line discussion forum that "[t]he negatives are not deleted scenes, they are very much a part of the novel but they are all splintered from it in some way" (Hall 2007b). All this suggests that a self envisioned as coherent and whole may only be a precarious, porous construct, a sign of the body struggling to maintain its physical and mental integrity.[155]

The dispersal or mobility of the work's constituent parts not only points to the disintegration of mind and body (liberature's characteristic thanatic impulse), but also to the dynamic and elusive nature of information. In fact, many facets of the work (the index, the flipbook section, images, photos, varied typography, and paratexts) belong to a multimodal information system that is activated by the reader in a non-trivial effort to maintain order during reading. Other liberatic works demonstrate the same property, as if the reader's intense and prolonged engagement with the work could counteract its inevitable destruction.

Recalling Derrida's metaphorical description of the effect of genre, we can see how he anticipated a theme that is prominent in many liberatic works. These hybrids – works that have "degenerated" from the perspective of more traditional genre classification – often explore themes of mental and physical degeneration, and dying. Their material and stylistic layers reflect a deterioration from the culturally accepted norm towards an abnormal condition that is deregulated, dysfunctional, defective. This is the main subject of Johnson's *Albert Angelo, House Mother Normal*, and *The Unfortunates*, as well as being a central theme in Federman's *Double or Nothing* and *Voice in the Closet*. It is also important for Danielewski's *House of Leaves* and *Revolutions*, not to mention *Oka-leczenie*.

---

[155] Hall's novel has been interpreted quite convincingly as an allegory for Alzheimer's disease (Pressman 2009: 472).

Thirlwell's *Kapow!* begins with Rustam, a taxi driver in Cairo who comes across a seemingly dead man, and subsequently saves him from actual death. Moreover, the book deals with the Arab spring, the revolution which disturbed and destroyed the prior social order, and in turn brought about chaos, war, and death.

Liberatic works also address dying as a cognitive and psychological experience, but do not attempt to describe this experience by setting the story in a strange, fantastic world (as is often the case with narratives dealing with the theme), but to recreate it as an experience during which the extinguishing mind loses control over the body. Hence, the disintegrated, incoherent, materially fragmented or discontinuous forms of the book: unbound signatures (*The Unfortunates*, *Composition no 1*), gradually fading or diminishing amounts of text (Orszulewski's *Jezus nigdy nie był taki blady*, *House Mother Normal*), elements "falling out of the confined shape" of the book in the form of an accordion insert (*Kapow!*, Fajfer's poem "Balkon") or into other media and the Internet (*The Raw Shark Texts*). Their de-generation is reflected in their departure from the generic conventions they simultaneously evoke and erase. It is communicated through "mutilated" structures of organisation whose traditional cohesive mechanisms are impaired. But this gives rise to the material metaphor, which – when per/con/ceived – is capable of evoking an intense feeling of presentification, of bringing the "dead letter of experiment" to life.

Conclusion

Liberature: what's in the name?

> What's in a name? That which we call a rose
> By any other name would smell as sweet.
> Shakespeare, *Romeo and Juliet* (act II, scene ii, 1–2)

"Almost always a form appears earlier than the critical name for it," claims Fowler based on the evidence of his decades-long study of empirical genres. He adds that "[t]he absence of a genre label is of course no argument against the genre's existence; after all architectural orders themselves went unnamed for more than 1500 years" (2003: 187). As I have described, first came book-bound works, then came the name liberature, "cepted" from a critical reflection on writing and reading. The idea, originating in a fusion of LITERATURE and BOOK, was tentatively framed in terms of genre. My argument has been that it is both conceivable and helpful to think about it in this way since genre is one of the fundamental means by which we organise knowledge about literature. Carolyn Miller notes that "our 'stock of knowledge' is based upon types" and explains that a new category may emerge and be accepted as,

> ...useful only in so far as it can be brought to bear upon new experience: the new is made familiar through the recognition of relevant similarities; those similarities become constituted as a type. A new type is formed from typifications already on hand when they are not adequate to determine a new situation. If a new typification proves continually useful for mastering states of affairs, it enters the stock of knowledge and its application becomes routine. (Miller 1994: 25)

For the pragmatic scholar, the ultimate test of genre viability is its use. This generates a web-like structure of associations that simultaneously delineates the semantic field of the concept. As regards liberature, even those who are skeptical about its generic dimension admit that it is a handy term, and use it. They apply it in analyses of actual works, acknowledging that it does tell us something theoretically important about literary discourse. First of all, they agree that it highlights the multimodality and multimediality of literature. Secondly, they acknowledge that it foregounds the book as a spatial means of organising literary discourse – a semantically charged, non-transparent interface. Of course, these features have always been present in literature. Some authors applied them in delibrate ways in literary works of different periods, but they are coming to the fore today under the pressure of electronic media. In response to the increased presence of such works, scholars, writers, poets, and artists have proposed a number of terms that aim to capture their specificity. Liberature, formulated on the brink of the new millenium, points to the fact that the book itself functions as a sign that needs to be read in its embodied totality. It reveals and underlines the latent potential of the book as a valid and engaging medium of literary expression, which however demands an expanded, multimodal literacy. Additionally, it illuminates the liberating effect such "writingreading" can have on both authors and audiences. As scholars researching the artists' book and practitioners of the art point out, the book can at last reveal its aesthetic potential, liberated from its obligation to serve as the major medium for storing and disseminating information. Liberature, on the other hand, bears witness to the fact that this potential need not be activated exclusively by visual artists, but also by writers who see their practice as material, embodied, and performative.

This is often perceived as a form of nostalgia or resistance against "the death" of the printed book. While death or loss feature prominently in most works referred to as liberature, I believe that such works also communicate their affinity with similar artistic texts created using other writing technologies. In this sense, liberature foregrounds book-bound technotexts as a distinct category of creative writing. At the same time the selected form of the book draws on rich symbolism. It is akin to the materialised content of the mind, a piece of architecture inhabited like a house or used for storing knowledge and memories, like a museum or a gallery, or puzzling and trapping the readers as they wander through its maze.

As for the classificatory function of the genre, it is better understood in terms proposed by Boon and Miller, as a kind of "ethnomethodological" procedure, intended "to explicate the knowledge that practice creates. This approach insists that the *'de facto'* genres, the types we have names for in everyday language, tell us something theoretically important about discourse" (Miller 1994: 23). Though certainly not as common as the novel or the sonnet, liberature is illuminating in this respect. When the label is applied to a work, it signals that the author resorts to material rhetoric, and prompts the readers to pay attention to non-linguistic codes. It is these "new" variables that are instrumental in describing liberature in generic terms. They have not gone entirely unnoticed in literary genre studies, but were downplayed or ignored for various reasons. For example, the genre(s) the author gestures towards in literary texts (and paratexts)[156] are entangled with the effect they intend their work to have, yet the fear of the intentional fallacy has trained generations of readers to disregard them. But they are important for hermeneutic readings and reader-response-led approaches.[157] Rhetorical-functional studies bring such features back into the picture, indicating how authorial signals may be related to the shape of a work, and consequently to genre(s) attributed to them by readers. An author's deliberate use of material rhetoric can be treated as a kind of paratext and a potential genre marker, as for example in the case of the layout of visual poems. Besides, in line with McGann's understanding of the bibliographical code, a work's material rhetoric constitutes yet another "voice" in the polyphony of primary speech genres combined in a literary work, and can therefore be described in terms of style. The specific shaping of the semiotic medium (that is language as writing/print inscribed in a book[158]) can be seen as the material equivalent to essential, non-verbal aspects of oral communication that are absent or downplayed in everyday writing (Assman 1994: 26) but foregrounded in artistic forms. The material form of the book can be described as a kind of rhetorical gesture[159] accompanying a verbal message, intended to add emphasis or illustrate the point.

So it seems that material features of bookish interfaces can be used to differentiate between artistic text types.[160] Indeed, as Frow states, "the for-

---

[156] Polish scholar Sanisław Balbus describes these as traces of authorial instructions for reading ("ślady instrukcji autorskiej"), which activate generic frameworks for understanding. During reading the reader then "tests" a text for features that either confirm or confront familiar generic conventions (Balbus 2007: 164).

[157] Cf. Eco's discussion of *intentio operis*, *intentio auctoris* and *intentio lectoris* (1992: 64).

[158] Again, let me stress that I mean here a codex or any other form of the book: an accordion structure, a scroll, a collection of pages or signatures, etc., in short, any physical, reproducible object or collection of objects serving as the space of inscription.

[159] I use the term in the sense of "the visible bodily action" that is expressive of a thought or feeling (Kendon 2004: 7–8).

[160] That is texts not only in the narrower sense of the term, i.e. a text as verbal message, but in a broader sense meaning any "message generated by the system of cultural codes" (Nöth 1995: 331).

mal organisation of a genre comprises a repertoire of ways of shaping the material medium in which it works" (2015: 81). This is in fact the premise underlying the concepts of *electronic literature* and visual and concrete poetry. Poetry in general can be linked to this notion, because of its distinct layouts. Deliberate choices regarding medial submodes can also be described in terms of style (hence, suggestions that liberature is a kind of poetics, see Dąbrowska 2013: 250–264, 160–161). It is this kind of extended conceptual framework that allows Gibbons to classify multimodal literature as a genre, and the multimodal novel as its book-bound subgenre. Likewise, liberature can be delineated as a type of literature bound to the printed book in a meaningful way according to the deliberate design of the author. As Miller notes, genre classification is useful only insofar as it is able to illuminate the way discourse works, "if it reflects the experience of the people who create and interpret" it (21). Due to the reconceptualisation of genre – which shifts our understanding of genre away from a description of a set of formal characteristics, and towards an understanding of genre as a repeated verbal behavior that is meaningful in social situations – we can think of genres as ways of doing things in the world. Thus, Fajfer's work and his "proclamation" of a "new literary genre" was evidently both a Bourdieusian intervention in the literary field (Bazarnik 2015a) as well as an "invention" of a new text type,[161] intended to boost multimodal ways of writing, which as we have stressed, have always been practiced but were downplayed by idealist conceptualisations of language as disembodied communications between disembodied minds.

An increasing number of similar "interventions," described by Pressman as the "aesthetic of bookishness," corroborates Miller's claim that a genre is "an index to cultural patterns" that illuminates ways in which texts are encountered, created, and understood (Miller 1994: 32). What was once considered playful, "gimmicky," contrived or experimental (cf. Malmgren 1985: 46) is coming to be recognised as a legitimate part of the literary repertoire, an acceptable option for contemporary writers and poets who wish to create narratives and express lyrical reflections. The growing number of such "cultural utterances" bears witness to the fact that this marginal, exceptional, eccentric practice has been shifting closer to the centre. Quite expectedly, the increase in such works has stimulated a need to classify and order them. Technotexts, readingwriting, multimodal literature, book-bound novels, liberature – all these terms respond to this need. Each term foregrounds

---

[161] Cf. Bawarshi's article "Genres as Forms of In(ter)vention" that focuses on this duplicity of genre function.

slightly different aspects of the works it claims to describe, and each modulates readers' expectations in a slightly different way.

Evidently, these conceptual changes are happening under the pressure and impact of technological changes. Contemporary writing tools facilitate and encourage multimodal and multimedial writing, no wonder then that contemporary authors resort to it. But more interesting, I believe, is the fact that the new writing technologies have simultaneously revealed the hidden potential of print, this arguably obsolete medium. The affordances actualised in the material rhetoric of the book may be considered stylistic and generic markers, as is evident in description of liberature, definition of multimodal literature, and the "book" as a subcategory of the novel. Frow concludes his monograph by stressing that "[c]ritical engagement with genre is central to the critical examination of our culture and our social world" because "through the use of genre we learn who we are, and encounter the limits of our world" (Frow 2015: 167 and 166 respectively). The genre I have outlined in this book addresses these questions, inviting a reconsideration of the concept of subjectivity, as well as socio-cultural and even political consequences of aesthetic choices. These vast questions perhaps call for a separate, more philosophically oriented study than this humble outline. So let me conclude by restating that what we can learn from liberature conceived of as a genre is that literature may be an embodied art, in parallel with sculpture, installation, the happening, and theatre, that it may be performative, too, engaging the reader in an aesthetic, intellectual and physical way. But it is still literature insofar as it wants to reach its audience through the word (so language remains its fundamental medium), as widely as possible (through multiple copy editions), and as intimately as possible (through the unique materiality of the book). Secondly, it proves once more that literature is a space for transgression, subversion, experimentation and change, which can still be practiced in the allegedly old-fashioned medium of the printed book. Finally, freed from its traditional obligations, literature in the form of the book has come into its own. It remains for the reader to judge whether it smells as sweetly under the name of liberature as under any other name.

Bibliography

Primary sources

Apollinaire, Guillaume (1966 [1918]). *Calligrammes.* Paris: Gallimard.

Bartnicki, Krzysztof (2010). *Prospekt emisyjny.* Kraków: Ha!art. Liberatura, vol. 14.

Bazarnik, Katarzyna, and Zenon Fajfer (2003). *(O)patrzenie.* Kraków: Krakowska Alternatywa [renamed as Korporacja Ha!art in 2004]. Liberatura, vol. 1.

Bazarnik, Katarzyna, and Zenon Fajfer (2012). *Sonnet of Sonnets.* Kraków: Korporacja Ha!art & Oakland: Eucalyptus Press.

Bednarczyk, Andrzej (1995). *Świątynia kamienia. Temple of Stone.* Trans. Barbara Kutryba. Kraków: Krakowski Oddział Literatów Polskich. Numbered and signed ed. Copy no 179.

Bervin, Jen (2004). *Nets.* New York: Ugly Duckling Press.

Blake, William (2001). *The Complete Illuminated Books.* Introd. by David Bindman. London: Thames and Hudson in association with the William Blake Trust.

Carson, Anne (2010). *Nox.* New York: New Directions Book.

Cendrars, Blaise, and Sonia Delaunay-Terk (2009 [1913]). *La Prose du Transsibérien et de la petite Jehanne de France.* New Haven, London: Beineke Rare Book and Manuscript Library.

Chopin, Henri (1961, 1970). *Le dernier roman du monde: (histoire d'un chef occidental ou oriental).* [Bruxelles]: Éditions Cyanuur. [Print and vinyl record].

Conrad, Joseph (1994 [1899]). *Heart of Darkness.* London: Penguin.

Cortázar, Julio (1987 [1963]). *Hopscotch.* Trans. Gregory Rabassa. New York: Pantheon.

Danielewski, Mark Z. (2000). *House of Leaves.* Full colour ed. New York: Pantheon Books.

Dante Alighieri (1988 [1320]). *La Divina Commedia.* Commentary Eugenio Camerini, illustr. by Gustave Doré. [n pl.]: Fratelli Melita Editori.

Dunajko, Paweł (2010). [ ] [anepigraph]. Kraków: Korporacja Ha!art. Liberatura, vol. 13.

Eliot, Thomas Stearns (1963). *Collected Poems 1909–1962.* London, Boston: Faber.

Fajfer, Zenon (dir.) (1992). *Madam Eva, Ave Madam.* Kraków: Zenkasi Theatre. 26 June, PDPS, ul. Zielna 41, Kraków. Performance.

Fajfer, Zenon (2004). *Spoglądając przez ozonową dziurę.* Kraków: Korporacja Ha!art. Liberatura, vol. 2.

Fajfer, Zenon (2007a [2004]). "Ars poetica" (Polish version) [in:] *Techsty. Magazyn* 3. http://www.techsty.art.pl/magazyn3/fajfer/Ars_poetica_polish.html (access: 3 November 2015).

Fajfer, Zenon (2007b [2005]). "Ars poetica" (English version) [in:] *Techsty. Magazyn* 3. http://www.techsty.art.pl/magazyn3/fajfer/Ars_poetica_english.html (access: 3 November 2015).

Fajfer, Zenon (2010). *dwadzieścia jeden liter / ten letters*. Trans. Katarzyna Bazarnik. Kraków: Korporacja Ha!art. Liberatura, vol. 10–11. Print and DVD.

Fajfer, Zenon (2013). *Powieki*. Szczecin: Forma. Print and CD.

Fajfer, Zenon (2014). "Powieki" [in:] *Techsty. Magazyn* 1.9. http://techsty.art.pl/powieki/ (access: 9 July 2014).

Fajfer, Zenon (2015a). *Widok z głębokiej wieży*. Szczecin: Forma.

Fajfer, Zenon (2015b). *Widok z głębokiej wieży* [View from the Deep Tower]. Teresa Nowak (dir.). Katowice: Rialto, 25 April. https://www.youtube.com/watch?v=IFKwPkhzGDU (access: 16 June 2016). Performance.

Fajfer, Zenon, and Katarzyna Bazarnik (2000). *Oka-leczenie*. Kraków: private limited ed.

Fajfer, Zenon, and Katarzyna Bazarnik (2009 [2000]). *Oka-leczenie*. Kraków: Korporacja Ha!art. Liberatura, vol. 8.

Federman, Raymond (1971). *Double or Nothing*. Chicago: The Swallow Press.

Federman, Raymond (1998). *Double or Nothing*. 3rd ed. Boulder, Normal, Ill.: Fiction Collective Two.

Federman, Raymond (2010). *Podwójna wygrana jak nic*. Trans. Jerzy Kutnik. Kraków: Korporacja Ha!art. Liberatura, vol. 16.

Federman, Raymond (1979). *The Voice in the Closet*. Madison: Coda Press.

Foer, Jonathan Safran (2010). *The Tree of Codes*. London: Visual Editions.

Gass, William H. (1995). *The Tunnel*. Normal. Il.: Dalkey Archive Press.

Gass, William H. (2006). *THE TUNNEL read by William H. Gass*. Dalkey Archive Press. CD-Audio.

Gass, William H. (1989 [1968]). *Willie Masters' Lonesome Wife*. Normal, Il.: Dalkey Archive.

Grudin, Robert (1992). *Book. A Novel*. New York: Random House.

Hall, Steven (2007a). *The Raw Shark Texts*. Edinburgh: Canongate.

Hardy, Thomas (1992 [1891]). *Tess of the d'Urbervilles*. New York: Bantam Books.

Herbert, George (1991). *The Complete English Poems*. John Tobin (ed.). London: Penguin.

Johnson, Bryan Stanley (1973). *Aren't You Rather Young to be Writing Your Memoirs?*. London: Hutchinson.

Johnson, Bryan Stanley (1999 [1969]). *The Unfortunates*. London: Picador.

Johnson, Bryan Stanley (2004a). *B.S. Johnson Omnibus*. London: Picador.

Johnson, Bryan Stanley (2004b [1964]). *Albert Angelo* [in:] Johnson 2004a.

Johnson, Bryan Stanley (2004c [1966]). *Trawl* [in:] Johnson 2004a.

Johnson, Bryan Stanley (2004d [1971]). *House Mother Normal* [in:] Johnson 2004a.

Johnson, Bryan Stanley (2008). *Nieszczęśni*. Trans. Katarzyna Bazarnik. Kraków: Korporacja Ha!art. Liberatura, vol. 5.

Joyce, James (1989 [1939]). *Finnegans Wake*. London: Faber.

Joyce, James (1998 [1922]). *Ulysses*. Ed. with introduction and notes by Jeri Johnson. Oxford: Oxford UP. (A facsimile edition reproduced from copy no 785 in the Bodleian Library).

Mallarmé, Stéphane (1994 [1897]). "A Throw of the Dice/Un Coup de Dés" [in:] *Collected Poems*. Trans. with a commentary by Henry Weinfield. Berkeley: University of California Press, 124–145.

Mallarmé, Stéphane (1998). *Poésies et autres textes*. Paris: Le Livre de Poche.

Mallarmé, Stéphane (2005 [1897]). *Rzut kośćmi nigdy nie zniweczy przypadku*. Trans. Tomasz Różycki. Kraków: Korporacja Ha!art. Liberatura, vol. 3.

Meersman, Philip (2014). *This is Belgian Chocolate. Manifestations of Poetry*. New York: Three Room Press.

Müller, Herta (2003). *Der König verneigt sich und tötet*. München: Hanser.

Müller, Herta (2010 [1993]). *Strażnik bierze swój grzebień / Der Wächter nimmt seinen Kamm*. Trans. Artur Kożuch. Kraków: Korporacja Ha!art. Liberatura, vol. 15.

Nowakowski, Radosław (2001). *Hasa Rapasa*. Dąbrowa Dolna: Ogon słonia.

Nowakowski, Radosław (2002). *Traktat kartkograficzny*. Dąbrowa Dolna: Liberatorium. Signed copy no. 22.

Nowakowski, Radosław (2003). *Sienkiewicza Street in Kielce*. Kielce: Biuro Wystaw Artystycznych.

Orszulewski, Dariusz (2013). *Jezus nigdy nie był taki blady*. Kraków: Korporacja Ha!art. Liberatura, vol. 21.

Perec, George (1988 [1978]). *Life Instruction Manual*. Trans. David Bellos. Boston: David R. Godin.

Queneau, Raymond (1961). *Cent Mille Milliards de Poèmes*. Paris: Gallimard.

Sałaj, Zbigniew (1997). *Miękka książka* [Soft Book]. One-of-a-kind book object. Book Art Museum, Łódź, Poland.

Smith, Ali (2015 [2014]). *How to Be Both*. London: Penguin, Random House UK.

Szczerbowski, Robert (2013). *Antologia: Kompozycje. Księga żywota. Æ*. Kraków: Korporacja Ha!art. Liberatura, vol. 20.

Sterne, Laurence (1990 [1759–1767]). *The Life and Opinions of Tristram Shandy, Gentleman*. The World's Classics. Ed. with an Introduction and Notes by Ian Campbell Ross. Oxford: Oxford UP.

Thirlwell, Adam (2012). *Kapow!*. London: Visual Editions. No. 4.

Williams, Emmettt (ed.) (2013 [1967]). *An Anthology of Concrete Poetry*. New York: Primary Information.

Secondary sources

Aarseth, Espen (1997). *Cybertext: Perspective on Ergodic Literature*. Baltimore: Johns Hopkins UP.

Adamowicz, Elza (2009). "The *livre d'artiste* in the Twentieth-century France" [in:] *French Studies* 63.3, 189–198. Web (access: 16 February 2016).

Arendt, Hannah (1969). "Introduction. Walter Benjamin: 1892-1940" [in:] *Illuminations*. Walter Benjamin. Trans. Harry Zohn. Hannah Arendt (ed.). New York: Shoken Books, 1–51.

Artemeva, Natasha, and Aviva Freedman (eds.) (2016). *Genre Studies around the Globe: Beyond the Three Traditions*. [No place]: Trafford Publishing. E-book.

Assman, Jan (1994). "Ancient Egypt and the Materiality of the Sign" [in:] *Materialities of Communication*. Trans. William Whobrey. Hans Ulrich Gumbrecht and K. Ludwig Pfeiffer (eds.). Standford: Stanford UP, 15–31.

Attridge, Derek (2004). *Singularity of Literature*. New York: Routledge.

Auken, Sune (2015). "Genre and Interpretation" [in:] Sune, Lauridsen, and Rasmussen (eds.), 154–183.

Auken, Sune, Palle Schantz Lauridsen, and Anders Juhl Rasmussen (eds.) (2015). *Genre and....* Valby: Ekbátana. Copenhagen Studies in Genre, vol. 2. Pdf (access: 22 November 2015).

Bakhtin, Mikhail M. (1981). *The Dialogic Imagination. Four Essays*. Trans. Caryl Emerson, and Michael Holquist. Michael Holquist (ed.). Austin: University of Texas Press.

Bakhtin, Mikhail M. (1996). *Speech Genres and Other Late Essays*. Trans. Vern W. McGee. Caryl Emerson, and Michael Holquist (eds.). Austin: University of Texas Press.

Balbus, Stanisław (2007 [1999]). "Zagłada gatunków" [in:] Ostaszewska and Cudak (eds.), 156–171.

Baldry, Anthony, and Paul J. Thibault (2006). *Multimodal Transcription and Text Analysis: A Multimedia Toolkit and Coursebook with Associated On-line Course*. London, Oakville, CT: Equinox.

Bawarshi, Anis (2000). "The Genre Function" [in:] *College English*, 62.3, 335–360. JSTOR (access: 18 January 2015).

Bawarshi, Anis (2001). "The Ecology of Genre" [in:] *Ecocomposition: Theoretical and Pedagogical Approaches*. Sidney I. Dobrin and Christian R. Weisser (eds.). Albany: State University of NY Press, 69–79. *Googlebooks* (access: 18 January 2015).

Bawarshi, Anis (2003). *Genre and the Invention of the Writer: Reconsidering the Place of Invention in Composition*. Logan: Utah State UP. Pdf. *DigitalCommons@USU*, Book 141 (access: 6 April 2016).

Bawarshi, Anis (2008). "Genres as Forms of In(ter)vention" [in:] *Originality, Imitation, and Plagiarism: Teaching Writing in the Digital Age*. Martha Vicinus, and Caroline Eisner (eds.). Ann Arbor: University of Michigan Press, 79–89.

Bazarnik, Katarzyna (2002a). "Dlaczego od Joyce'a do liberatury (Zamiast wstępu)" [in:] Bazarnik 2002c (ed.), v–xvi.

Bazarnik, Katarzyna (2002b). "*Książka jako przedmiot* Michela Butora, czyli o liberaturze przed liberaturą" [in:] Bazarnik 2002c (ed.), 171–194.

Bazarnik, Katarzyna (ed.) (2002c). *Od Joyce'a do liberatury. Szkice o architekturze słowa*. Kraków: Universitas.

Bazarnik, Katarzyna (2004). "Liberature. The Body of the Book. *Willie Masters' Lonesome Wife* by William H. Gass" [in:] *Ways of Looking at a Blackbird. Essays in British and American*

Literature and Studies in Honor of Prof. Irena Przemecka. Grażyna and Andrzej Branny (eds.). Kraków: Instytut Filologii Angielskiej UJ, 253–261.

Bazarnik, Katarzyna (2005a). "Liberatura: ikoniczne oka-leczenie literatury" [Liberature: an iconic mut-I-lation of literature] [in:] Małgorzata Dawidek Gryglicka (ed.). *Tekst-tu-ra. Wokół nowych form tekstu literackiego i tekstu jako dzieła sztuki.* Kraków: Korporac-ja Ha!art, 23–40.

Bazarnik, Katarzyna (2005b). "Liberature – What's in a Name" [in:] Bazarnik, and Fajfer, 9–10.

Bazarnik, Katarzyna (2006). "Popsuta przestrzeń" [in:] *Autoportret. Pismo o dobrej przestrzeni* 17, 4–7.

Bazarnik, Katarzyna (2007a). "Joyce, Liberature and Writing of the Book" [in:] *Hypermedia Joyce Studies* 8.2. http://hjs.ff.cuni.cz/archives/v8_2/main/essays.php?essay=bazarnik (access: 25 March 2015).

Bazarnik, Katarzyna (2007b). "Liberature: a New Literary Genre?" [in:] *Insistent Images.* Elżbieta Tabakowska, Christina Ljungberg, and Olga Fischer (eds.). Amsterdam, Phila-delphia: John Benjamins, 189–206.

Bazarnik, Katarzyna (2009). "Some comments on liberature and artists' books" [in:] Bib-lioteka OK'ART. Book Art Museum website, Łódź, Poland (access: 30 March 2016).

Bazarnik, Katarzyna (2010a). "Chronotope in Liberature" [in:] *James Joyce and After. Writer and Time.* Katarzyna Bazarnik, and Bożena Kucała (eds.). Newcastle: Cambridge Schol-ars Publishing, 117–132.

Bazarnik, Katarzyna (2010b). "Liberature or on the Origin of (Literary) Species" [in:] Fajfer 2010a, 151–163.

Bazarnik, Katarzyna (2010c). "Materialność jako wyznacznik gatunkowy liberatury" [Ma-teriality as the generic parameter of liberature] [in:] Michał Ostrowicki (ed.). *Materia sz-tuki.* Kraków: Universitas, 109–118.

Bazarnik, Katarzyna (2011). *Joyce & Liberature.* Prague: Litteraria Pragensia.

Bazarnik, Katarzyna (2012a). リベラトゥラーテキストと書物の形を統合する新しい文学ジャン ル（久山宏一訳）[Liberature. The Literary Genre Integrating Text with the Form of the Book] [in:] *Journal of the Department of Contemporary Literary Studies,* University of Tokyo, Japan. Trans. Koichi Kujama. 『れにくさ. Renyxa. Реникса 3, winter, 207–225.

Bazarnik, Katarzyna (2012b). "Liberatura – rewitalizacja książki" [Liberature –regenera-tion of the Book] [in:] Monika Górska-Olesińska (ed.). *Liberatura, e-literatura i… Remiksy, remediacje, redefinicje.* Opole: Wydawnictwo Uniwersytetu Opolskiego, 9–18.

Bazarnik, Katarzyna (2014). "Introduction: Modernist Roots of Liberature" [in:] Bazarnik, and Curyłło-Klag (eds.), 1–14.

Bazarnik, Katarzyna (2015a). "Liberatura w polu produkcji kulturowej" [Sociological Con-texts of Liberature] [in:] *Teksty Drugie* 3, 57–76.

Bazarnik, Katarzyna (2015b). "Liberature: Literature in the space of the book" [in:] *Les Espaces du Livre / Spaces of the Book.* Isabelle Chol, and Jean Khalfa (eds.). Bern: Peter Lang, 25–42.

Bazarnik, Katarzyna (2016). "Hydra czy hybryda. Liberatura jako gatunek (jednak) litera-cki" [A Hydra or a Hybrid? Liberature as a Literary Genre (after all)] [in:] *Er(r)go. Teoria-Literatura-Kultura* 32.1, forthcoming.

Bazarnik, Katarzyna, and Izabela Curyłło-Klag (eds.) (2014). *Incarnations of Material Textuality. From Modernism to Liberature.* Newcastle upon Tyne: Cambridge Scholars Publishers.

Bazarnik, Katarzyna, and Zenon Fajfer (2005a). "A Brief History of Liberature" [in:] Bazarnik, and Fajfer 2005b, 12–23. Rep. in Fajfer 2010a, 85–92.

Bazarnik, Katarzyna, and Zenon Fajfer (2005b). *Liberature.* Kraków: Artpartner.

Bazarnik, Katarzyna, and Zenon Fajfer (2009). "Liberature: literature in the form of the book" [in:] *Traditional and emerging formats of artists books: Where do we go from here?*, conference materials. Sarah Bodmand, and Tom Sowden (eds.). Centre for Fine Print Research. University of the West of England. Web (access: 1 May 2010).

Bazerman, Charles (1994). "Systems of Genres and the Enactment of Social Intentions" [in:] Freedman, and Medway (eds.), 67–85.

Beebee, Thomas Olivier (1994). *The Ideology of Genre. A Comparative Study of Generic Instability.* University Park: Pennsylvania State UP.

Benton, Megan L. (2007). "The Book as Art" [in:] Eliot, and Rose (eds.), 493–507.

Bense, Max (1971). "Concrete Poetry" [in:] Solt (ed.), 73–74.

Bhabha, Homi, K. (1994). *The Location of Culture.* London, New York: Routledge.

Blanchot, Maurice (2000). "The Book to Come" [in:] Rothenberg, and Clay (eds.), 141–159.

Bolecki, Włodzimierz, and Ireneusz Opacki (2000). *Genologia dzisiaj.* Warszawa: IBL.

Bolter, Jay David (1991). *Writing Space. The Computer, Hypertext and the History of Writing.* Hillsdale, NJ, Hove and London: Lawrence Erlbaum Associates.

Boon, Mieke (2012). "Scientific Concepts in the Engineering Sciences: Epistemic Tools for Creating and Intervening with Phenomena" [in:] *Scientific Concepts and Investigative Practice.* Uljana Feest, and Friedrich Steinle (eds.). Berlin, Boston: Walter de Gruyter, 219–244. *Googlebooks* (access: 2 May 2016).

Bourdieu, Pierre (1995). *Rules of Art: Genesis and Structure of the Literary Field.* Trans. Susan Emanuel. Stanford: Stanford UP.

Bray, Joe (2015). "Concrete Poetry and Prose" [in:] Bray, Gibbons, and McHale (eds.), 298–309.

Bray, Joe, and Alison Gibbons (eds.) (2011). *Mark Z. Danielewski.* Manchester, New York: Manchester UP.

Bray, Joe, Alison Gibbons, and Brian McHale (eds.) (2015). *The Routledge Companion to Experimental Literature.* London, New York: Routledge.

Brooke-Rose, Christine (1991). *Stories, Theories and Things.* Cambridge: Cambridge UP.

Butor, Michel (2000a [1963]). "Le livre comme objet" [in:] *Essais sur le roman.* Michel Butor. Paris: Gallimard, 130–157.

Butor, Michel (2000b [1963]). "Sur la page" [in:] *Essais sur le roman.* Michel Butor. Paris: Gallimard, 125–129.

de Campos, Augusto, Decio Pignatari, and Haroldo de Campos (1970 [1958]). "Pilot Plan" [in:] Solt (ed.), 71–72.

Caraher Brian G. (2006). "Chapter I. Re-framing Genre Theory. Genre Theory: Cultural and Historical Motives Engendering Literary Genre" [in:] *Genre Matters: Essays in Theory and Criticism*. Dowd, Garin, Jeremy Strong, and Lesley Stevenson (eds.). Bristol: Intellect, 29–39. *EBSCO. eBook Academic Collection* (access: 15 December 2014).

Carrión, Ulises (1985). "The New Art of Making Books" [in:] *Artists' Books: A Critical Anthology and Sourcebook*. Joan Lyons (ed.). Layton, Utah: Gibbs M. Smith & Visual Studies Workshop, 31–43. Retrieved from: Harry Reese's course page "Art 112 • Artists' Books. EVERYTHING IN THE WORLD. A BOOK ARTS READER," The Department of Art, University of California, Santa Barbara. http://www.arts.ucsb.edu/faculty/reese/classes/artistsbooks/Ulises%20Carrion,%20The%20New%20Art%20of%20Making%20Books.pdf (access: 19 February 2016).

Chappell, Duncan (2003). "Typologising the artist's book" [in:] *Art Libraries Journal* 28.4, 12–20.

Chessmaster, Conic (ed.) (2010). *Perec instrukcja obsługi*. Kraków: Ha!art. Liberatura, vol. 9.

Chopin, Henri (1971 [1967]). "Why I Am the Author of Sound Poetry and Free Poetry" [in:] Solt (ed.), 80–82.

Chuderski, Adam, and Józef Bremer, (eds.) (2011). *Pojęcia. Jak reprezentujemy i kategoryzujemy świat*. Kraków: Universitas.

Cohn, Ralph (1989). "Do Postmodern Genres Exist?" [in:] *Postmodern Genres*. Marjorie Perloff (ed.). Norman, London: University of Oklahoma Press.

Colie, Rosalie Littell (1973). *The Resources of Kind: Genre Theory in the Renaissance*. Barbara K. Lewalski (ed.). Berkley, Los Angeles, CA: University of California Press. *Googlebooks* (access: 15 January 2015).

Collins, Viki Tollar (1999). "The Speaker Respoken: Material Rhetoric as Feminist Methodology" [in:] *College English*, 61.5, 545–573. JSTOR (access: 15 November 2015).

"Copyright for Researchers" (2014). NTU Library. Nottingham Trent University. https://www4.ntu.ac.uk/library/document_uploads/166648.pdf (access: 30 January 2016).

Couturier, Maurice (1991). *Textual Communication: A Print-based Theory of the Novel*. London: Routledge.

Croce, Benedetto (1995 [1902; 1909]). "The Activity of Externalization. Technique and the Theory of the Arts" [in:] *Aesthetic as Science of Expression and General Linguistic*. Trans. Douglas Ainslie, with a new introduction by John McCormick. New Brunswick, NJ.: Transaction, 111–117. *Googlebooks* (access: 9 June 2014).

Cuber, Marta (2003). "Rozmówki polsko-niepolskie". *Ha!art. Interdyscyplinarny Magazyn Kulturalno-Artystyczny* 2.15, [no pagination].

Cudak, Romuald (ed.). (2009). *Polska genologia. Gatunek w literaturze współczesnej*. Warszawa: Wydawnictwo Naukowe PWN.

Dawidek Gryglicka, Małgorzata (ed.) (2005). *Tekst-tura. Wokół nowych form tekstu literackiego i tekstu jako dzieła sztuki*. Kraków: Korporacja Ha!art.

Dawidek Gryglicka, Małgorzata (2012). *Historia tekstu wizualnego. Polska po 1967 roku.* Kraków: Korporacja Ha!art.

Dąbrowska, Elżbieta (2013). "6.7. Styl liberacki – między liberaturą a medium elektronicznym – sztuka interaktywna" [in:] *Style współczesnej polszczyzny. Przewodnik po stylistyce polskiej.* Ewa Malinowska, Jolant Nocoń, and Urszula. Żydek-Bednarczuk (eds.). Kraków: Universitas, 160–162.

Derrida, Jacques (1974). *Glas.* Paris: Éditions Galilée.

Derrida, Jacques (1992). "The Law of Genre" [in:] *Acts of Literature.* Trans. Avital Ronell, with editorial revisions. Derek Attridge (ed.). New York, London: Routledge, 221–252.

Devitt, Amy J. (2009). "Re-fusing Form in Genre Studies" [in:] Giltrow, and Stein, 27–48.

Dickson, Barbara (1999). "Reading Maternity Materially. The Case of Demi Moore" [in:] *Rhetorical Bodies.* Jack Selzer, and Sharon Crowley (eds.). Madison: The University of Wisconsin Press, 297–313. *Googlebooks* (access: 15 November 2015).

Dowd, Garin (2006). "Introduction: Genre Matters in Theory and Criticism" [in:] Dowd, Strong, and Stevenson, 11–27.

Dowd, Garin and Natalia Rulyova (eds.) (2015). *Genre Trajectories. Identifying, Mapping, Projecting.* Basingstoke: Palgrave Macmillan.

Dowd, Garin, Jeremy Strong, and Lesley Stevenson (eds.) (2006). *Genre Matters: Essays in Theory and Criticism.* Bristol: Intellect. EBSCO. *eBook Academic Collection* (access: 15 December 2014).

Drucker, Johanna (1994). *The Visible Word: Experimental Typography and Modern Art, 1909–1923.* Chicago: Chicago UP.

Drucker Johanna (1998). *Figuring the Word: Essays on Books, Writing, and Visual Poetics.* New York: Granary Books.

Drucker, Johanna (2000). "The Artist's Book as Idea and Form" [in:] Rothenberg, and Clay, 376–388.

Drucker, Johanna (2004 [1994]). *The Century of Artists Books.* New York: Granary Books.

Drucker Johanna (2009). "Entity to Event: From Literal, Mechanistic Materiality to Probabilistic Materiality" [in:] *Parallax* 15.4, 7–17. Taylor and Francis Online (access: 31 October 2015).

Drucker, Johanna (2013a). *Diagrammatic Writing.* Eindhoven: Onomatopee, Cabinet Project, No. 97.

Drucker Johanna (2013b). "Performative Materiality and Theoretical Approaches to Interface" [in:] *Digital Humanities Quarterly* 7.1 (access: 31 October 2015).

Dubrow, Heather (1982). *Genre.* London, New York: Methuen.

Duff, David (ed.) (2000). *Modern Genre Theory.* London, New York: Routledge.

Dziadek, Adam (2014). *Projekt krytyki somatycznej.* Warszawa: Instytut Badań Literackich PAN.

Eagleton, Terry (2012). *The Event of Literature.* New Haven, London: Yale UP.

Eco, Umberto (1992). *Interpretation and Overinterpretation.* Stefan Collini (ed.). Cambridge: Cambridge University Press.

Eliot, Simon, and Jonathan Rose (eds.) (2007). *A Companion to the History of the Book.* Malden, Oxford, Carlton: Blackwell.

Eliot, Thomas Stearns (1975 [1919]). "Tradition and Individual Talent" [in:] *Selected Prose of T. S. Eliot*. With an introduction by F. Kermode. New York: Harcourt Brace Jovanovich, and Farrar, Straus, and Giroux, 37–44.

Ellmann, Richard (1983). *James Joyce*. Oxford, New York: Oxford UP.

Emerson, Lori (2014). *Reading Writing Interfaces From the Digital to the Bookbound*. Minneapolis, London: University of Minneapolis Press.

Fajfer, Zenon (1999). "Liberatura. Aneks do słownika terminów literackich" [in:] *Dekada Literacka* 5–6, 30 June, 8–9. Rep. in Fajfer 2010a, 22–28.

Fajfer, Zenon (2008 [1999]). "Liberatur. Appendiks til en håndbog over litterære termer". Trans. Anna Mrozewicz. *Den Blå Port* 79, October, 13–19.

Fajfer, Zenon (2010a). *Liberatura czyli literatura totalna / Literature or Total Literature. Collected Essays 1999–2009*. Trans. and ed. Katarzyna Bazarnik. Kraków: Korporacja Ha!art. Liberatura, vol. 12.

Fajfer, Zenon (2010b [1999]). "Liberature. Appendix to a Dictionary of Literary Terms" [in:] Fajfer 2010a, 22–28. Rep. in Bazarnik and Fajfer 2005, 2–7; Fajfer 2011, 298–300; and Bazarnik and Curyłło-Klag, 121–126.

Fajfer, Zenon (2010c [2001]). "Liberature or Total Literature (Appendix to the 'Appendix to the Dictionary of Literary Terms')" [in:] Fajfer 2010a, 29–41. Rep. in Bazarnik and Curyłło-Klag, 127–138.

Fajfer, Zenon (2010d [2002]). "lyric, epic, dramatic, liberature" [in:] Fajfer 2010a, 43–49. Rep. in Bazarnik and Curyłło-Klag, 139–146.

Fajfer, Zenon (2010e [2003]). "Liberature: Hyperbook in the Hypertext Era" [in:] Fajfer 2010a, 50–59.

Fajfer, Zenon (2010f [2003]). "(N)on Description of Liberature" [in:] Fajfer 2010a, 60–65.

Fajfer, Zenon (2010g [2004]). "How to Distinguish between Liberature and Literature (selected anatomical details)" [in:] Fajfer 2010a, 81–84.

Fajfer, Zenon (2010h [2004]). "Joyce – Unwelcome Guest in Plato's Republic" [in:] Fajfer 2010a, 68–80.

Fajfer, Zenon (2010i [2005]). "Liberum Veto? (an authorial commentary to my article 'Liberature. Appendix to a Dictionary of Literary Terms')" [in:] Fajfer 2010a, 110–114.

Fajfer, Zenon (2010j [2005]). "The Muse of Liberature (or Who's Afraid of Widow Wadman)" [in:] Fajfer 2010a, 115–122.

Fajfer, Zenon (2010k [2005]). "Towards Liberature" [in:] Fajfer 2010a, 93–109.

Fajfer, Zenon (2010l [2009]). "How Liberature Redefines the Artist's Book" [in:] Fajfer 2010a, 134–140.

Fajfer, Zenon (2011). "Liberature" [in:] *Vlak. Contemporary Poetics and the Arts* 2, May, 298–300.

Fajfer, Zenon (2016). "Wśród przeczytanych łąk, asonansów... O literaturze totalnej trochę innym głosem" [Reading about Meadows and Assonances... A Slightly Different Voice on Total Literature] [in:] *Er(r)go. Teoria–Literatura–Kultura* 32.1, forthcoming.

Fajfer, Zenon, and Katarzyna Bazarnik (2010 [2005]). "Two Throws of the Dice or The Special and General Theory of Liberature" [in:] Fajfer 2010a, 123–126.

Fanning, Christopher (2002). "On Sterne's Page: Spatial Layout, Spatial Form, and Social Spaces in *Tristram Shandy*" [in:] *Laurence Sterne*. Ed. and introduced by Marcus Walsh. London: Longman, 178–200.

Federman, Raymond (1981 [1975]). "Surfiction – Four Propositions in Form on an Introduction" [in:] *Surfiction. Fiction Now… and Tomorrow*. Raymond Federman (ed.). 2nd enlarged edition. Chicago: Swallow Press, 5–15.

Fishelov, David (1993). *Metaphors of the Genre. The Role of Analogies in Genre Theory*. University Park: Pennsylvania State UP.

Fishelov, David (1999). "The Birth of a Genre" [in:] *European Journal of English Studies* 3.1, 51–63. Taylor and Francis Online (access: 1 April 2014).

Fowler, Alastair (1982). *Kinds of Literature. An Introduction to the Theory of Genres and Modes*. Oxford: Oxford UP.

Fowler, Alastair (1990). "Genre" [in:] *Encyclopedia of Literature and Criticism*. Martin Coyle, Peter Garside, Malcolm Kelsall, and John Peck (eds.). London: Routledge, 151–163. *Questia* (access: 14 June 2014).

Fowler, Alastair (2003). "The Formation of Genres in the Renaissance and After" [in:] *New Literary History* 34.2, Theorising Genres issue, 185–200. JSTOR (access: 7 June 2014).

Freedman, Aviva, and Peter Medway (eds.) (1994). *Genre and the New Rhetoric*. London, Bristol, PA: Taylor and Francis.

Frow, John (2006). *Genre*. London: Routledge.

Frow, John (2015 [2006]). *Genre*. 2nd ed. London: Routledge.

Gabora, Liane, Eleanor Rosch, and Diederik Aerts (2008). "Toward an Ecological Theory of Concepts" [in:] *Ecological Psychology* 20.1, 84–116. Francis and Taylor Online (access: 3 May 2016).

Gass, William H. (1970). "The Medium of Fiction" [in:] *Fiction and the Figures of Life*. New York: Alfred A Knopf, 27–34.

Gass, William H. (1997a). *Finding a Form*. Ithaca: Cornell UP.

Gass, William H. (1997b). "The Book As a Container of Consciousness" [in:] Gass 1997a, 327–352.

Gass, William H. (1997c). *Habitations of the Word*. Ithaca: Cornell UP.

Gass, William H. (1997d). "On reading to Oneself" [in:] Gass 1997c, 227–228.

Gass, William H. (1997e). "Representation and the War for Reality" [in:] Gass 1997c, 111–112

Gass, William H. (1997f). "Tropes of the Text" [in:] Gass 1997c, 141–159.

Gass, William H. (no date). "Designing The Tunnel" [in:] *Context*, 18. Dalkey Archive Press website (access: 30 January 2016).

Gaver, William W. (1991). "Technology affordances" [in:] *CHI'91. Proceedings of the SIGCHI Conference on Human Factors in Computing Systems. Reaching through technology*, 79–84. ACM Digital Library (access: 20 January 2016).

Gavins, Joanna (2007). *Text World Theory: An Introduction*. Edinburgh: Edinburgh UP. *EB-SCOhost. eBook Academic Collection* (access: 13 February 2016).

Gazda, Grzegorz (ed.) (2012). *Słownik rodzajów i gatunków literackich* [A Dictionary of Literary Kinds and Genres]. Warszawa: Wydawnictwo Naukowe PWN.

de Geest, Dirk, and Hendrik van Gorp (1999). "Literary Genres from a Systemic Functional Perspective" [in:] *European Journal of English Studies*, 3.1, 33–50. EBSCO (access: 21 November 2009).

Genette, Gérard (1992 [1979]). *The Architext: An Introduction*. Trans. Jane E. Levin, with a foreword by Robert Scholes. Berkley, LA, Oxford: University of California Press. *Googlebooks* (access: 10 June 2014).

Genette, Gérard (1997a). *Paratexts. Thresholds of Interpretation*. Trans. Jane E. Levin, foreword by Richard Macksey. Cambridge: Cambridge UP.

Genette, Gérard (1997b). *The Work of Art. Immanence and Transcendence*. Trans. G.M. Goshgarian. Ithaca: Cornell UP.

Gibbons, Alison (2008). "Multimodal Literature 'Moves' Us: Dynamic Movement and Embodiment in *VAS: An Opera in Flatland*" [in:] *Hermes. Journal of Language and Communication Studies* 41, 107–124 (access: 24 February 2016).

Gibbons, Alison (2011). "This is not for you" [in:] Bray, and Gibbons, 17–32.

Gibbons, Alison (2012). *Multimodality, Cognition, and Experimental Literature*. New York, London: Routledge.

Gibbons, Alison (2015). "Multimodal Literature and Experimentation" [in:] Bray and Gibbons, 420–435.

Giltrow, Janet, and Dieter Stein (eds.) (2009). *Genres in the Internet. Issues in the Theory of Genre*. Amsterdam, Philadelphia: John Benjamins.

Głowiński, Michał (2007). "Gatunek literacki i problemy poetyki historycznej" [Literary genre and the problems of historical poetics] [in:] Ostaszewska, and Cudak 2007 (eds.), 69–91.

Głowiński, Michał, Teresa Kostkiewiczowa, Aleksandra Okopień-Sławińska, and Janusz Sławiński (1989). *Słownik terminów literackich* [A Dictionary of Literary Terms]. 2nd enlarged and corrected ed. Wrocław, Warszawa, Krakow, Gdańsk, Łódź: Ossolineum.

Gomringer, Eugen (1970a [1954]). "From Line to Constellation" [in:] Solt (ed.), 67.

Gomringer, Eugen (1970b [1958]). "Max Bill and Concrete Poetry" [in:] Solt (ed.), 68–69.

Gonigroszek, Dorota (2015). "*Hybrid cars, hybrid theories, hybrid nails*. Corpora analyses "hybridized" with psycho-and sociolinguistic investigations" [in:] *Hybrids and Hybridity*. Alina Kwiatkowska, and Agnieszka Stanecka (eds.). Piotrków Trybunalski: Naukowe Wydawnictwo Piotrkowskie, 209–225.

Górska-Olesińska, Monika (ed.) (2012). *Liberatura, e-literatura i… Remiksy, remediacje, redefinicje*. Opole: Wydawnictwo Uniwersytetu Opolskiego.

Greg, Walter Wilson (1950/1951). "The Rationale of Copy-text" [in:] *Studies in Bibliography* 3, 19–36. JSTOR (access: 24 January 2016).

Grochowska, Alina (2007). "Czy język haseł przedmiotowych Biblioteki Narodowej nadąża za rozwojem dziedzin i ich terminologią" [Does the language of subject terms of the National Library of Poland keep up to date with the development of academic fields and their terminology?] [in:] EBIB, the Electronic Portal of the Polish Librarians Association, 22 Nov. http://www.ebib.info (access: 10 March 2011).

Gumbrecht, Hans Ulrich (2004). *Production of Presence: What Meaning Cannot Convey.* Stanford, Ca: Stanford UP. *EBSCOhost. eBook Academic Collection* (access: 19 November 2015).

Gumbrecht, Hans Ulrich, and K. Ludwig Pfeiffer (eds.) (1994). *Materialities of Communication.* Trans. William Whobrey. Standford: Stanford UP.

Hall, Steven (2007b). "What are *The Raw Shark Texts* Negatives?". Steven-Hall.org. Discussion forum » Book 1 – The Raw Shark Texts » Crypto-Forensics ». 15 August, 05:05:14. http://forums.steven-hall.org/yaf_postst52_What-are--Raw-Shark-Texts-Negatives. aspx (access: 3 July 2016).

Hamilton, Mary (2005). "Book Review: Discourses in Place: Language in the Material World: Reading and Writing in One Community" [in:] *Visual Communication* 4.3, October, 378–382. *Sage journals* (access: 2 February 2016).

Harmon, William, and C. Hugh Holman (1996). *A Handbook to Literature. 7th Edition.* Upper Saddle River, NJ: Prentice Hall.

Hayles, N. Katherine (1999). *How We Became Posthuman: Virtual Bodies in Cybernetics, Literature, and Informatics.* Chicago: University of Chicago Press.

Hayles, N. Katherine (2002). *Writing Machines.* Cambridge, London: MIT Press.

Hayles, N. Katherine (2006). "The Time of Digital Poetry: From Object to Event" [in:] *New Media Poetics. Contexts, Technotexts, and Theories.* Adalaide Morris, and Thomas Swiss (eds.). Cambridge, MA., London: MIT Press.

Hayles, N. Katherine (2011). "Material Entanglements: Steven Hall's *The Raw Shark Texts* as Slipstream Novel" [in:] *Science Fiction Studies* 38.1, 115–133. JSTOR (access: 27 April 2015).

Hayman, David (1970). *Ulysses: The Mechanics of Meaning.* Englewood Cliffs: Prentice Hall.

Hermansson, Gunilla (2013). "Expressionism, Fiction and Intermediality in Nordic Modernism" [in:] Posman, Reverseau, Ayers, Bru, and Hjartarson, 207–220.

Heuckelom, Kris van (2012). "(S)Tree(t) of (Cro)cod(il)es. Jonathan Safran Foer 'okalecza' Brunona Schulza" ["(S)Tree(t) of (Cro)cod(il)es. Jonathan Safran Foer 'mutilates' Bruno Schulz] [in:] *Literatura polska w świecie. T. 4: Oblicza światowości.* Romuald Cudak (ed.). Katowice: Wydawnictwo Gnome, 15–29.

Higgins, Dick (2001 [1985; 1966]). "Intermedia" with an Appendix by Hannah Higgins [in:] *Leonardo* 34.1, 49–54 (access: 18 January 2016).

Hitchings, Henry (2009). *The Secret Life of Words: How English Became English.* New York: Picador. *Googlebooks* (access: 22 February 2015).

Hix, Harvey Lee (2002). *Understanding William H. Gass.* Columbia: University of South Caroline Press. *Googlebooks* (access: 30 January 2016).

Bibliography

Holland, Norman Norwood (2009). *Literature and the Brain*. Gainesville, Fl.: PsyArt Foundation. *Googlebooks* (access: 12 November 2015).

Husárová, Zuzana, and Nick Montfort (2012). "Shuffle Literature and The Hand of Fate" [in:] *The Electronic Book Review: Electropoetics*, 5 August. *MLA International Bibliography* (access: 18 February 2016).

Hybrid. Oxford Dictionaries site. Oxford UP. http://www.oxforddictionaries.com/definition/english/hybrid?searchDictCode=all (access: 19 February 2015).

Ingarden, Roman (1973 [1937]). *The Cognition of the Literary Work*. Trans. Ruth Ann Crowley, and Kenneth R. Olson. Evanstone: Northwestern UP.

Ingarden, Roman (1989 [1962]). *The Ontology of the Work of Art*. Trans. Raymond Meyer with John T. Goldthwait. Athens, Ohio: Ohio UP.

Iser, Wolfgang (1972). "The Reading Process: A Phenomenological Approach" [in:] *New Literary History*, On Interpretation: I, 3.2, Winter, 279–299. JSTOR (access 18 August 2008).

Jankowicz, Grzegorz (2003). Rev. of *Oka-leczenie* [in:] *Ha!art. Interdyscyplinarny magazyn kulturalno-artystyczny* 2.15, [no pagination].

Jankowicz, Grzegorz (moderator) (2010). "Od *Oka-leczenia* do liberatury", panel with Katarzyna Bazarnik, Zenon Fajfer, Agnieszka Przybyszewska, and Jan Gondowicz. Bunkier Sztuki, pl. Szczepański 3a, Krakow, 20 Jan 2010 [in:] *Ha!art. Postdyscyplinarny magazyn o nowej kulturze* 30, 5–14.

Jauss, Hans Robert (2001). "The Identity of the Poetic Text in the Changing Horizon of Understanding" [in:] *Reception Study: From Literary Theory to Cultural Studies*. James L. Machor, and Philip Goldstein (eds.). New York, London: Routledge. *Googlebooks* (access: 15 January 2016).

Jelsbak, Torben (2005). *Ekspressionisme: modernismens formelle gennembrud i dansk malerkunst og poesi*. Copenhagen: Spring.

Johnson, Bryan Stanley (1973). "Introduction" [in:] *Aren't You Rather Young to be Writing Your Memoirs?*. London: Hutchinson, 11–31.

Johnson, Jeri (1992). "Introduction" [in:] James Joyce, *Ulysses*. Jeri Johnson (ed.). Oxford: Oxford UP, ix–xxxvii.

Kalaga, Wojciech (2010a). "Liberature: Word, Icon, Space" [in:] Fajfer 2010a, 9–19.

Kalaga, Wojciech (2010b). "Tekst hybrydyczny. Polifonie i aporie doświadczenia wizualnego" [in:] *Kulturowe wizualizacje doświadczenia*. Włodzimierz Bolecki, and Adam Dziadek (eds.). Warszawa: IBL and Fundacja "Centrum Międzynarodowych Badań Polonistycznych," 74–104.

Kamisińska, Dorota (2006). "'Typographus computericus' – czyli od Wyspiańskiego do liberatury" [in:] *Autoportret. Pismo o dobrej przestrzeni* 17, 26-29.

Kant, Immanuel (1998 [1781]). *The Critique of Pure Reason*. Trans. and ed. Paul Guyer, and Allen W. Wood. Cambridge: Cambridge UP.

Kantor, Tadeusz (1993). *A Journey Through Other Spaces: Essays and Manifestos, 1944-1990*. Trans. and ed. Michał Kobiałka. Berkley, Los Angeles: University of California Press. *Googlebooks* (access: 11 November 2015).

Kato, Ariko (2012). "Manipulation of Narrative/History. Visual Elements in the Books of Jonathan Safran Foer" [in:] 『れにくさ. Renyxa. Реникса 3, winter, 226–242.

Kato, Ariko (2014). "Book as a New Genre: The Book Illustrations of Bruno Schulz" [in:] Bazarnik, and Curyłło-Klag (eds.), 15–29.

Kaufman, Michael (1994). Textual Bodies: Modernism, Postmodernism and Print. Lewisburg: Bucknell UP.

Kelm, Rebecca S. (1992). "Book reviews: Fiction" [Review of Robert Grudin's Book] [in:] Library Journal 117.12, 124. Academic Search Complete (1 August 2016).

Kendon, Adam (2004). Gesture: Visible Action as Utterance. Cambridge: Cambridge UP. Googlebooks (access: 25 February 2016).

Kenner, Hugh (2004). "The Arranger" [in:] James Joyce's Ulysses. A Casebook. Derek Attridge (ed.). Oxford, NY: Oxford UP. 17–32.

Khalfa, Jean (2001). The Dialogue Between Painting and Poetry: Livres D'artistes, 1874–1999. Cambridge: Black Apollo Press.

Kluszczyński, Ryszard W. (1996). "Interaktywność – właściwość odbioru czy nowa jakość sztuki/kultury" [Interactivity – a Property of Reception or a New Quality of Art/Culture] [in:] Estetyczne przestrzenie współczesności. Anna Zeidler-Janiszewska (ed.). Warszawa: Instytut Kultury.

Kostelanetz, Richard (2000). A Dictionary of the Avant-Gardes. 2nd ed. New York: Schirmer Books.

Kress, Gunther (2010). Multimodality: a Social Semiotic Approach to Contemporary Communication. London, New York: Routledge.

Kress, Gunther, and Theo van Leeuwen (1996). Reading Images: The Grammar of Visual Design. London, New York: Routledge.

Kress, Gunther, and Theo van Leeuwen (2001). Multimodal Discourse. The Modes and Media of Contemporary Communication. London: Hodder.

Kucała, Bożena (2012). Intertextual Dialogue with the Victorian Past in the Contemporary Novel. Frankfurt am Main, Berlin, Bern, Bruxelles, New York, Oxford, Warszawa, Wien: Peter Lang.

Kuře, Josef (2009). "Etymological background and further clarifying remarks cocenring chimera and hybrids" [in:] CHIMBRIDS – Chimeras and Hybrids in Comparative European and International Research. Scientific, Ethical, Philosophical and Legal Aspects. Jochen Taupitz, and Marion Weschka (eds.). Heidelberg, London, New York: Springer, 7–20. Googlebooks (access: 19 February 2015).

Kutnik, Jerzy (1986). The Novel as Performance. The Fiction of Ronald Sukenick and Raymond Federman. Carbondale, Edwardsville: Southern Illinois UP.

Ladorucki, Jacek (2009). "O inlibrizacji czyli książkowym żywocie dzieł literackich" [On inlibrisation or the bookish life of literary works] [in:] Pasja książki. Studia poświęcone pamięci profesora Janusza Dunina. Jacek Ladorucki, and Magdalena Rzadkowolska (eds.). Łódź: Wydawnictwo Literatura, 214–224.

Lakoff, George (2004). Don't Think of an Elephant!: Know Your Values and Frame the Debate: the Essential Guide for Progressives. White River Junction, VT: Chelsea Green Publishing.

Lakoff, George, and Mark Johnson (2003 [1980]). *Metaphors We Live By*. Chicago, London: University of Chicago Press.

Litz, A. Walton (1974). "The Genre of *Ulysses*" [in:] *The Theory of the Novel. New Essays*. John Halperin (ed.). New York, London, Toronto: Oxford UP, 109–120.

Machin, David (2013). "What is multimodal critical discourse studies?" [in:] *Critical Discourse Studies* 10.4, 347–355. Taylor and Francis Online (access: 2 Feb 2016).

Mahaffey, Viki (1991). "Intentional Error: The Paradox of Editing Joyce's *Ulysses*" [in:] *Representing Modernist Texts. Editing as Interpretation*. G. Bornstein (ed.). Ann Arbor: the University of Michigan Press.

Mallarmé, Stéphane ([1895], 1982). "The Book: A Spiritual Instrument" [in:] Stéphane Mallarmé, *Selected poetry and prose*. Trans. Bradford Cook. Mary Ann Caws (ed.). New York: New Directions Publishing, 80–84.

Mallarmé, Stéphane (1994 [1897]). "Preface. Préface" [in:] Collected Poems. Trans. with a commentary by Henry Weinfield. Berkeley: University of California Press, 121–123.

Malmgren, Carl Darryl (1985). *Fictional Spaces in the Modernist and Postmodernist American Novel*. Lewisburg: Bucknell UP.

Manguel, Alberto (1996). *A History of Reading*. New York: Viking. *Open Library* (access: 16 January 2016).

Manovich, Lev (2001). *The Language of New Media*. Cambridge, Ma., London: the MIT Press.

Marecki, Piotr (ed.) (2003). *Liternet.pl*. Kraków: Rabid.

Matuszyk, Łukasz (2016). "Liberackie ciało i jego *Oka-leczenie*" [in:] *Er(r)go. Teoria–Literatura–Kultura* 32.1, forthcoming.

Maziarczyk, Grzegorz (2013). *The Novel as Book*. Lublin: Wydawnictwo KUL.

McGann, Jerome (1991). *The Textual Condition*. Princeton: Princeton UP.

McGann, Jerome (1993). *Black Riders. The Visible Language of Modernism*. Princeton: Princeton UP.

McHale, Brian (1987). *Postmodernist Fiction*. New York and London: Methuen.

McKenzie, Donald Francis (1999). *Bibliography and the Sociology of Texts*. Cambridge: Cambridge UP.

McLuhan, Marshall (2001 [1964]). *Understanding Media*. London, New York: Routledge.

Mitchell, W. J. Thomas (1994). *Picture Theory: Essays on Verbal and Visual Representation. Picture Theory*. Chicago: University of Chicago Press.

Medin, Douglas L., and Cynthia Aguilar (1999). "Categorization" [in:] *MITECS: The MIT Encyclopedia of the Cognitive Sciences*. http://ato.ms/MITECS/Entry/medin.html (access: 16 February 2015.

Miller, Carolyn R. (1994). "Genre as Social Action" [in:] Freedman, and Medway (eds.), 20–36.

Moeglin-Delcroix, Anne (1997). *Esthétique du livre d'artiste. Une introduction à l'art contemporain*. Paris: Jean Michel Place/Bibliothèque nationale de France.

Nöth, Winfried (1995). *Handbook of Semiotics*. Bloomington, Indianapolis: Indiana UP.

O'Connor, Timothy, and Hong Yu Wong (2015 [2002]). "Emergent Properties" revised [in:] *The Stanford Encyclopedia of Philosophy*. Edward N. Zalta (ed.). Summer 2015 Edition.

http://plato.stanford.edu/archives/sum2015/entries/properties-emergent/ (access: 12 June 2016).

Olczyk, Jacek (2006). "'Księga jest więc jak Bóg: konieczna, obecna, nieistniejąca.' O nieukończonym dziele Stéphane'a Mallarmégo" [in:] Autoportret. Pismo o dobrej przestrzeni 17, 20-23.

Ong, Walter J. (2012). Orality and Literacy. The Technologizing of the Word. 30th Anniversary Ed. with additional chapters by John Hartley. London, New York: Routledge.

Opacki, Ireneusz (2000 [1963]). Royal Genres. Trans. David Malcolm. Duff, 118–126.

Opacki, Ireneusz (2007 [1963]). "Krzyżowanie się postaci gatunkowych jako wyznacznik ewolucji poezji" [in:] Ostaszewska, and Cudak 2007 (eds.), 92–114.

Ostaszewska, Danuta, and Romuald Cudak (eds.) (2007). Polska genologia literacka. Warszawa: Wydawnictwo Naukowe PWN.

Ostaszewska, Danuta, and Romuald Cudak (eds.) (2008). Polska genologia lingwistyczna. Warszawa: Wydawnictwo Naukowe PWN.

Otty, Lisa (2008). "Signals and Noise: Art, Literature and the Avant-garde." Unpublished PhD dissertation. The University of Edinburgh. Edinburgh Research Archive. Pdf.

Otty, Lisa (2013). "Small Press Modernists" [in:] Posman, Reverseau, Ayers, Bru, and Hjartarson (eds.). Berlin, Boston: De Gruyter, 128–143.

Pavel, Thomas (2003). "Literary Genres as Norms and Good Habits" [in:] New Literary History, Theorising Genres, 34.2, 201–210. JSTOR (access: 7 June 2014).

Perloff, Marjorie (ed.) (1988). Postmodern Genres. Normans, London: University of Oklahoma Press.

Perloff, Marjorie (2003 [1986]). The Futurist Moment: Avant-Garde, Avant Guerre, and the Language of Rupture. Chicago: Chicago University Press.

Phillpot, Clive (1982). "Books, Bookworks, Book Objects, Artists' Books" [in:] Artforum 20.9, May, 77–79.

Phillpot, Clive (1986). "Artists' Booklet" [in:] Printed Matter 1986/87 Catalogue. New York: Printed Matter, Inc. Essays. http://www.printedmatter.org/about/booklets.cfm (access: 25 February 2005).

Posman, Sarah, Anne Reverseau, David Ayers, Sascha Bru, and Benedikt Hjartarson (2013). The Aesthetics of Matter Modernism, the Avant-Garde and Material Exchange. Berlin, Boston: De Gruyter.

Pressman, Jessica (2006). "House of Leaves: Reading the Networked Novel" [in:] Studies in American Fiction 34.1, 107–122. Questia (access: 20 August 2016).

Pressman, Jessica (2009). "The Aesthetic of Bookishness in Twenty-First Century Literature" [in:] Michigan Quarterly Review 48.4, 465–482. ProQuest (access: 14 March 2014).

Pressman, Jessica (2014). Digital Modernism. Making It New in New Media. Oxford, New York: Oxford UP.

"Prospectus (finance)" [in:] Wikipedia. https://en.wikipedia.org/wiki/Prospectus_(finance) (access: 7 May 2016).

Przybyszewska, Agnieszka (2007a). "E-liberatura." Materials to The Companion of the Literary Genres [in:] Zagadnienia Rodzajów Literackich [The Problems of Literary Genres] 50.1–2, 247.

Przybyszewska, Agnieszka (2007b). "Liberatura." Materials to *The Companion of the Literary Genres* [in:] *Zagadnienia rodzajów literackich* [The Problems of Literary Genres] 50.1–2, 255–258.

Przybyszewska, Agnieszka (2007c). "W pudełku i na wadze – o przestrzeni śmierci i przestrzeni tekstu w utworach Brayana [sic] S. Johnsona oraz Zenona Fajfera i Katarzyny Bazarnik" [In the box and on the scales: on the spaceof death and the spce of text in the works of B. S. Johnson as well as Zenon Fajfer and Katarzyna Bazarnik] [in:] *Kulturowe obrazy śmierci od przełomu romantycznego do dziś*. Izabela Grzelak, and Tomasz Jermalonek (eds.). Łódź: Piktor, 207–222.

Przybyszewska, Agnieszka (2012). "Liberatura/Literatura totalna" [in:] *Słownik rodzajów i gatunków literackich* [A Dictionary of Literary Kinds and Genres]. Grzegorz Gazda (ed). Warszawa: Wydawnictwo Naukowe PWN, 521–526.

Przybyszewska, Agnieszka (2014a). "Close Reading of the Liberatic Canon. On *Oka-leczenie* by Zenon Fajfer and Katarzyna Bazarnik" [in:] Bazarnik, and Curyłło-Klag (eds.), 81–114.

Przybyszewska, Agnieszka (2014b). "Ku literaturze grywalnej. (Kilka uwag wstępnych)" [Towards Playable Literature (Some Preliminary Remarks)] [in:] *Przegląd Kulturoznawczy* 2.20, 127–147. Scientific Journals Online, *Cultural Studies Review* (access: 14 March 2016).

Przybyszewska, Agnieszka (2015). *Liberackość dzieła literackiego* [Liberariness of the literary work]. Łódź: Wydawnictwo Uniwersytetu Łódzkiego.

"Punctuation" (1999) [in:] J.A. Cuddon. *The Penguin Dictionary of Literary Terms*. Rev. C.E. Preston. London: Penguin, 711–714.

Ranocchi, Emiliano (2012). "Liberatura między awangardą i tradycją. Bilans pierwszego dziesięciolecia" [Between liberature and the avant-garde. Report on the first decade] [in:] *Liberatura, E-literatura i... Remiksy, Remediacje, Redefinicje*. Monika Górska-Olesińska (ed.). Opole: University of Opole Press, 19–36.

Ranocchi, Emiliano (2013). "Liberatura tra avanguardia e tradizione. Bilancio del primo decennio" [in:] *Avanguardie e tradizioni nel XX e XXI sec. Tra Polonia, Italia e Europa. Atti del Convegno dei polonisti 22–23 aprile 2010*. Marina Ciccarini, Leszek Kuk, and Luigi Marinelli (eds.). Roma: Accademia Polacca delle Scienze, 255–275.

Ranocchi, Emiliano (2014). "Liberature and Person: An Anthropological Question" [in:] Bazarnik, and Curyłło-Klag (eds.), 107–118.

Rinck, Fanny, and Françoise Boch (2012). "Enunciative Strategies and Expertise Levels in Academic Writing: How Do Writers Manage Point of View and Sources?" [in:] *University Writing: Selves and Texts in Academic Societies*. Montserrat Castelló, and Christiane Donahue (eds.). Bingley: Emerald, 111–127. *Googlebooks* (access: 20 February 2015).

Rosmarin, Adena (1985). *Power of Genre*. Minneapolis, Mn.: University of Minnesota Press.

Rosch, Eleanor (1978). "Principles of Categorization" [in:] *Cognition and Categorization*. Eleanor Rosch, and Barbara B. Lloyd (eds.). Hillsdale, NJ: Lawrence Erlbaum; New York, London: Halsted Press, 27–48.

Rothenberg, Jerome, and Steven Clay (eds.) (2000). *A Book of the Book*. New York: Granary Books.

Royce, Terry D., and Wendy L. Bowcher. (2007). *New Directions in the Analysis of Multimodal Discourse*. Mahwah, NJ, London: Lawrence Erlbaum Associates.

Runkle, Matt (2011). "The Liberating Bond: An Interview with Katarzyna Bazarnik & Zenon Fajfer" [in:] San Francisco Center for the Book blog. https://sfcb.org/blog/2011/12/28/the-liberating-bond-an-interview-with-katarzyna-bazarnik-zenon-fajfer/ (access: 9 July 2016).

Rypson, Piotr (2000). *Książki i strony. Polska książka awangardowa i artystyczna w XX wieku.* Warszawa: Centrum Sztuki Współczesnej Zamek Ujazdowski.

Schenkenberg, Stephen (2007). "Basking in Hell: Returning to William H. Gass's *The Tunnel*" [in:] *The Quarterly Conversation*, 6 (winter), [no pagination]. http://quarterlyconversation.com/william-h-gass-the-tunnel-review (access: 30 January 2016).

Scherer, Jacques (1977). *Le « Livre » de Mallarmé*. Paris: Gallimard.

Schulz, Christoph Benjamin (2015). *Poetiken des Blätterns.* Hildesheim, Zurich, New York: Olms.

Shklovsky, Victor (1965). "Art as Technique" [in:] *Russian Formalist Criticism. Four Essays.* Trans. Lee T. Lemon, and Marion J. Reis. University of Nebraska Press: Lincoln & London.

Skierkowska, Elżbieta (1960). *Wyspiański – artysta książki.* Wrocław: Ossolineum.

Slote, Sam (2004). *Ulysses in the Plural: the Variable Editions of Joyce's Novel.* Dublin: The National Library of Ireland.

Sławek, Tadeusz (1989). *Między literami. Szkice o poezji konkretnej.* Wrocław: Wydawnictwo Dolnośląskie.

Sławek, Tadeusz (2003). "Biorąc książkę do ręki" [Picking up a book] [in:] *Ha!art* 15.2, 16–18.

Solt, Mary Ellen (1971) (ed.). *Concrete Poetry. A World View.* Bloomington, London: Indiana UP.

Stamirowska, Krystyna (2006). *B. S. Johnson's Novels: A Paradigm of Truth.* Kraków: Universitas.

Staśko, Maja, and Dawid Gostyński (2015). "Liberatura. Próba wiary, że wszystko ma sens," interview with Zenon Fajfer [in:] *eleWator* 13.3, 128–135.

Steinmetz, Sol (2005). *Dictionary of Jewish Usage: A Guide to the Use of Jewish Terms.* Lanham, Boulder, New York, Toronto, Oxford: Rowman & Littlefield. *Googlebooks* (access: 3 November 2015).

Stöckl, Hartmut (ed.) (2004). "In between modes. Language and image in printed media" [in:] Kaltenbacher, Cassily, and Eija (eds.), 11–30. *EBSCOhost. eBook Academic Collection* (access: 24 February 2016).

Stockwell, Peter (2002). *Cognitive Poetics: An Introduction.* London, New York: Routledge.

Stockwell, Peter (2009). *Texture: A Cognitive Aesthetics of Reading.* Edinburgh: Edinburgh UP. *EBSCOhost. eBook Academic Collection* (access: 22 November 2015).

Swales, John M. (1990). *Genre Analysis: English in Academic and Research Settings.* Cambridge: Cambridge UP.

Tabaczyński, Michał (2011). *Liber NAUTICA. Cztery szkice o ciele i piśmie.* Bydgoszcz: Liberatak – Miejski Ośrodek Kultury.

Tabakowska, Elżbieta (2011). "W co przechodzi ludzkie pojęcie?" [in:] *Pojęcia. Jak reprezentujemy i kategoryzujemy świat.* Adam Chuderski, and Józef Bremer (eds.). Kraków: Universitas, 199–213.

Tabakowska, Elżbieta (2016). "'Ception': Language and the Grammar of Concepts" [in:] *Beyond Words: Crossing Borders in English Studies*. Vol. 2. Justyna Leśniewska, and Mateusz Urban (eds.). Kraków: Tertium, 9–22.

Talmy, Leonard (1996). "Fictive Motion in Language and-Ception" [in:] *Language and Space*. P. Bloom et al. (eds.). Cambridge, Ma.: MIT Press, 211–276.

Talmy, Leonard (2000). *Toward a Cognitive Semantics*. Vol. 1: *Concept Structuring Systems*. Cambridge, Ma.: MIT Press.

Taxidou, Olga (2013). *The Mask: A Periodical Performance by Edward Gordon Craig*. London, New York: Routledge. *Googlebooks* (access: 28 August 2016).

Therrien, Carl (2014). "Interface" [in:] *The Johns Hopkins Guide to Digital Media*. Benjamin J. Robertson, Lori Emerson, and Marie-Laure Ryan (eds.). Baltimore: Johns Hopkins UP. *EBSCOhost. eBook Academic Collection* (access: 6 August 2015).

Todorov, Tzvetan (1990). *Genres in Discourse*. Trans. Catherine Porter. Cambridge: Cambridge UP.

de Tollenaere, Kris, Jeanine Eerdekens, Pascal Lefèvre, and Sofie Vandoninck (2010). *Woord & Beeld verhalen. Transitionaliteit tussen woord en beeld in fictieverhalen voor volwassenen*. Cahiers van het IvOK 19. Leuven: Acco.

de Tollenaere, Kris, and Jeanine Eerdekens (2014). "The Hybrid Book Genre of Word & Image Narratives: Results of an Artistic Research Project" [in:] Bazarnik, and Curyłło-Klag, 59–72.

Ulbæk, Ib (2015). "Genre and Categorization" [in:] Auken, Lauridsen, and Rasmussen (eds.), 422–454.

Warren, Minton (1884). "On the Etymology of Hybrid (Lat. Hybrida)" [in:] *The American Journal of Philology* 5.4, 501–502 (access: 19 February 2015).

White, Hayden (2003). "Commentary: Good of Their Kind" [in:] *New Literary History*. Theorizing Genres I 34. 2, 367–376. JSTOR (access: 7 June 2014).

Wilk, Eugeniusz, and Monika Górska-Olesińska (eds.) (2011). *Od liberatury do e-literatury*. Opole: Wydawnictwo Uniwersytetu Opolskiego.

Wysłouch, Seweryna (2007). "Nowa genologia – rewizje i reinterpretacje" [in:] Ostaszewska, and Cudak (2007), 288–305.

Ventola, Eija, Cassily Charles, and Martin Kaltenbacher (eds.) (2004). *Perspectives On Multimodality*. Amsterdam: John Benjamins. *EBSCOhost. eBook Academic Collection* (access: 24 February 2016).

Young, Janis (2009). "Expanding the Power of the Library's Family of Vocabularies: Genre/Form Headings" [in:] The Library of Congress "Digital Future and You" series. Washington D.C., 2 July. Lecture. The Library of Congress Webcasts. https://www.loc.gov/today/cyberlc/feature_wdesc.php?rec=4627 (access: 30 January 2016).

Zadeh, Lofti A. (1965). "Fuzzy Sets" [in:] *Information and Control* 8, 338–353. The Berkley Initiative in Soft Computing, University of California at Berkley. Pdf (access: 8 June 2014).

Websites

Boluk Stephanie, Leonardo Flores, Jacob Garbe, and Anastasia Salter (eds.) (2016). *Electronic Literature Collection 3*. The Electronic Literature Organization (ELO). http://collection.eliterature.org/3/.

Borràs, Laura, Talan Memmott, Rita Raley, Brian Stefans (eds.) (2011). *Electronic Literature Collection 2*. The Electronic Literature Organization (ELO). http://collection.eliterature.org/2/.

Catalogues of the National Library. The National Library of Poland. Warszawa. http://alpha.bn.org.pl/search*.

Editions at Play. Digital publishers' website. http://visual-editions.com/google-creative-labs.

Genre Studies Network. University of Birmingham, Department of Modern Languages, Russian Studies Section. http://www.birmingham.ac.uk/schools/lcahm/departments/languages/sections/russian/research/genre-studies-network.aspx.

GXB "Genre Across Borders. An international, interdisciplinary network of researchers, theories and resources." The Arts Computing Office, the University of Waterloo, Canada. http://genreacrossborders.org/.

Hayles, N. Katherine, Nick Montfort, Scott Rettberg, and Stephanie Strickland (eds.) (2006). *Electronic Literature Collection 1*. The Electronic Literature Organization (ELO). http://collection.eliterature.org/1/index.html.

"Henri Chopin." Jean-Dominique CARRE Archives. http://archives.carre.pagesperso-orange.fr/Chopin%20Henri.html.

"Liberatura." Korporacja Ha!art Publishing House series. Publisher's and foundation website. www.ha.art.pl/wydawnictwo/linie-wydawnicze/586-liberatura.html.

Liberature Reading Room. Website of the collection in Wojewódzka Bibliotek Publiczna w Krakowie. www.liberatura.pl.

Oxford Dictionaries. Language Matters. Oxford University Press. http://www.oxforddictionaries.com/.

Research Group for Genre Studies. University of Copenhagen, Department of Nordic Studies and Linguistics. http://genre.ku.dk/.

Visual Editions. Great Looking Stories. Publisher's website. http://visual-editions.com/ (VE pre-2005 website at http://2005.visual-editions.com/).

Author and subject index

Aarseth, Espen 53, 55

accordion 17, 164, 167

Adamowicz, Elza 42

Aerts, Diederik 111, 127, 128, 131, 132, 147

affordance 85

Aguilar, Cynthia 111

Apollinaire Guillaume (Wilhelm Apolinary Kostrowicki) 34

Arendt, Hannah 143

Aristotle 78, 109, 117

Arranger 61, 72

Artemeva, Natasha 113

artist's book 21, 41, 42, 44, 46, 120, 132, 147, 159

Ascott, Roy 53

asemic writing 18

Assman, Jan 139, 167

Attridge, Derek 80, 81

Auken, Sune 111, 115

autonomous theatre 85

Bakhtin, Mikhail Mikhailovich 80, 115, 116, 136

Balbus, Stanisław 150, 152, 167

Baldry, Anthony 98

Barthes, Roland 110

Bartnicki, Krzysztof 138, 155

Bateman, John 102

Bawarshi, Anis 37, 117, 120, 132, 148, 157, 168

Bazarnik, Katarzyna 13, 17, 19, 34, 35, 43, 45, 63, 67, 75, 78, 88, 99, 101, 103, 133, 136, 137, 141, 148, 168

Bazerman, Charles 37, 120, 148

Bednarczyk, Andrzej 102

Beebee, Thomas O. 109, 125, 152

Bellaman, Richard E. 146

Benjamin, Walter 143

Bense, Max 90, 93

Benton, Megan L. 41

Bervin, Jen 102, 133

Bhabha, Homi 27, 28

bibliographical code 21, 35, 64, 79, 167

Bieszczad, Liliana 53, 54

Blake, William 34, 41

Blanchot, Maurice 95, 110

Bloom, Harold 65

Boch, Françoise 15

Bolecki, Włodzimierz 113

Bolter, Jay David 52

book-in-the-box 46

bookishness 21, 54, 100, 119, 121, 130, 136, 156, 168

Boon, Mieke 130, 131, 166

Bourdieu, Pierre 37, 160

Bowcher, Wendy L. 98

Branny, Andrzej 70

Branny, Grażyna 70

Bray, Joe 65, 90, 91, 92

Bremer, Józef 127

Brooke-Rose, Christine 14, 15, 92

de Campos, Augusto 90

de Campos, Haroldo 90

Caraher, Brian G. 113, 125

Carrión, Ulises 93, 95, 133

Carroll, Lewis 67

Carson, Anne 49, 141

Cassily, Charles 96

Cendrars, Blaise (Frédéric Sauser) 34, 49

Chartin, J.-J. 110

Chopin, Henri 84, 92

Chuderski, Adam 127

Clark, Andy 117, 118

code 19, 34, 43, 81, 87, 95, 96, 149, 151

codex 15, 17, 18, 44, 45, 46, 47, 49, 51, 55, 58, 67, 99, 100, 135, 155, 162, 167

Coetzee, John Maxwell 14

Cohn, Ralph 110

Coleridge, Samuel Taylor 88

Collins, Viki Tollar 36

conceptual metaphor 60, 63, 65, 66, 67, 145

concrete 32, 34, 65, 67, 90, 91, 92, 93, 95, 99, 100, 101, 102, 104, 105, 127, 158, 168

Conrad, Joseph (Józef Konrad Korzeniowski) 28

Cortázar, Julio 45, 64

Couturier, Maurice 63, 92, 102

Craig, Edward Gordon 68

Croce, Benedetto 109

Cuber, Marta 25, 41, 150

Cudak, Romuald 105, 113

Danielewski, Mark Z. 49, 65, 66, 92, 93, 133, 138, 141, 156, 160, 163

Dante, Alighieri 34

Dąbrowska, Elżbieta 138, 168

De Geest, Dirk 145, 146

deixis 49, 59, 60

Delaunay-Terk, Sonia 34, 49

Derrida, Jacques 77, 124, 125, 138, 163

De Tollenaere, Kris 79

Dickson, Barbara 36

Dowd, Garin 110, 113, 114, 118, 121, 125, 128

Drucker, Johanna 41, 43, 52, 55, 62, 69, 80, 81, 83, 86

Dunajko, Paweł 160

Dziadek, Adam 36

Eco, Umberto 14, 87, 167

Eerdekens, Jeanine 79

Eliot, Thomas Stearns 15, 28

Ellmann, Richard 154

emanational form 18, 31

Emerson, Lori 21, 36, 54, 121

Fajfer, Zenon 13, 16, 17, 18, 19, 20, 21, 28, 31, 32, 33, 34, 35, 36, 37, 41, 43, 44, 45, 46, 49, 54, 58, 68, 75, 82, 83, 84, 85, 87, 88, 89, 90, 93, 95, 96, 97, 99, 102, 103, 104, 105, 119, 121, 126, 128, 129, 131, 132, 133, 137, 138, 140, 141, 148, 153, 160, 164, 168

Federman, Raymond 14, 36, 48, 63, 92, 101, 129, 141, 155, 160, 163

Fielding, Henry 92

Fishelov, David 109, 111, 145, 146, 157

Fish, Stanley 80

Foer, Jonathan Safran 108, 120

Fowler, Alastair 96, 109, 115, 116, 117, 133, 137, 138, 139, 145, 146, 150, 151, 152, 154, 157, 165

Freedman, Aviva 112, 118, 157

Frow, John 9, 21, 109, 113, 116, 123, 124, 135, 136, 137, 138, 152, 160, 167, 169

fuzzy set 130, 146

Gabora, Liane 111, 127, 128, 131, 132, 146, 147

Gass, William H. 9, 14, 57, 62, 63, 64, 65, 67, 69, 70, 71, 72, 74, 75, 76

Gaver, William W. 85

Gavins, Joanna 79

Gazda, Grzegorz 103, 113

Geeraerts, Dirk 145

Genette, Gerard 97, 109, 151, 152, 154, 155, 156

genre 13, 14, 20, 21, 27, 34, 37, 41, 46, 48, 63, 82, 88, 89, 90, 91, 92, 95, 96, 99, 100, 102, 103, 104, 105, 109, 110, 111, 112, 113, 114, 115, 116, 117, 118, 120, 123, 124, 125, 129, 130, 131, 133, 135, 136, 137, 138, 139, 140, 145, 146, 147, 148, 149, 150, 151, 152, 153, 157, 158, 160, 163, 165, 166, 168, 169

Gesamtkunstwerk 68

Gibbons, Alison 21, 63, 65, 66, 70, 79, 86, 89, 98, 99, 100, 101, 102, 103, 105, 133, 156, 168

Giltrow, Janet 112, 114

Głombiowski, Karol 32

Głowiński, Michał 32, 152

Goldberg, Samuel Louis 149

Gomringer, Eugen 90

Gonigroszek, Dorota 26

Goytisolo, Juan 64

Gray, Alasdair 92, 147

Greg, Walter Wilson 35

Grochowska, Alina 158, 159

Grotowski, Jerzy 85

Gumbrecht, Hans Ulrich 21, 77, 78, 79, 81, 83, 84, 86

Günthner, Susanne 116

Hallet, Wolfgang 86

Hall, Steven 100, 133, 138, 141, 156, 160, 161, 162, 163

Hamilton, Mary 46

Hayles, N. Katherine 21, 32, 36, 52, 53, 65, 83, 101, 121, 161, 162

Hayman, David 61

Herbert, George 34

Hermansson, Gunilla 41

Higgins, Dick 88, 89, 92, 148, 157

Hirsch, Eric Donald 145

Hitchings, Henry 26

Hitler, Adolf 71

Hix, Harvey Lee 71, 73

Homer 140

Husárová, Zuzana 46

hybrid 13, 15, 16, 17, 25, 26, 27, 31, 34, 42, 46, 87, 89, 98, 102, 130, 149, 154

hybridity 13, 25, 26, 27, 28, 87, 125, 150, 152, 156

hypertext 45, 55, 89, 102, 136

iconicity 100

Ingarden, Roman 63, 67, 80

inlibrisation 51

interface 52, 53, 62, 129, 136, 166

intermedia 36, 87, 88, 90

Iser, Wolfgang 47, 80

Iwasiów, Inga 14

Jankowicz, Grzegorz 41, 150

Jasieński, Bruno 34

Jauss, Hans Robert 115, 151

Jelsbak, Torben 41

Johnson, Bryan Stanley 50, 57, 58, 59, 60, 61, 62, 63, 66, 96, 140, 141

Johnson, Jeri 154

Johnson, Mark 57, 66

Joyce, James 26, 34, 58, 63, 69, 75, 76, 79, 92, 148, 149, 151, 154, 155

Kalaba, Robert 146

Kalaga, Wojciech 11, 19, 26, 53, 54, 55, 69, 85, 86, 87, 98, 129

Kaltenbacher, Martin 96

Kamisińska, Dorota 34
Kant, Immanuel 9, 126
Kantor, Tadeusz 68, 85
Kato, Ariko 34, 120, 129
Kaufman, Michael 71, 75
Kenner, Hugh 61
Kerbrat-Orecchioni, Catherine 15
Khalfa, Jean 42
Kleiber, George 145
Kluszczyński, Ryszard 54
Kostelanetz, Richard 92
Kostkiewiczowa, Teresa 32
Kożuch, Artur 159
Kress, Gunther 96, 97, 98
Kucała, Bożena 110
Kuře, Josef 25
Kutnik, Jerzy 86

Ladorucki, Jacek 51
Lakoff, George 57, 66, 89, 145
Lalewicz, Janusz 32
Langacker, Ronald W. 145
Lefèvre, Pascal 79
liberariness 21, 91, 103, 104, 130
liberary 103, 130
liberatic 21, 25, 26, 34, 35, 37, 46, 49, 53,
    57, 65, 69, 78, 84, 85, 89, 93, 95, 96,
    97, 98, 100, 103, 104, 120, 130, 137,
    138, 140, 141, 143, 153, 156, 163
liberature 13, 16, 17, 19, 20, 21, 25, 26,
    27, 34, 35, 37, 41, 43, 44, 52, 53, 54,
    55, 57, 58, 68, 78, 80, 82, 83, 85, 86,
    87, 88, 89, 90, 91, 92, 95, 96, 97, 98,
    99, 100, 101, 103, 104, 105, 111, 116,
    117, 119, 120, 121, 123, 124, 126,
    128, 129, 130, 131, 132, 135, 136,
    137, 138, 140, 141, 143, 147, 150,
    152, 153, 155, 157, 158, 159, 160,
    163, 165, 166, 167, 168, 169
Linati, Carlo 154

Litz, Walton Arthur 149, 150
livre d'artiste 42
Locke, John 71, 140

Machin, David 96
Magritte, René 156
Mahaffey, Vicky 67, 68
Mallarmé, Stéphane 9, 34, 75, 83, 118,
    119, 160
Malmgren, Carl Darryl 46, 48, 168
Manguel, Alberto 149, 150
Marinetti, Filippo Tommaso 34
Markiewicz, Henryk 32
materiality 19, 20, 32, 33, 36, 37, 41,
    48, 52, 53, 54, 57, 64, 65, 81, 83, 87,
    96, 97, 99, 100, 101, 105, 125, 129,
    132, 169
material metaphor 51, 61, 71, 72, 80,
    140, 164
material rhetoric 33, 36, 37, 41, 49, 51,
    57, 58, 59, 62, 72, 79, 82, 119, 153,
    155, 167, 169
Maziarczyk, Grzegorz 63, 96, 99, 105
McGann, Jerome 20, 35, 69, 154, 167
McKenzie, Donald Francis 20
McLuhan, Marshall 34
Medin, Douglas L. 111
medium 20, 32, 34, 36, 43, 47, 48, 52, 54,
    55, 61, 75, 86, 88, 89, 95, 96, 98, 99,
    103, 104, 116, 117, 132, 135, 161,
    166, 167, 168, 169
Medway, Peter 112, 118, 157
Meersman, Philip 102, 133, 138
Mehrlingsbuch 16
metafictive 99, 101
metatextual 43, 48, 61, 77, 136, 155
Miller, Carolyn 37, 109, 111, 116, 118,
    148, 165, 166, 167, 168
Milton, John 20
Minsky, Marvin 161

Author and subject index

Mitchell, William John Thomas 81, 125

mode 36, 37, 43, 96, 97, 98, 99, 137, 152
   peripheral semantic m. 155

Moeglin-Delcroix, Anne 42

monomediality 96

Montfort, Nick 46

Mrozewicz, Anna 31

Müller, Herta 102, 129, 141, 159

multimediality 166

multimodality 36, 87, 96, 102, 130, 166

multimodal literature 21, 79, 86, 87, 96, 98, 99, 101, 105, 130, 133, 168, 169

Nancy, Jean-Luc 83

Nöth, Winfried 100, 167

Nowakowski, Radosław 49, 97, 129, 138, 160

Okopień-Sławińska, Aleksandra 32

Ong, Walter Jackson 97

Opacki, Ireneusz 27, 113

Orszulewski, Dariusz 129, 138, 141, 164

Otty, Lisa 41

Palmer, Stephen 126

paratext 64, 65, 154, 155, 156, 163, 167

Pavel, Thomas 151

Pavič, Milorad 14

Perec, Georges 65

performative 34, 62, 74, 80, 82, 85, 86, 100, 148, 155, 166, 169

Perloff, Marjorie 41

Phillpot, Clive 45

Pignatari, Decio 90

Plato 34

Pope, Alexander 140

Porter, Katherine Anne 64

Pound, Ezra 57, 69

presentification 77, 78, 81, 164

Pressman, Jessica 21, 36, 100, 101, 119, 121, 163, 168

Przyboś, Julian 34

Przybyszewska, Agnieszka 19, 20, 32, 34, 37, 83, 91, 95, 103, 104, 105, 110, 114, 129, 131, 132, 137, 138, 141, 147, 152

Queneau, Raymond 137, 138

Ranocchi, Emiliano 35, 36, 68, 129, 155

Rasmussen, Anders Juhl 115

readingwriting 21, 54, 121, 130, 168

Rinck, Fanny 15

Rosch, Eleanor 111, 126, 127, 128, 131, 132, 145, 146, 147

Rose, Jacqueline 14

Rosmarin, Adena 109

Royce, Terry D. 98

Rulyova, Natalia 110, 113, 114, 118, 121

Rypson, Piotr 32, 42

Sałaj, Zbigniew 42, 43

Scarry, Elaine 49

Schulz, Bruno 34

Schulz, Christoph Benjamin 67

scroll 46, 51, 135, 167

Shakespeare, William 66, 165

shuffle literature 46

Skwarczyńska, Stefania 32

Slote, Sam 69, 154

Sławek, Tadeusz 32, 53, 75, 84, 90, 91, 124

Sławiński, Janusz 32

Smith, Ali 143

Solt, Mary Ellen 90, 93

space 18, 20, 27, 28, 32, 45, 46, 47, 48, 49, 63, 64, 73, 74, 75, 85, 91, 92, 125, 128, 135, 136, 156, 161, 163, 169
   compositional s. 46, 47, 48, 52, 67, 76, 92, 99, 100, 138, 154, 162
   conceptual s. 146
   event-space 62

fictional s. 52, 64, 136
iconic s. 46, 47
material s. 64, 153
mental s. 49, 59
performative s. 85
qualified s. 90, 92
s. of inscription 46, 47, 51, 55, 87, 126
s. of the book 13, 34, 46, 48, 74, 76, 85, 136, 162
s. of the literary work 85
s. of the page 69
s. of writing 52
technological s. 54, 57
textual s. 17, 135
writing s. 85
Space 26
space-time 93, 95
Stamirowska, Krystyna 11, 60
Stein, Dieter 112, 114
Steinmetz, Sol 18
Sterne, Laurence 34, 91, 118, 140, 141
Stevenson, Lesley 113
Stöckl, Helmut 97
Stockwell, Peter 48, 49, 59, 60
Strong, Jeremy 113
Strzemiński, Władysław 34
Swales, John 109, 145, 157
Szczerbowski, Robert 129, 133, 160

Tabakowska-Muskat, Elżbieta 126, 127, 128, 130, 131
Talmy, Leonard 126, 127
Taylor, John R. 145
technotext 130

textimage 86
texture 36, 48, 49, 59, 61, 72, 96
Theocritus 139
Therrien, Carl 52
Thibault, Paul J. 98
Thirlwell, Adam 49, 50, 120, 133, 164
time 20, 32, 72, 135, 136, 139, 161
fictional t. 136
reading t. 136
space-time 93, 95
total literature 68
transgenre 26, 87, 98

Ulbæk, Ib 104, 111, 123, 129, 145, 146, 147

Vandoninck, Sofie 79
Van Gorp, Hendrik 145, 146
Van Heukelom, Kris 120, 129
Van Leeuwen, Theo 96, 98
Virgil 139

Watt, Ian 63, 92
Weitz, Morris 146
White, Hayden 109
Wilkoszewska, Krystyna 53
Williams, Emmett 90
Wysłołuch, Seweryna 116, 147
Wyspiański, Stanisław 34, 68

Young, Janis 57, 140, 154, 158

Zadeh, Lofti A. 146
Zbierski, Teodor 32
Zeidler-Janiszewska, Anna 54

EDITOR-IN-CHIEF
Anna Poinc-Chrabąszcz

TECHNICAL EDITOR
Gabriela Niemiec

PROOFREADER
Alicja Dziura

TYPOGRAPHIC DESIGN
Marta Jaszczuk

Jagiellonian University Press
Editorial Offices: ul. Michałowskiego 9/2, 31-126 Krakow
Phone: +48 12 663 23 80, +48 12 663 23 82, Fax: +48 12 663 23 83

GPSR Authorized Representative: Easy Access System Europe, Mustamäe tee
50, 10621 Tallinn, Estonia, gpsr.requests@easproject.com

www.ingramcontent.com/pod-product-compliance
Lightning Source LLC
Chambersburg PA
CBHW061747120626
46550CB00005B/1916